The Possibilities of Transnational Activism

History of International Relations, Diplomacy, and Intelligence

Series Editor

Katherine A. S. Sibley
Saint Joseph's University

Editorial Board

Mark T. Berger, Naval Postgraduate School
Klaus W. Larres, University of Ulster
Erin Mahan, Office of the Historian,
U.S. State Department
Rorin Platt, Campbell University
Geoffrey Roberts, University College Cork
Jeremi Suri, University of Wisconsin
Thomas Zeiler, University of Colorado at Boulder

VOLUME 2

The Possibilities of Transnational Activism

The Campaign for Disarmament between the Two World Wars

By

Thomas Richard Davies

MARTINUS NIJHOFF PUBLISHERS

LEIDEN • BOSTON
2007

This book is printed on acid-free paper.

Library of Congress Cataloging-in-Publication Data

A C.I.P. record for this book is available from the Library of Congress

On the cover. (i) 'Pour le désarmement des nations' (1932 poster by Jean Carlu with photographer André Vigneau). © ADAGP, Paris, and DACS, London, 2007.

(ii) Photograph of the public at the World Disarmament Conference in 1932. © League of Nations Archives, UNOG Library, 2007.

ISSN 1874-0294
ISBN 978 90 04 16258 7

PRINTED IN THE NETHERLANDS

To the memory of
Richard Andrew Davies
(1950–2007)

CONTENTS

PART V

ASSESSMENT—THE POSSIBILITIES OF TRANSNATIONAL ACTIVISM

APPENDICES

ACKNOWLEDGEMENTS

Many people and organisations helped me during the course of writing this book. I am especially grateful to my doctoral supervisor, Martin Ceadel, who inspired my interest in this subject and who carefully guided me through the research for the thesis on which this book is based. I am also very grateful to everyone who provided me with advice on the manuscript, especially Jonathan Wright for his comments on draft chapters. Andrew Barros, Carl Bouchard, Timothy Garton Ash, Norman Ingram, Peter Jackson, Carolyn Kitching, Kalypso Nicolaidis, Ali Parchami, Marta Reuter and Adam Roberts have also provided me with very helpful advice. I am particularly grateful to Lorna Lloyd and Neil MacFarlane, who provided excellent feedback as the examiners of my doctoral thesis and who have given me invaluable advice subsequently.

I would like to express my gratitude to the staff of the libraries and archives I consulted, especially the very helpful staff of the League of Nations Archives in Geneva, who kindly gave me permission to use their photograph of the public at the World Disarmament Conference on the cover of this book. For the cover reproduction of 'Pour le désarmement des nations,' I am grateful to the estate of Jean Carlu and DACS.

The research on which this book is based was made possible by financial support from Oxford University's Department of Politics and International Relations and Magdalen College's Student Support Fund. I am also very grateful for the support of my friends outside academia, especially Asif Huq for accommodation in London and New York. Above all, I am indebted to my family, especially my mother for her help with the index. She, my late father, and my sister have given me far more than can be written here.

LIST OF ABBREVIATIONS

Add. MSS	Additional Manuscripts (British Library)
BDFA	*British Documents on Foreign Affairs*
CGT	*Confédération Générale du Travail*
CIAMAC	*Conférence Internationale des Associations de Mutilés et Anciens Combattants* (= International Conference of Disabled Soldiers and Ex-Servicemen)
CID	Committee of Imperial Defence
CRLA	Conference for the Reduction and Limitation of Armaments (= World Disarmament Conference)
CSDN	*Conseil Supérieur de la Défense Nationale*
DBFP	*Documents on British Foreign Policy*
DCCIO	Disarmament Committee of Christian International Organisations
DCSIO	Disarmament Committee of Students' International Organisations
DCWIO	Disarmament Committee of Women's International Organisations
DDF	*Documents Diplomatiques Français*
DTMA	Draft Treaty of Mutual Assistance
FIDAC	*Fédération Interalliée des Anciens Combattants* (= Interallied Federation of Ex-Servicemen)
FoR	Fellowship of Reconciliation
FPA	Foreign Policy Association
FRUS	*Papers relating to the Foreign Relations of the United States*
FUI	*Fédération Universitaire Internationale pour la Société des Nations* (= International Federation of University League of Nations Societies)
IAW	International Alliance of Women for Suffrage and Equal Citizenship
ICA	International Co-operative Alliance
ICBL	International Campaign to Ban Landmines
ICD	Interorganization Council on Disarmament
ICG	International Consultative Group (for Peace and Disarmament)
ICI	Imperial Chemical Industries

ICW	International Council of Women
ICWG	International Co-operative Women's Guild
IFLNS	International Federation of League of Nations Societies
IFoR	International Fellowship of Reconciliation
IFSS	International Federation of Socialist Students
IFTU	International Federation of Trade Unions
IFULNS	International Federation of University League of Nations Societies
IFUW	International Federation of University Women
INGO	International Non-Governmental Organisation
IPB	International Peace Bureau
IPU	Inter-Parliamentary Union
ISS	International Student Service
JDC	Joint Disarmament Commission (of the International Federation of Trade Unions and the Labour and Socialist International)
LCWIO	Liaison Committee of Women's International Organisations
LDH	*Ligue des Droits de l'Homme*
LDM	*Ligue des Mères et des Educatrices pour la Paix*
LNA	League of Nations Association (USA)
LNU	League of Nations Union (Great Britain)
LSI	Labour and Socialist International
MAE	*Ministère des Affaires Étrangères*
NCCCW	National Committee on the Cause and Cure of War
NCPW	National Council for Prevention of War
NGO	Non-Governmental Organisation
NPC	National Peace Council
SDN	*Société des Nations* (= League of Nations)
TMC	Temporary Mixed Commission
UFAC	*Union Fédérale des Anciens Combattants*
UMI	University Microfilms International
WIL	Women's International League (Great Britain)
WILPF	Women's International League for Peace and Freedom
WSCF	World Student Christian Federation
YMCA	Young Men's Christian Association
YWCA	Young Women's Christian Association

PART ONE

PURPOSE AND METHOD

CHAPTER ONE

TRANSNATIONAL ACTIVISM: UNTESTED ASSERTIONS

The post-Cold War era has witnessed transnational activism on a scale
unseen since the 1930s. In 1997, for example, a coalition of three
hundred non-governmental organisations claimed responsibility for
the agreement of 122 countries to a treaty banning landmines.[1] Four
years later, representatives of 1,396 civil society organisations participated in the first World Social Forum.[2] And on 2 July 2005, a petition
demanding governmental action to wipe out world poverty acquired
the names of 30 million people within a single day.[3] Developments such
as these have led some academics to speak of the rise of 'global civil
society' and to make elaborate claims about its significance. In one of
the most influential articles on the subject, Jessica Tuchman Matthews
has claimed that 'increasingly, NGOs are able to push around even the
largest governments... The steady concentration of power in the hands
of states that began in 1648 with the Peace of Westphalia is over.'[4]

One of the principal purposes of this book is to go beyond such
sweeping claims and to discover if there are any specific assertions
about the role of transnational activism in international affairs that
can be justified empirically. It carries out this task by examining the
evidence from a campaign just as substantial as those that have taken
place in the post-Cold War era, but for which all of the necessary
governmental and non-governmental primary sources are available: the
global campaign for general disarmament that took place in the period
between the two World Wars. This campaign claimed to have mobilised
non-governmental organisations with a combined membership as high

---

[1] Ann M. Florini (ed.), *The Third Force: The Rise of Transnational Civil Society* (Washington, DC, 2000), p. 2.

[2] Guenther Schoenleitner, 'World Social Forum: Is Another World Possible?' in John
Clark (ed.), *Globalizing Civic Engagement: Civil Society and Transnational Action* (Sterling, VA,
2003), p. 129.

[3] Kumi Naidoo, *Reflections on the G8 Summit*, written on 13 July 2005 and published
on the website http://www.whiteband.org/specialIssues/G8/gcapnews.2005-07-
14.5388032995/en on 14 July 2005.

[4] Jessica T. Matthews, 'Power Shift: The Rise of Global Civil Society,' *Foreign Affairs*,
76/1 (1997), pp. 50, 53.

as half of the population of the world at the time,[5] yet until now it has been neglected by both historians and political scientists.

This opening chapter briefly outlines the evolution of the existing literature on transnational activism and summarises the claims that have been made in it. The subsequent chapter describes the purposes of this book. It shows how this book uses the evidence of the interwar disarmament campaign to test the claims made in the existing literature, in order to reveal if there are any general assertions about the role of transnational activism in world affairs that can be justified empirically. It also shows how this book fills an important gap in the historical literature on the development of interwar international relations.

The Development of Academic Literature on 'Transnational Activism'

At the same time as the global disarmament campaign reached its peak in the early 1930s, an American academic, Lyman Cromwell White, produced a thesis arguing that 'in the study of international organization, concentration in the field of public or official organizations has left neglected an important field of private international organizations, of which there are thousands, covering practically all the things that human beings are interested in. . . . [S]ome of these private organizations are more important than many of the public international organizations and exert a greater influence on international affairs.'[6] According to a Quaker specialist on international affairs, Bertram Pickard, private, or unofficial, international organisations constituted 'the Greater League of Nations.'[7]

After the Second World War, private international organisations became known as 'international non-governmental organisations' (INGOs), following the terminology of Article 71 of the United Nations Charter. The Economic and Social Council of the United

---

[5] Philip Noel-Baker, *The First World Disarmament Conference, 1932–1934, And Why It Failed* (Oxford, 1979), pp. 73–4.

[6] Quotation from George A. Finch's review of Lyman Cromwell White's *The Structure of Private International Organizations* (Philadelphia, PA, 1933) in *American Journal of International Law*, 27/4 (1933), pp. 810–1.

[7] Bertram Pickard, *The Greater League of Nations: A Brief Survey of the Nature and Development of Unofficial International Organisations* ([Zurich], 1936).

Nations defined an INGO as 'any international organisation which is not established by intergovernmental agreement.'[8]

Until the late 1960s, academic attention on international non-governmental organisations was limited. By the early 1970s, however, US political scientists including Robert Keohane, Joseph Nye and Samuel Huntington had developed a body of literature studying the role of 'transnational actors' and 'transnational relations' in world politics.[9] The term 'transnational actor' was applied to 'corporate bodies other than the state' with which people across national borders identify themselves.[10]

By the 1980s, scholarly attention was being paid to specific types of transnational actor, such as 'transnational pressure groups' that 'exist in order to influence public opinion and preferably also public policy.'[11]

Since the end of the Cold War, academic literature on transnational actors has become particularly commonplace. James Rosenau's 1990 study of 'turbulence in world politics' claims that a post-international politics has emerged, characterised by a 'bifurcation in which the state-centric system now co-exists with an equally powerful, though more decentralized, multi-centric system' composed of transnational 'sovereignty-free' actors.[12]

A substantial body of literature claiming the existence of a 'global civil society' has also been produced, which argues that there is now 'an international rule of law guaranteed by a range of interlocking institutions, including—but not only—states, and…citizens' networks who monitor, contest and put pressure on these institutions.'[13] Other

---

[8] Lyman Cromwell White and Marie Ragonetti Zocca, *International Non-Governmental Organizations: Their Purposes, Methods, and Accomplishments* (New Brunswick, 1951), p. 3.

[9] Robert Keohane and Joseph Nye (eds.), *Transnational Relations and World Politics* (Cambridge, MA, 1971) and Samuel P. Huntington, 'Transnational Organizations in World Politics,' *World Politics*, 25 (1973), pp. 333–58.

[10] Arnold Wolfers, *Discord and Collaboration: Essays on International Politics* (Baltimore, 1962).

[11] Quotation from Martin Ceadel, *Semi-Detached Idealists: The British Peace Movement and International Relations, 1854–1945* (Oxford, 2000), p. 3. The principal work on transnational pressure groups is Peter Willetts (ed.), *Pressure Groups in the Global System: The Transnational Relations of Issue-Oriented Non-Governmental Organisations* (London, 1982).

[12] James N. Rosenau, *Turbulence in World Politics: A Theory of Change and Continuity* (Princeton, NJ, 1990), p. 11, quoted in Thomas Risse, 'Transnational Actors and World Politics' in Walter Carlsnaes, Thomas Risse and Beth A. Simmons (eds.), *Handbook of International Relations* (London, 2002), p. 258.

[13] Mary Kaldor, 'Global Civil Society,' in David Held and Anthony McGrew (eds.), *The Global Transformations Reader: An Introduction to the Globalization Debate*, second edition, (Cambridge, 2003), p. 560. On global civil society, see also Mary Kaldor, *Global Civil*

accounts of 'global civil society' simply mean by it transnational 'activities by voluntary associations to shape policies, norms and/or deeper social structures.'[14] The terms 'third sector' and 'third force' have also been introduced to describe these activities.[15]

As well as witnessing an expansion in the number of terms used to describe transnational non-governmental activities in general, the post-Cold War period has also seen a multiplication in the different types of transnational actors subjected to scholarly investigation. In 1998, for example, Margaret Keck and Kathryn Sikkink published to wide acclaim a work delineating the role in world politics of 'transnational advocacy networks,' defined as transnational 'forms of organisation characterised by voluntary, reciprocal and horizontal patterns of communication and exchange,' which 'are organised to promote causes, principled ideas, and norms.'[16] Sociologists, on the other hand have emphasised the role of 'transnational social movements,' defined as transnational 'efforts by clusters of relatively marginalized actors to promote some form of social or political change.'[17]

A broader concept that has been elaborated in recent years is that of 'transnational activism,' which forms the subject of this book.[18] Activism has been defined as 'political activities that are: (1)...of a contentious nature; (2) challenging or supporting certain power structures; (3) involving non-state actors; and (4) taking place (at least partly) outside formal political arenas.'[19] An important characteristic of activism is 'a focus on public (as opposed to private) goals. Activity that only aims at promoting one's own private interests is not activism.'[20] Another vital feature of most activism is the 'targeting [of] formal political institutions'

Society: An Answer to War (Cambridge, 2003), John Keane, *Global Civil Society?* (Cambridge, 2003), and the annual *Global Civil Society Yearbooks* produced by the Centre for the Study of Global Governance in London.

[14] Jan Aart Scholte, *Globalization: A Critical Introduction* (Basingstoke, 2000), p. 277.

[15] See Florini, *Third Force, passim*.

[16] Margaret Keck and Kathryn Sikkink, *Activists Beyond Borders: Transnational Advocacy Networks in World Politics* (Ithaca, NY, 1998), p. 8.

[17] Jackie Smith, Charles Chatfield and Ron Pagnucco (eds.), *Transnational Social Movements and World Politics: Solidarity beyond the State* (Syracuse, NY, 1997), p. 59.

[18] Recent studies of transnational activism include Sidney Tarrow, *The New Transnational Activism* (Cambridge, 2005) and Nicola Piper and Anders Uhlin (eds.), *Transnational Activism in Asia: Problems of Power and Democracy* (London, 2004).

[19] Nicola Piper and Anders Uhlin, 'New Perspectives on Transnational Activism' in Piper and Uhlin (eds.), *Transnational Activism in Asia*, p. 4.

[20] Piper and Uhlin, 'New Perspectives on Transnational Activism,' p. 4.

in order to secure its goals.[21] Activism is transnational when it has one
or more of the following features: (1) when it has a 'focus on transnational issues;' (2) when the activist organisations are transnational in
structure; (3) when 'transnational methods and strategies' are applied;
(4) when the targets of activism are located in several countries; and
(5) when the activists 'hold transnational views and consider themselves
as "global citizens."'[22]

Untested Assertions

Much of the post-Cold War literature on global civil society and
transnational activism has made considerable claims about the power
of non-governmental organisations in international affairs. Jessica Tuchman Matthews' assertion that 'NGOs are able to push around even the
largest governments'[23] is just one example of this.[24] Matthew Evangelista has gone as far as to argue that non-governmental organisations
'contributed to...the end of the Cold War.'[25]

Another prominent feature of much of the literature on transnational
activism is the assumption that its impact is positive. As Jan Aart Scholte
has pointed out, with an idealism similar to that present among liberals in the period between the two World Wars, 'many [present-day]
advocates of progressive social change have...championed the "third
sector" as an arena of virtue that overcomes domination in government
and exploitation in the market.'[26]

As well as this tendency to make sweeping claims about activist
impact, a further notable feature of many contemporary works on transnational activism has been pointed out by Richard Price: a tendency

---

[21] Piper and Uhlin, 'New Perspectives on Transnational Activism,' p. 4.

[22] Piper and Uhlin, 'New Perspectives on Transnational Activism,' p. 5.

[23] Matthews, 'Power Shift,' p. 22; the full quotation is on page 3.

[24] For a concise survey of similar literature, see the annotated bibliography by Yahya
A. Dehqanzada in Florini, *Third Force*, pp. 241–76.

[25] Quotation from Thomas Risse-Kappen (ed.), *Bringing Transnational Relations Back
In: Non-State Actors, Domestic Structures and International Institutions* (Cambridge, 1995),
p. 280; the argument is most fully outlined in Matthew Evangelista, *Unarmed Forces:
The Transnational Movement to End the Cold War* (Ithaca, NY, 1999).

[26] Quotation from Scholte, *Globalization*, p. 277, citing David C. Korten, *Getting to
the 21st Century: Voluntary Action and the Global Agenda* (Hartford, CT, 1990) and Richard
A. Falk, *On Humane Governance: Toward a New Global Politics* (Cambridge, 1995).

simply to produce 'a long menu describing what transnational activists do and how they do it.'[27]

An important recent development is the publication of a more sophisticated body of literature that has also sought to answer the question: 'under what…circumstances do transnational coalitions and actors who attempt to change policy outcomes in a specific issue-area succeed or fail to achieve their goals?'[28]

This literature has come to no agreement as to what the circumstances that affect achievement of activist goals are.[29] Furthermore, those authors who have sought to test the criteria affecting achievement of activist goals have assessed only a limited range of these factors.[30]

On the next two pages of this chapter, therefore, a table has been produced that compiles all of the main factors cited in the literature, together with a number of factors that have yet to be analysed.[31] The criteria listed in this table relate to the domestic and international environments in which activists operate, as well as to the characteristics of activists themselves and the issues they promote.

---

[27] Richard Price, 'Transnational Civil Society and Advocacy in World Politics,' *World Politics*, 55 (2003), p. 586.

[28] Quotation from Thomas Risse-Kappen, 'Bringing Transnational Relations Back In: Introduction' in Risse-Kappen, *Bringing Transnational Relations Back In*, p. 5. In addition to the volume by Risse-Kappen, the principal works that have addressed this question include: Joe Bandy and Jackie Smith (eds.), *Coalitions Across Borders: Transnational Protest and the Neoliberal Order* (Lanham, MD, 2005); Susan Burgerman, *Moral Victories: How Activists Provoke Multilateral Action* (Ithaca, NY, 2001); Michael Edwards and John Gaventa (eds.), *Global Citizen Action* (London, 2001); Alan Thomas, Susan Carr and David Humphreys (eds.), *Environmental Policies and NGO Influence: Land Degradation and Sustainable Resource Management in Sub-Saharan Africa* (London, 2001); Azeez Mehdi Khan, *Shaping Policy: Do NGOs Matter? Lessons from India* (New Dehli, 1997); Bas Arts, *The Political Influence of Global NGOs: Case Studies on the Climate and Biodiversity Conventions* (Utrecht, 1998); Ann Marie Clark, Elisabeth J. Friedman and Kathryn Hochstetler, 'The Sovereign Limits of Global Civil Society: A Comparison of NGO Participation in UN World Conferences on the Environment, Human Rights, and Women,' *World Politics*, 51/1 (1998), pp. 1–35; Price, 'Transnational Civil Society and Advocacy in World Politics;' Risse, 'Transnational Actors and World Politics;' and Keck and Sikkink, *Activists Beyond Borders*.

[29] Contrast, for example, the conclusions of Arts, *Political Influence of Global NGOs*, with those of Clark, Friedman and Hochstetler in 'Sovereign Limits of Global Civil Society.'

[30] Risse-Kappen, *Bringing Transnational Relations Back In*, for example, assesses only the role of international institutions and domestic structures (see esp. pp. 14–32).

[31] The contents of table one are derived from, *inter alia*, the books and articles listed in footnote 28.

Table 1. Factors Facilitating or Inhibiting Achievement of Transnational Activist Objectives.

	FACTORS *FACILITATING* ACHIEVEMENT OF ACTIVIST OBJECTIVES	FACTORS *INHIBITING* ACHIEVEMENT OF ACTIVIST OBJECTIVES
CHARACTERISTICS OF THE INTERNATIONAL ENVIRONMENT	1) 'Existence of international codes and legislation' that provide legitimacy for activist objectives.[32] 2) 'The presence of international governmental organisations…that facilitate network development.'[33]	1) Existence of 'international political conflict.'[34] 2) Presence of global economic crisis.
CHARACTERISTICS OF THE NATIONAL ENVIRONMENT	3) Existence of an 'open' political system.[35] 4) Presence of 'a key element of the domestic political elite, one capable of exerting its authority over armed elements,' that is sensitive to activist demands.[36]	3) Existence of a 'closed' political system. 4) Existence of substantial opposition in government structures. 5) Existence of substantial non-governmental opposition.
CHARACTERISTICS OF THE ACTIVISTS THEMSELVES	5) Leadership of 'active individuals.'[37] 6) The existence of 'well-organised national movements.'[38] 7) The presence of 'an active international campaign.'[39] 8) Activist 'expertise,' 'experience, professionalism & work record.'[40]	6) Susceptibility to accusations of having a 'hidden' or self-serving agenda.[41] 7) *Promotion of an inconsistent/ incoherent programme.*

---

[32] Jennifer Chapman, 'What Makes International Campaigns Effective? Lessons from India and Ghana' in Edwards and Gaventa, *Global Citizen Action*, p. 263.

[33] Bandy and Smith, *Coalitions Across Borders*, p. 232.

[34] Bandy and Smith, *Coalitions Across Borders*, p. 236.

[35] John D. McCarthy, 'The Globalization of Social Movement Theory,' in Pagnucco, Chatfield and Smith, *Transnational Social Movements*, p. 255.

[36] Burgerman, *Moral Victories*, p. 5.

[37] Chapman, 'What Makes International Campaigns Effective?,' p. 263.

[38] Bandy and Smith, *Coalitions Across Borders*, p. 233.

[39] Chapman, 'What Makes International Campaigns Effective?,' p. 263.

[40] Khan, *Shaping Policy*, pp. 19–20.

[41] Khan, *Shaping Policy*, p. 21.

Table 1 (*cont.*)

	FACTORS *FACILITATING* ACHIEVEMENT OF ACTIVIST OBJECTIVES	FACTORS *INHIBITING* ACHIEVEMENT OF ACTIVIST OBJECTIVES
CHARACTERISTICS OF THE ISSUE-AREA TARGETED	9) ' "Low politics" issue-areas such as environmental and economic issues.'[42]	8) 'High politics' issue-areas such as security. 9) Activist objectives that, if achieved, would bring about fundamental change in international relations.[43]

---

[42] Risse-Kappen, *Bringing Transnational Relations Back In*, p. 305.

[43] The nature of fundamental change in international relations is outlined on page 166.

CHAPTER TWO

THE INTERWAR DISARMAMENT CAMPAIGN:
A TEST CASE

This chapter sets out the purposes of this book. It shows how this
book, by using the evidence of the interwar disarmament campaign
to test the assertions outlined in chapter one, reveals if there are any
general propositions about the role of transnational activism in world
affairs that can be empirically supported. This chapter also describes
the important contribution that this book makes to the literature on
the evolution of international relations in the period between the two
World Wars. The methodology and sources used in this book, and the
structure of the chapters that follow, are also described.

THE INTERWAR DISARMAMENT CAMPAIGN AS A CASE STUDY OF TRANSNATIONAL ACTIVISM

The global campaign for disarmament that took place in the period
between the two World Wars is a uniquely valuable case study. It is
an exceptionally clear example of transnational activism as defined on
pages six and seven of the first chapter: the contentious transnational
public goal of general disarmament was promoted by numerous global
non-state actors which used transnational methods to target actors in
many countries. Furthermore, the scale of the campaign was remarkable: in terms of the proportion of the world's population that participated directly or indirectly in the campaign, it has arguably never
been matched before or since.[1]

A study of the interwar disarmament campaign also has two distinct
advantages over studies of contemporary transnational activism. First,
all of the necessary activist and governmental sources are available for
consultation. And secondly, there is the benefit of distance in time from
the events described. This enables an examination of the complete history of the movement and its impact from a less partial perspective.

---

[1] For a full assessment of the comparative scale of the campaign, see chapter 11.

Simply by providing an assessment of the evolution and impact of the campaign for disarmament between the two World Wars, this book is an important addition to the literature on transnational activism. This is because of the crucial differences between this study of the interwar disarmament campaign and the other case studies of transnational activist campaigns that have already been undertaken.

The first difference lies in the goals of the movement under examination. Many of the case studies of transnational activism that have so far been undertaken have been of campaigns with highly limited objectives, such as environmental standards or the Ottawa landmines convention.[2] The movement studied in this book, on the other hand, attempted *fundamentally* to change the nature of international relations by campaigning for a global convention for general and comprehensive disarmament.

Secondly, this book also differs from the small number of studies that *have* examined activist campaigns that promoted more ambitious objectives, such as Matthew Evangelista's investigation of the organisations that he claims 'contributed to…the end of the Cold War.'[3] Whereas the organisations studied by Evangelista were only one element among many necessary for a complete explanation of the end of the Cold War, the organisations studied in this book represented the *principal* driving force behind the movement for the creation of a multilateral disarmament convention.

A third way in which this book differs from the majority of studies of activist influence is that it is concerned as much with the *failures*

---

[2] On the International Campaign to Ban Landmines, see Don Hubert, *The Landmine Ban: A Case Study in Humanitarian Advocacy* (Providence, RI, 2000); Maxwell A. Cameron, Robert J. Lawson and Brian W. Tomlin (eds.), *To Walk Without Fear: The Global Movement to Ban Landmines* (Toronto, 1998); Kenneth Anderson, 'The Ottawa Convention Banning Landmines, the Role of International Non-Governmental Organizations and the Idea of International Civil Society,' *European Journal of International Law*, 11/1 (2000), pp. 91–120; Nicole Short, 'The Role of NGOs in the Ottawa Process to Ban Landmines,' *International Negotiation*, 4/3 (1999), pp. 483–502; Motoko Mekata, 'Building Partnerships toward a Common Goal: Experiences of the International Campaign to Ban Landmines' in Ann M. Florini, (ed.), *The Third Force: The Rise of Transnational Civil Society* (Tokyo, 2000), pp. 143–76; and Richard Price, 'Reversing the Gun Sights: Transnational Civil Society Targets Landmines,' *International Organization*, 52/3 (2000), pp. 613–44.

[3] Quotation from Thomas Risse-Kappen (ed.), *Bringing Transnational Relations Back In: Non-State Actors, Domestic Structures and International Institutions* (Cambridge, 1995), p. 280; the argument is most fully outlined in Matthew Evangelista, *Unarmed Forces: The Transnational Movement to End the Cold War* (Ithaca, NY, 1999).

as with the successes of the global campaign for disarmament in the period between the two World Wars. As Thomas Risse has noted of the existing literature: although 'there are many single case-studies of successful transnational campaigns... we know much less about failed campaigns.'[4] This is an important problem with the existing literature, since for those who wish to learn how to conduct a successful campaign, it is essential to know what may prevent achievement of objectives.

It should be noted that there are a very small number of works that have investigated campaign failures, such as Sarah E. Mendelson and John K. Glenn's work on democracy-building in the former Soviet bloc which describes how, despite activist success in the establishment of democratic institutions, activists failed to influence the way in which the institutions subsequently functioned.[5] Another example is David Cortright and Ron Pagnucco's examination of the failure of the 1980s nuclear freeze campaign.[6] However, neither of these campaigns was comparable in scale to that of the campaign for disarmament in the period between the two World Wars.

Furthermore, this book is much more ambitious in its objectives than simply providing a case study of an activist campaign and its influence. It seeks also to answer a fundamentally important question about global civil society and transnational activism that has not yet been answered: are there any general propositions about the role of transnational activism in world affairs that can be justified empirically?

The literature summarised in chapter one has produced a number of propositions that have yet to be tested. For example, is the claim that global civil society is 'an arena of virtue that overcomes domination in government'[7] justifiable? That particular question involves a normative judgement to which no definitive answer can be given on the basis of empirical data alone. However, the more sophisticated literature from

---

[4] Thomas Risse, 'Transnational Actors and World Politics' in Walter Carlsnaes, Thomas Risse and Beth A. Simmons (eds.), *Handbook of International Relations* (London, 2002), p. 264.

[5] Sarah E. Mendelson and John K. Glenn (eds.), *The Power and Limits of NGOs: A Critical Look at Building Democracy in Eastern Europe and Eurasia* (New York, 2002).

[6] David Cortright and Ron Pagnucco, 'Limits to Transnationalism: *The 1980s Freeze Campaign*' in Jackie Smith, Charles Chatfield, and Ron Pagnucco (eds.), *Transnational Social Movements and World Politics: Solidarity beyond the State* (Syracuse, NY, 1997), pp. 159–74.

[7] Quotation from Jan Aart Scholte, *Globalization: A Critical Introduction* (Basingstoke, 2000), p. 277, citing David C. Korten, *Getting to the 21st Century: Voluntary Action and the Global Agenda* (Hartford, CT, 1990) and Richard A. Falk, *On Humane Governance: Toward a New Global Politics* (Cambridge, 1995).

which table one is derived provides a set of empirically testable propositions as to which factors influence achievement of activist objectives. The assessment in Part V of this book therefore examines each of the factors listed in table one using the evidence provided by the interwar disarmament campaign, and addresses the question: are the factors listed in table one, either individually or in combination, sufficient conditions for achievement of or failure to achieve activist objectives? It finds that only one proposition (highlighted in italics in table one) is supported by the evidence provided in this book, and represents the only generalisation that can be made about the role of transnational activism in world politics on the basis of the evidence supplied in this book.

The Contribution of this Book to the Historiography of the Interwar Years

Although this study is intended to provide new insights into the role of transnational activism in world affairs, it is also intended to fill a significant gap in the historical literature on the international relations of the period between the two World Wars. Even though the pursuit of general disarmament was one of the principal problems with which statesmen had to deal during the period 1919–1934, there are very few studies of the subject. Furthermore, despite the scale and significance of the transnational non-governmental campaign for general disarmament, it has been almost entirely neglected in the existing historical literature. One of the principal reasons for this is the failure of the movement for general disarmament to result in a convention embodying that ideal.[8] The more successful movement for naval disarmament, by comparison, has received considerable attention.[9]

---

[8] For example, the principal disarmament activist of the interwar years, Viscount Cecil of Chelwood, scarcely mentions his pro-disarmament activities in his autobiography, *A Great Experiment* (London, 1941), choosing instead to concentrate on his more successful work.

[9] On the history of naval disarmament between the two World Wars, see Christopher Hall, *Britain, America and Arms Control, 1921–1937* (London, 1987); Richard W. Fanning, *Peace and Disarmament: Naval Rivalry and Arms Control, 1922–1933* (Lexington, KY, 1995); C. Leonard Hoag, *Preface to Preparedness: The Washington Disarmament Conference and Public Opinion* (Washington, DC, 1941); and Robert Gordon Kaufman, *Arms Control during the Pre-Nuclear Era: The United States and Naval Disarmament between the two World Wars* (New York, 1990).

The principal focus for those historians who have examined the pursuit of general disarmament in the period between the two World Wars has been the evolution of the disarmament policies of particular states. On British policy, for example, there are several works by Carolyn Kitching, Dick Richardson and David Shorney.[10] On German policy, there are substantial books written by Edward W. Bennett and Sten Nadolny;[11] while on the United States, there is the work of Merze Tate, Fred Herbert Winkler and David Cornelius Deboe.[12] As for French disarmament policy, there is a body of literature by Maurice Vaïsse, Lamri Chirouf, John L. Hogge II, Peter Jackson, and the author of this book.[13] There are also a few studies of the evolution of the inter-war disarmament negotiations from an international perspective.[14]

---

[10] Carolyn Kitching, *Britain and the Geneva Disarmament Conference: A Study in International History* (Basingstoke, 2002); Carolyn Kitching, *Britain and the Problem of International Disarmament, 1919–1934* (London, 1999); Dick Richardson and Carolyn Kitching, 'Britain and the World Disarmament Conference,' in P. Catterall and C. J. Morris (eds.), *Britain and the Threat to Stability in Europe, 1918–1945* (Leicester, 1993), pp. 35–56; Dick Richardson, 'The Geneva Disarmament Conference, 1932–1934' in Dick Richardson and Glyn Stone (eds.), *Decisions and Diplomacy: Essays in Twentieth Century International History: In Memory of George Grun and Esmonde Robertson* (London, 1995), pp. 60–82; Dick Richardson, *The Evolution of British Disarmament Policy in the 1920s* (London, 1989); and David Shorney, *Britain and Disarmament, 1916–1931* (PhD thesis, University of Durham, 1980).

[11] Edward W. Bennett, *German Rearmament and the West, 1932–1933* (Princeton, NJ, 1979) and Sten Nadolny, *Abruestungsdiplomatie, 1932/3: Deutschland auf der Genfer Konferenz im Uebergang von Weimar zu Hitler* (Munich, 1978).

[12] Merze Tate, *The United States and Armaments* (Cambridge, MA, 1948); Fred Herbert Winkler, *The United States and the World Disarmament Conference, 1926–1935: A Study of the Formulation of Foreign Policy* (PhD thesis, Northwestern University, 1957); and David Cornelius Deboe, *The United States and the Geneva Disarmament Conference, 1932–1934* (PhD thesis, Tulane University, 1969).

[13] Maurice Vaïsse, *Sécurité d'abord: la politique française en matière de désarmement, 9 décembre 1930–17 avril 1934* (Paris, 1981); Lamri Chirouf, *The French Approach to Disarmament, 1920–1930: Policy Making Process, Principles and Methods* (PhD thesis, Southampton University, 1989); John L. Hogge II, *Arbitrage, Sécurité, Désarmement: French Security and the League of Nations, 1920–1925* (DPhil thesis, New York University, 1994); Peter Jackson, 'France and the Problems of Security and Disarmament after the First World War,' *The Journal of Strategic Studies*, 29/2 (2006), pp. 247–280; and Thomas R. Davies, 'France and the World Disarmament Conference of 1932–34,' *Diplomacy & Statecraft*, 15/4 (2004), pp. 765–780.

[14] John W. Wheeler-Bennett, *Disarmament and Security since Locarno, 1925–1931: Being the Political and Technical Background of the General Disarmament Conference, 1932* (London, 1932); John W. Wheeler-Bennett, *The Disarmament Deadlock* (London, 1934); John W. Wheeler-Bennett, *Information on the Reduction of Armaments* (London, 1925); Adelphia Dane Bowen, *The Disarmament Movement, 1918–1935* (PhD thesis, Columbia University, 1956); Major-General Arthur Cecil Temperley, *The Whispering Gallery of Europe* (London, 1938); Farajollah Ardalan, *The League of Nations and Disarmament: National Policies and Concepts of Sovereignty, Security and Peace, 1919–1934* (PhD thesis, University of Akron,

However, little reference is made in any of this literature to the role of the international non-governmental campaign for disarmament. In fact, in several of these works the role of non-governmental activism is deliberately neglected.[15]

The one body of literature that has investigated the activities of the interwar disarmament campaign is that on the history of the peace movement in the period between the two World Wars. Martin Ceadel, Donald Birn and Cecelia Lynch have outlined the activities of the British peace movement in the promotion of disarmament,[16] while Charles Chatfield and Cecelia Lynch have described the activities of the US peace movement.[17]

Of these authors, only Cecelia Lynch has systematically examined the impact of peace activism on government policy and investigated the global as well as the national peace movement's activities in the promotion of disarmament. However, Lynch's primary concern with national peace movement activity means that only five pages of her principal work, *Beyond Appeasement*, are dedicated to the study of the global disarmament campaign.[18] Furthermore, the role of the secondary peace movement[19] both nationally and internationally, and of the disarmament campaign in France, has been neglected by all of these authors.[20]

1980); Subhakanta Behera, *The Politics of Disarmament, 1919–1939: A Study of the World Disarmament Conference* (Vidyapuri, 1990); Maurice Vaïsse, 'Security and Disarmament: Problems in the Development of the Disarmament Debates, 1919–1934' in R. Ahmann, A. M. Birke and M. Howard (eds.), *The Quest for Stability: Problems of West European Security, 1918–1957* (London, 1993), pp. 173–200; Andrew Webster, 'The Transnational Dream: Politicians, Diplomats and Soldiers in the League of Nations' Pursuit of International Disarmament, 1920–1938,' *Contemporary European History*, 14/4 (2005), pp. 493–518; and B. J. C. McKercher, 'Of Horns and Teeth: The Preparatory Commission and the World Disarmament Conference, 1926–1934' in B. J. C. McKercher (ed.), *Arms Limitation and Disarmament: Restraints on War, 1899–1939* (Westport, CT, 1992), pp. 173–201.

[15] See, for example, Kitching, *Britain and the Geneva Disarmament Conference*, p. 210.

[16] Martin Ceadel, *Semi-Detached Idealists: The British Peace Movement and International Relations, 1854–1945* (Oxford, 2000); Donald Birn, *The League of Nations Union, 1918–1945* (Oxford, 1981); and Cecelia Lynch, 'A Matter of Controversy: The Peace Movement and British Arms Policy in the Interwar Period' in McKercher, *Arms Limitation and Disarmament*, pp. 61–82.

[17] Charles Chatfield, *For Peace and Justice: Pacifism In America, 1914–1941* (Knoxville, TN, 1971); and Cecelia Lynch, *Beyond Appeasement: Interpreting Interwar Peace Movements in World Politics* (Ithaca, NY, 1999).

[18] Lynch, *Beyond Appeasement*, pp. 183–7.

[19] On the distinction between the primary and secondary peace movements, see chapter 4.

[20] Norman Ingram's study of the French peace movement, *The Politics of Dissent: Pacifism in France 1919–1939* (Oxford, 1991) makes almost no reference to the disarmament campaign in France.

The most comprehensive assessment of the activities of the interwar disarmament campaign is contained in an account of the World Disarmament Conference of 1932–34 by one of the leading activists, Philip Noel Baker.[21] However, as Carolyn Kitching has noted, it is a 'rather idiosyncratic analysis…influenced, not unnaturally, by his position as personal assistant to the President of the Disarmament Conference.'[22]

This book, on the other hand, examines from a less partial perspective both the transnational disarmament campaign and the national campaigns in Britain, France and the United States; investigates the promotion of disarmament by the secondary as well as the primary peace movement; and draws conclusions on the impact of activism on government policy on the basis of a systematic examination of national and international official records.

CLASSICAL METHOD

Analysing Activist Influence

Since this book not only describes the evolution and activities of the interwar disarmament campaign, but also examines the *influence* of the campaign, it is necessary to make clear from the outset *how* this influence is examined. As Robert Dahl has pointed out, 'no matter how precisely one defines influence and no matter how elegant the measures and methods one proposes, the data within reach even of the most assiduous researcher require the use of operational measures that are at best somewhat unsatisfactory.'[23] The method used in this book is therefore 'classical' in Hedley Bull's terms, i.e. it 'is characterised above all by explicit reliance on judgement and by the assumption that if we confine ourselves to strict standards of verification and proof there is very little of significance that can be said about international relations.'[24]

'Influence' in this book refers to the actions and policies of governments that can be shown to have been (at least partly) a response to

---

[21] Philip Noel-Baker, *The First World Disarmament Conference, 1932–1934, And Why It Failed* (Oxford, 1979), pp. 73–4.

[22] Kitching, *Britain and the Geneva Disarmament Conference*, p. 2.

[23] Robert A. Dahl, *Who Governs? Democracy and Power in an American City* (New Haven, CT, 1961), p. 330.

[24] Hedley Bull, 'International Theory: The Case for a Classical Approach,' *World Politics*, 18 (1966), p. 361.

activist pressure. This definition has been selected because it includes responses to activism that fall short of achievement of activist objectives, since the interwar disarmament campaigners failed to achieve their principal goal of the creation of an 'international convention' that would provide for 'a substantial reduction in armaments.'[25] The focus on impact upon *government* action and policy has been chosen because governments were the main actors targeted by the interwar disarmament activists.

The claims made in this book about activism's influence are derived from the reasons cited by senior policymakers for their decisions in official and private correspondence.[26] This research has an important advantage over that on contemporary transnational activism in that all the necessary primary sources are open for consultation. In contrast, most existing approaches to the study of activist influence, including the 'EAC (Ego-perception, Alter-perception, Causal analysis)' method adopted by Bas Arts in the most systematic existing effort to analyse NGO influence, rely almost entirely on the least reliable form of evidence: interviews with activists and policymakers.[27]

Since this book adopts the classical method, *judgement* has been used in order to determine whether or not references in the primary sources to the role of activism in influencing outcomes are reliable. Stated concerns about the role of activism have been balanced against all the other factors expressed as being important, as well as those not explicitly mentioned, and judgement has been used in distinguishing genuine reasons from excuses. For example, activism is described in this book as the principal reason for French War Minister Joseph Paul-Boncour's introduction of the 'Constructive Plan' of November 1932 because it is the principal reason cited in his private as well as his

---

[25] Articles 1 and 2 of the Budapest Resolution in International Federation of League of Nations Societies, *XV Plenary Congress of the International Federation of League of Nations Societies, Budapest, 1931* (Brussels, 1931), pp. 156–7. The complete text of this resolution is provided in appendix vi of this book.

[26] This method has been used in the case of all claims of activist influence in chapters 7–9, on which the conclusions of this book are primarily based. In the case of the introductory chapters 3, 5 and 6, claims of activist influence are derived from a combination of primary and secondary sources: secondary sources are mainly used in the case of the naval disarmament process since there is already a considerable body of secondary literature on naval disarmament.

[27] Bas Arts, *The Political Influence of Global NGOs: Case Studies on the Climate and Biodiversity Conventions* (Utrecht, 1998), pp. 80–3.

official correspondence, and because there is no satisfactory alternative explanation.[28]

Chronological Organisation

Parts III and IV of this book are organised chronologically. There are three principal reasons for the adoption of this method of organisation. First, since no comprehensive study of the history of disarmament activism in the interwar years exists, a chronological account is necessary to fill the gap in the historical literature. Secondly, a chronological account is the only effective way to provide a 'thick description' of the influence of disarmament activism on particular outcomes. Thirdly, presenting the material in a chronological fashion in Parts III and IV ensures that the analysis in Part V can be written concisely, since the detailed justification of the empirical examples (of activist influence, etc.) cited in the analysis in Part V will already have been provided in the earlier chapters.

Testing General Propositions on Transnational Activism

As was indicated on page thirteen, this book is intended to provide more than simply a detailed outline of one activist campaign and its influence. The assessment in Part V seeks to discover if there are any general propositions about the role of transnational activism in world politics that survive being tested against empirical evidence.

The set of factors that are supposed to facilitate or inhibit achievement of activist objectives listed in table one has been adopted as the set of propositions to be tested, since these represent the principal assertions put forward in the most advanced literature to have been produced on the subject to date.

The method that is used in Part V to test the propositions is as follows. Each proposition is examined in turn to see if the evidence from the experience of the interwar global disarmament campaign supports or disproves it. Any proposition that is disproved by the evidence of the interwar disarmament campaign cannot be considered to be a justifiable generalisation about the role of transnational activism in world affairs

---

[28] See chapter 9 for a detailed explanation of the origins of the Paul-Boncour plan.

and is rejected.[29] In the case of the factors listed in table one as facilitative of achievement of activist objectives, all those that are shown to have been present in the case of the interwar disarmament campaign are rejected as sufficient conditions for the realisation of activist goals (since the interwar disarmament campaigners failed to achieve their primary objective of a global disarmament convention).

Those propositions that are not disproved by the evidence of the interwar disarmament campaign are then tested against the evidence provided in other existing studies of transnational activist influence. In the case of the factors cited as inhibitive of achievement of activist goals, all those that are shown in other existing studies of transnational activist influence to have been present in the case of campaigns that successfully achieved their objectives are rejected as sufficient conditions for the prevention of achievement of activist goals.

The one proposition that survives being tested against the evidence of both the interwar disarmament campaign and the other existing studies of activist influence may alone be considered to be a general truth about the role of transnational activism in world affairs. It should preserve this status until a satisfactory counterexample can be found.

Since this book adopts the classical method, judgement on the basis of the available evidence is the approach used throughout the proposition-testing process. The interwar disarmament campaign has been selected as the principal case study for the reasons outlined at the beginning of this chapter: it is a particularly clear example of transnational activism, all of the necessary activist and governmental sources are available for consultation, and an impartial assessment is possible due to the distance in time from the events described.

---

[29] The evidence of the interwar global disarmament campaign is sufficient to reach this conclusion because it is arguably what Harry Eckstein has referred to as a 'critical case' in the sense of being a case that you would least expect to disprove these propositions (See Harry Eckstein, 'Case Study and Theory in Political Science,' in Fred I. Greenstein and Nelson W. Polsby (eds.), *Handbook of Political Science*, vol. 7, *Strategies of Inquiry* (Reading, MA, 1975), pp. 79–138). For instance, in the case of the factors cited in table one as facilitating achievement of activist objectives, chapter 11 shows that these factors were often present to a greater degree in this case than in any other, so this is a case you would least expect to result in an outcome contradictory to the proposition that these factors facilitate achievement of activist objectives.

SOURCES CONSULTED

Well over forty international non-governmental organisations representing between 200,000 and a billion people of a hundred nationalities participated in the global disarmament campaign of the interwar years. The governments of nearly every state in the international system were targeted. It has therefore been necessary to limit the sources consulted to those relating to the most significant activists and governments.

With respect to the transnational activist bodies, the focus has been limited to the organisations that: (i) participated in the main body that co-ordinated the global disarmament campaign (the International Consultative Group for Peace and Disarmament); and/or (ii) participated in the special session of the World Disarmament Conference of 6 February 1932 at which the principal INGO demands were presented. In the case of the actors the activists targeted, concentration has been limited to the institutions of the League of Nations and the governments of Great Britain, France and the United States, which were the principal states that the campaigners believed were fundamental to ensuring realisation of their objectives. Since the global campaign grew out of the national campaigns in Great Britain and the United States, and since the governments of Great Britain, the United States and France were the three principal targets of the global campaign, domestic activism within each of these three countries has also been assessed.

The principal primary sources on the transnational dimension of the disarmament movement that were consulted were the archives of the principal global organisations that co-ordinated the disarmament campaign, namely the International Consultative Group for Peace and Disarmament, the Disarmament Committees of Women's, Students' and Christian Organisations, the International Federation of League of Nations Societies, the Women's International League for Peace and Freedom, the World Alliance for Promoting International Friendship through the Churches, the Labour and Socialist International, and the International Federation of Trade Unions. The archives of a number of organisations that played a less prominent role in the disarmament campaign, such as the International Co-operative Women's Guild, the International Student Service and the World's YMCAs and YWCAs, were also consulted.

The main archival sources that were examined on the domestic campaigns in Great Britain, France and the United States were the records of the principal national peace societies and the national co-ordinating bodies. In the case of the British campaign, the archives of the principal peace organisation—the League of Nations Union—were consulted, as well as the records of the National Peace Council and the British branch of the Women's International League for Peace and Freedom. In the case of the US campaign, the archives of the Interorganization Council on Disarmament, the National Council for Prevention of War and the US branch of the Women's International League for Peace and Freedom were assessed.

Since many of these archives are incomplete, especially with respect to the activities of the disarmament campaign in France, the principal activist periodicals were also examined. The most useful resource on the activities of the French disarmament movement was the leading journal of the pacificist peace movement in France, *La Paix par le Droit*; while one of the most helpful sources on the global campaign during the World Disarmament Conference was the journal of the Disarmament Information Committee, simply entitled *Disarmament*. Pamphlets, autobiographies and other publications by the activists have also been assessed.

In addition to the records and publications of the organisations that promoted disarmament, the private papers of the leading individual activists have been consulted, including the papers of British campaigners such as Viscount Cecil of Chelwood, Gilbert Murray, Philip Noel Baker, Margery Corbett Ashby and Kathleen Courtney; French activists such as Henry de Jouvenel, Louise Weiss, Pierre Cot, Jules Prudhommeaux and Gabrielle Duchêne; and US campaigners such as James T. Shotwell and Laura Puffer Morgan.

Since this is a study of activist influence on government policy, national and international official records have also been examined. At the international level, the principal official sources consulted were the records of the League of Nations Secretariat, especially the Disarmament Section files. In the case of Great Britain, the main official sources that were assessed were the Cabinet minutes (CAB 23), the Foreign Office records (especially the general correspondence contained in FO 371), and the records of the Committee of Imperial Defence and its disarmament sub-committees. The principal French official sources that were consulted were the archives of the League of Nations section of the French Foreign Ministry and the records of the main disarmament decision-making body in France, the *Conseil Supérieur de la Défense Nationale*. In the case of US sources, the most useful official records that were examined were contained in the Department of State Decimal File (RG 59).

In addition to these unpublished primary sources, the main published official records on the subject have also been consulted, including the records of the meetings of League organs such as the Council, the Assembly, the Temporary Mixed Commission, the Preparatory Commission, and the World Disarmament Conference. Also examined were the published official documents of Great Britain, France and the United States, including *British Documents on Foreign Affairs*, *Documents on British Foreign Policy*, *Documents Diplomatiques Français* and *Papers Relating to the Foreign Relations of the United States*.

The most helpful resource with respect to determining which factors motivated statesmen's decisions was the private correspondence of the principal policymakers. The correspondence assessed includes that of: British Prime Ministers Stanley Baldwin and James Ramsay MacDonald; British Foreign Secretaries Sir John Simon, Sir Austen Chamberlain and the Marquess of Reading; French Prime Ministers Edouard Daladier, Edouard Herriot, Joseph Paul-Boncour and André Tardieu; US Presidents Herbert Hoover and Franklin D. Roosevelt; US Secretaries of State Henry Stimson and Cordell Hull; US Ambassadors Hugh Gibson and Norman Davis; the President of the World Disarmament Conference Arthur Henderson; and League of Nations Secretary-General Sir Eric Drummond. The memoirs of many of these and other statesmen have also been assessed.

As for the main secondary sources consulted, these fall into three principal categories: (i) general studies on the role of transnational activism/ INGOs in international politics; (ii) biographies of prominent activists and statesmen; and (iii) historical studies of three major aspects of the interwar years: (a) peace movement activity in Great Britain, France and the United States; (b) disarmament policy in Great Britain, France and the United States; and (c) the activities of international governmental and non-governmental organisations. The main collections used were located in the Bodleian Library in Oxford, the British Library and the British Library of Political and Economic Science in London, the French National Library in Paris, the Library of Contemporary International Documentation in Nanterre, the Library of Congress in Washington, DC, New York Public Library, Swarthmore College Peace Collection in Pennsylvania, the Hoover Institution Library in California, the International Institute of Social History in Amsterdam and the United Nations Library in Geneva.

Outline of this Book

This book is divided into five parts. The first part (chapters one and two) has introduced this book's purposes, its contribution to political science and international history, and the methodology and sources used.

The second part introduces the interwar disarmament campaign. Chapter three outlines the origins of the movement, while chapter four describes the characteristics of the principal non-governmental organisations that participated in the global campaign for disarmament.

The third and fourth parts outline the evolution of the disarmament movement and its impact in chronological sequence. Part III delineates the origins and growth of the campaign for disarmament between 1919 and 1930. Chapter five describes how the first national movements for disarmament emerged after the Paris Peace Conference, and investigates their impact on the Washington Naval Conference and the first initiatives for disarmament through the League of Nations. Then chapter six describes the development of disarmament activism during the period between 1926 and 1930, when the establishment of the Preparatory Commission for the World Disarmament Conference and the convening of the London Naval Conference proved to be significant stimuli for the emergence of a *transnational* campaign.

Part IV outlines the activities and influence of the global disarmament campaign during its peak years of 1931 to 1933. The seventh chapter describes how in 1931 *super*-international non-governmental organisations were established to co-ordinate the disarmament-promoting activities of numerous different international non-governmental organisations. Then the eighth and ninth chapters outline the impact of the transnational disarmament campaign upon developments at the World Disarmament Conference that opened in February 1932 and collapsed in October 1933.

The fifth and final part of this book is the concluding assessment. Chapter ten summarises the findings of the previous five chapters with respect to the influence achieved by the interwar disarmament campaign. After that, chapter eleven performs the crucial task using the evidence of the interwar disarmament campaign to discover whether or not there are any general propositions about the role of transnational activism in world politics that are justifiable. The material provided in the previous six chapters is used to test the propositions about the factors affecting achievement of activist goals contained in table one. The propositions that are not eliminated in this assessment are then tested against the empirical evidence provided in other studies of transnational activism. Finally, chapter twelve summarises the findings of chapter eleven and describes in depth the proposition that survives both tests and the possible lessons for transnational activism that arise from it.

PART TWO

BACKGROUND TO THE DISARMAMENT CAMPAIGN

CHAPTER THREE

ROOTS, PRECURSORS AND PRECEDENTS

Part II of this book provides the background material necessary to understand the campaign for disarmament that took place in the period between the two World Wars. In chapter four, the principal organisations that participated in the interwar disarmament campaign will be introduced. This chapter, on the other hand, describes the pre-1919 developments that helped to make the interwar movement possible. The first of these developments was the emergence in the late eighteenth century of the idea that war could be prevented. This was followed in the early nineteenth century by the foundation of the first national associations explicitly devoted to the promotion of peace. By the middle of the nineteenth century, the first international non-governmental organisations had been established, which greatly facilitated transnational activism. The first notable example of a transnational campaign for disarmament took place during the Hague Conferences of 1899 and 1907, which set several important precedents for the much larger campaign of the interwar years. Finally, the First World War witnessed the transformation of the peace movement and the establishment of many of the international non-governmental organisations that were to lead the interwar disarmament campaign.

EMERGENCE OF PEACE ACTIVISM

Martin Ceadel has pointed out that peace activism was made possible by intellectual developments in the eighteenth century, when the fatalistic assumption that war was inevitable began to be challenged by 'a belief that human agency could limit the incidence of war,' at least between 'civilised' countries.[1] A transnational dimension was evident even at this early stage, since the belief developed simultaneously throughout Europe and North America, with eighteenth-century philosophers including

---

[1] Martin Ceadel, *Semi-Detached Idealists: The British Peace Movement and International Relations, 1854–1945* (Oxford, 2000), p. 13.

Bentham, Kant and Rousseau outlining the possible mechanisms for preventing international conflict. Of high importance to these authors was the reduction and limitation of armaments. While Rousseau noted the financial savings to be gained by disarmament, Kant and Bentham had specific disarmament proposals: Kant advocated the abolition of standing armies, while Bentham proposed treaties to reduce and limit the armaments of all countries.[2]

An equally important development took place the following century, when the promotion of peace became organised for the first time when 'Peace Societies' were established simultaneously in Britain and the United States in the aftermath of the Anglo-American and Napoleonic Wars.[3] W. H. van der Linden has pointed out that initially disarmament was of little interest to these Christian pacifist organisations.[4] However, by the mid-nineteenth century the promotion of disarmament had become one of their primary goals and the principal modes of agitation for disarmament were developed, such as resolutions and petitions. Between 1845 and 1853, for instance, over 600,000 people signed petitions in support of disarmament in Britain, although the impact on government policy was negligible.[5]

As Ceadel has noted, Britain and the United States were exceptional in their geographical detachment from continental Europe and their liberal political cultures.[6] They therefore took the lead in developing a European movement. For example, Stephen Rigaud of Britain's Peace Society toured Europe and promoted the formation of the first continental peace associations, such as the *Société de la Paix de Paris*, established in 1844.[7] At the same time, the first attempts at transnational co-ordination of peace activism took place when British pacifists promoted a series

---

[2] See the text of Immanuel Kant's *Perpetual Peace* in Hans Reiss, (ed.), *Kant: Political Writings* (Cambridge, 1991), pp. 93–130; and the text of Jeremy Bentham's *Plan for a Universal and Perpetual Peace* and Jean-Jacques Rousseau's *Jugement sur le Projet de Paix Perpétuelle de l'Abbé de Saint-Pierre* in Frédéric Ramel (ed.), *Philosophie des Relations Internationales* (Paris, 2002), pp. 276–8 and 238–47.

[3] See Martin Ceadel, *The Origins of War Prevention: The British Peace Movement and International Relations, 1730–1854* (Oxford, 1996), and Wilhelmus Hubertus van der Linden, *The International Peace Movement, 1815–1874* (Amsterdam, 1987).

[4] van der Linden, *International Peace Movement*, p. 54.

[5] Christina Phelps Harris, *The Anglo-American Peace Movement in the Mid-Nineteenth Century* (New York, 1930), pp. 82, 171–2. See Also Merze Tate, *The Disarmament Illusion: The Movement for a Limitation of Armaments to 1907* (New York, 1942), p. 10.

[6] Ceadel, *Semi-Detached Idealists*, pp. 18–22.

[7] van der Linden, *International Peace Movement*, pp. 206–16.

of international peace congresses in Europe between 1843 and 1851, at which disarmament became an increasingly important priority.[8]

Despite the setbacks of the Crimean and American Civil Wars, the number of European peace associations expanded considerably after 1867. That year, the *Ligue Internationale et Permanente de la Paix* and the *Ligue Internationale de la Paix et Liberté*[9] were established in Paris and Geneva respectively. By the 1880s, peace associations had been established in Scandinavia and Italy, and the International Arbitration and Peace Association had been founded in Britain. 1887 saw the creation of the *Association de la Paix par le Droit*, a liberal internationalist organisation based in Nîmes, which was to be one of the few primary peace organisations established before the First World War to play a leading role in the interwar disarmament campaign. Finally, the early 1890s saw activism spread to central Europe, with the establishment of small peace societies in Germany and Austria inspired by the charismatic Austrian activist Bertha von Suttner.

EMERGENCE OF INTERNATIONAL NON-GOVERNMENTAL ORGANISATIONS

Before 1889, associations for the promotion of peace were primarily nationally-based organisations. However, the mid-nineteenth century witnessed another development of crucial importance for the emergence of transnational disarmament activism: the establishment of the first private international associations. As Lyman Cromwell White has pointed out: 'Contrary to what might be expected, the first INGOs to be organized were not primarily concerned with the betterment of international relations.'[10] In fact, 'probably the first true international non-governmental organisation to be established in the modern movement' was the World's Alliance of Young Men's Christian Associations.[11]

---

[8] van der Linden, *International Peace Movement*, pp. 148–53, 398ff.

[9] It should be noted that this organisation's claim to be a peace society was undermined by its initial revolutionist desires for 'one last war' to secure their goals. See Ceadel, *Semi-Detached Idealists*, pp. 80–1.

[10] Lyman Cromwell White and Marie Ragonetti Zocca, *International Non-Governmental Organizations: Their Purposes, Methods and Accomplishments* (New Brunswick, 1951), p. 4.

[11] White and Zocca, *International Non-Governmental Organizations*, p. 4. However, some have argued that the British and Foreign Anti-Slavery Society (created in London in 1823) was the first modern INGO (See Charles Chatfield, 'Intergovernmental and Non-Governmental Associations to 1945' in Jackie Smith, Charles Chatfield and Ron Pagnucco (eds.), *Transnational Social Movements and Global Politics: Solidarity Beyond the State* (Syracuse, NY, 1997), p. 21).

This organisation was international from its foundation in 1855, with member associations from Belgium, England, France, Germany, Holland, Scotland, Switzerland and the United States. It was joined in 1864 by the First Socialist International, in 1883 by the World Women's Christian Temperance Union, and in 1888 by the International Council of Women. All of these organisations (or their successors) were to play an important role in the disarmament campaign after the First World War.

By 1889, the first significant international non-governmental organisation for the promotion of peace had been established: the Inter-Parliamentary Union. Two years later, it was joined by the International Peace Bureau, which was created to co-ordinate the annual 'Universal Peace Congresses' that had been revived by the continental European peace movement. The Universal Peace Congresses organised by the Bureau became a focal point for a revival of disarmament activism in the decade following the publication of Suttner's famous pacifist novel, *Die Waffen Nieder!* (*Lay Down Your Arms!*), in 1889. At every Congress between 1889 and 1898, a resolution on disarmament was passed, including a resolution in 1891 calling for 'a Conference of European Powers in order to bring about a mutual, proportional and simultaneous disarmament.'[12] Five years later, women peace activists joined together in a *Ligue Internationale des Femmes pour le Désarmement Général*, which hosted a Congress of international journalists in support of disarmament in November 1896. By 1898, therefore, 'there existed in England, the United States, and to a lesser extent in France and Germany, an inchoate opinion in favour of the limitation of armaments, but this opinion did not exert a great influence upon governments.'[13]

THE HAGUE CONFERENCES

When Tsar Nicholas II issued his Rescript of 27 August 1898, which called for a conference for the limitation of armaments, it was greeted with great enthusiasm by the peace movement. The English activist W. T. Stead even claimed that the Tsar had been influenced by peace

---

[12] Bureau International de la Paix, *Bulletin Officiel du Troisième Congrès International de la Paix tenu à Rome, Novembre 1891* (Rome, 1891), pp. 173–4.

[13] Tate, *Disarmament Illusion*, pp. 158, 162.

movement resolutions, although historians have subsequently demonstrated that 'economic necessity' was the Tsar's primary motive.[14] Nevertheless, the First Hague Conference of 1899 provided the first major opportunity for peace activists to conduct a transnationally co-ordinated disarmament campaign, and the precedents set at this Conference assisted the efforts of the much larger disarmament campaign conducted during the World Disarmament Conference four decades later.

In the build-up to the First Hague Conference, several transnational initiatives were undertaken. One of the most notable was the effort by the German peace activist Margarethe Lenore Selenka to arrange the 'first worldwide Women's Peace Demonstration' three days before the Conference opened. Over five hundred centres were established in eighteen countries to organise the simultaneous women's peace demonstrations that were to be held on 15 May 1899 and at which identical resolutions were to be passed.[15] Other activities included the tours of Europe that were undertaken by Baroness von Suttner and W. T. Stead, both of whom succeeded in gaining audiences with senior politicians including the Tsar. Stead's subsequent initiative—the International Crusade of Peace—met with little success outside his own country, however. Stead had initially planned 'a great pilgrimage of peace throughout all nations, beginning in San Francisco and ending at St. Petersburg,' but he found that support was limited to the two hundred demonstrations that took place in Great Britain.[16]

Once the Conference had begun on 18 May 1899, numerous telegrams, resolutions, letters and pamphlets were sent by activists to delegates.[17] In addition, Bertha von Suttner made herself known at all the social events during the Conference and her salon became 'the focal point for all those interested in what was going on, for delegates, journalists and interviewers, who managed to find out a great deal

---

[14] Thomas K. Ford, 'The Genesis of the First Hague Peace Conference,' *Political Science Quarterly*, 51/3 (1936), p. 381. See also Dan L. Morrill, 'Nicholas II and the Call for the First Hague Conference,' *Journal of Modern History*, 46 (1974), pp. 296–313.

[15] Ute Kaetzel, 'A Radical Women's Rights and Peace Activist: Margarethe Lenore Selenka, Initiator of the First Worldwide Women's Peace Demonstration in 1899,' *Journal of Women's History*, 13/3 (2001), p. 51. Although this article describes the preparations for the demonstrations, it should be noted that there is no account of the actual events of 15 May 1899. It should also be noted that at the time it was not normal for women to be allowed to address public gatherings in many continental European countries.

[16] Ceadel, *Semi-Detached Idealists*, pp. 152–3; Tate, *Disarmament Illusion*, p. 210.

[17] See Andrew D. White's *Autobiography*, vol. 2 (London, 1905), p. 285, cited in Tate, *Disarmament Illusion*, p. 214.

of things and make them public despite the fact that the proceedings were officially secret.'[18] In addition to this, Frau Selenka was given the opportunity to present to the president of the Conference a petition containing over a million signatures gathered by women worldwide.[19]

Despite securing the establishment of a permanent court of arbitration, the First Hague Conference failed to achieve any agreement on the limitation of armaments and merely referred the issue to governments for further study. However, there was one development at the Conference which was to be of much greater importance to disarmament activism in the long-term: the establishment on 28 July of a special commission of the Conference to examine all the petitions and resolutions received by the Bureau, which set the legal precedent that made possible the presentation of the interwar disarmament movement's demands at the start of the World Disarmament Conference on 6 February 1932.[20]

Conflicts in the Far East and South Africa following the First Hague Conference failed to prevent the peace movement from continuing to promote disarmament. Resolutions on the issue were passed at every Universal Peace Congress between 1901 and 1906, as well as at the National Peace Congresses held for the first time in Britain, France and Italy in the early 1900s. The 1904 Universal Peace Congress held in Boston is of particular interest because, as the pre-eminent historian of pre-war disarmament Merze Tate has pointed out, US President Theodore Roosevelt 'promised the Universal Peace Congress to take the initiative in calling a new Conference to continue the work of that of 1899.'[21] The following year, Roosevelt offered the Russian Tsar the opportunity to take the lead in summoning the Second Hague Conference that took place in 1907.[22]

Pressure from members of the British peace movement was important in ensuring that British delegates Sir Henry Campbell-Bannermann and Sir Edward Grey insisted on the inclusion of the limitation of arma-

---

[18] Beatrix Kempf, *Suffragette for Peace: The Life of Bertha von Suttner* (London, 1972), p. 48.

[19] Brigitte Hamann, *Bertha von Suttner: A Life for Peace* (Syracuse, NY, 1996), p. 146; Calvin DeArmond Davis, *The United States and the First Hague Peace Conference* (Ithaca, NY, 1962), pp. 99–100.

[20] 'Précédents relatifs à la Présentation des Pétitions, Genève, le 3 février 1932,' cote 867, série SDN, French Foreign Ministry Archives, Paris.

[21] Tate, *Disarmament Illusion*, p. 298. He first made this promise in September 1904 in response to the demands of members of the Inter-Parliamentary Union at their St. Louis Congress.

[22] Tate, *Disarmament Illusion*, p. 302.

ments on the agenda of the Second Hague Conference despite Russian opposition.[23] However, the issue was bypassed at the Conference: as Tate points out, 'even before the final invitation had been issued the proposal for a limitation of armaments was moribund.'[24] Despite this, activists including Suttner and Stead formed a *Cercle International* during the Conference, which published a journal of proceedings and 'constituted a kind of unofficial conference going on alongside the Governments' Conference.'[25] Furthermore, the numerous resolutions received again caused the Bureau of the Conference to establish a committee for their consideration, thereby reaffirming the crucial precedent set at the First Hague Conference.

The Impact of the First World War

Although the outbreak of the First World War precipitated the decline of the pre-war peace movement, it was of considerable importance in the development of disarmament activism for three reasons. First, the experience of the conflict was something to which the disarmament movement could subsequently appeal to gain popular support for its objectives. Secondly, the peace movement was transformed by the war, with the replacement of the pre-war movement with a new and more efficiently organised international movement. And thirdly, the war stimulated a wave of new international non-governmental organisations in all spheres of human activity which were later to provide the basis for mass mobilisation behind the disarmament movement's goals.

The brutality of the First World War, and the unprecedented number of people directly affected by it, made it a vital tool for stirring up support for the campaign for disarmament in the aftermath of that conflict. The belief that the pursuit of general disarmament could help prevent another World War was one of the most persistent themes of activist propaganda throughout the period 1919 to 1933. The speech of Jean Dupuy of the Disarmament Committee of Students' International Organisations to the Special Session of the World Disarmament

---

[23] A. J. A. Morris, 'The English Radicals' Campaign for Disarmament and the Hague Conference of 1907,' *Journal of Modern History*, 43/3 (1971), pp. 367–93; Tate, *Disarmament Illusion*, p. 162 and chs. 16–17.

[24] Tate, *Disarmament Illusion*, p. 327.

[25] Caroline E. Playne, *Bertha von Suttner and the Struggle to Avert the World War* (London, 1936), p. 155.

Conference held on 6 February 1932 is just one example: 'we are convinced that it is our duty to work for a reduction of armaments, because we are convinced that that means working for organised peace and defending an ideal, an ideal sanctified by the death of numberless men on numberless battlefields, who were all convinced, no matter from what country they came, that they were dying to end war.'[26]

Although the experience of the First World War was to become a major reference point for the post-war disarmament campaign, it should be noted that disarmament was not the principal solution promoted by the peace movement during that conflict. Instead, the creation of a League of Nations was the primary goal of a new set of peace societies established during the First World War. At the end of the conflict, they collaborated to form the International Federation of League of Nations Societies, which, as the next chapter will show, replaced the International Peace Bureau as the principal peace INGO of the interwar years.

A further international peace organisation which emerged during the First World War was the Women's International League for Peace and Freedom. This was to play an equally important role in the interwar disarmament movement and reflected the increasing concern of the international women's movement with international affairs and the promotion of peace.

The women's movement was not alone: the end of the First World War was accompanied by the (re-)formation of many private international organisations in diverse fields of human activity which were also able subsequently to play an important function in supplying the disarmament movement with a broad basis of support. Three of the most important were: the International Federation of Trade Unions, which had approximately twenty million members; the eight million-strong Interallied Federation of Ex-Servicemen; and the International Confederation of Students, which had a million members.

---

[26] League of Nations, *Records of the Conference for the Reduction and Limitation of Armaments: Series A: Verbatim Records of Plenary Meetings: Volume I: February 2nd–July 23rd, 1932* (Geneva, 1932), p. 193.

CHAPTER FOUR

COMPOSITION

Whereas the previous chapter outlined the developments up to 1918 that helped to make the post-Great War disarmament movement possible, this chapter clarifies what exactly constituted the movement. It briefly introduces the principal transnational organisations involved in the promotion of arms reduction after the First World War, as well as the main national-level actors that participated in the campaign in Great Britain, France and the United States.

First, however, it is important to note the difficulties involved in determining what counted as a constituent of the non-governmental disarmament campaign, since the boundary between governmental and non-governmental was often indistinct. For instance, many of the leading figures in the arms limitation movement often officially represented their countries in discussions of disarmament: Lord Robert (later Viscount) Cecil of the League of Nations Union in Great Britain is the most notable example. Furthermore, some of the organisations discussed in this book crossed the boundary between governmental and non-governmental, such as the Labour and Socialist International, which contained national parties that occasionally participated in the governments of Britain and France in the period under consideration. One organisation that played a role in the movement for arms reduction, the Communist—or Third—International (also known as the Komintern), has had to be excluded from this study because its policies on disarmament were indistinguishable from those of the government of the Soviet Union.

The Transnational Organisations

The transnational organisations involved in the interwar disarmament campaign were both numerous and diverse. However, Martin Ceadel has pointed out that a distinction can be made between the 'primary' and 'secondary' peace movement. The 'primary' peace movement consisted of 'those associations and individual campaigners that worked for peace as an exclusive or predominant goal,' while the 'secondary' peace movement 'worked to abolish war as an expression of a broader associational purpose, whether religious, political or social.'[1] This section will therefore begin by describing the main 'primary' transnational organisations that promoted arms reduction in the interwar period.

Two of these organisations were of pre-war origin: the International Peace Bureau (IPB) and the Inter-Parliamentary Union (IPU). As the previous chapter has outlined, the International Peace Bureau was set up in Switzerland in 1891 by national peace societies to facilitate the organisation of annual 'Universal Peace Congresses.' These pre-war Congresses attracted wide interest, but, as the Bureau now admits, 'in the interwar period the IPB struggled to get its voice heard.'[2] The Inter-Parliamentary Union, on the other hand, remained an influential organisation in the interwar years.[3] Composed of approximately five thousand members of parliaments from over thirty nations, the IPU's ultimate goal was 'the future creation of a World Parliament, or of a House of Commons of the League of Nations.'[4] In the meantime, the organisation devoted itself to the promotion of arbitration and disarmament.[5] The IPU's Norwegian secretary-general, Christian Lange, was to play a crucial role in pushing for these as a delegate to the Assemblies of the League of Nations.[6]

With the outbreak of the First World War, the two main long-standing transnational peace organisations found themselves accompanied by a number of newcomers. Two of these were Christian groups: the World Alliance for Promoting International Friendship through the Churches and the International Fellowship of Reconciliation (IFoR). The International Fellowship of Reconciliation was started in England late in 1914 by Henry Hodgkin, a Quaker missionary. As it was a 'quietist'[7]

---

[1] Martin Ceadel, *Semi-Detached Idealists: The British Peace Movement and International Relations, 1854–1945* (Oxford, 2000), p. 8.

[2] http://www.ipb.org/web/noticia.php?id=69, last accessed on 30 April 2007.

[3] On the history of the IPU, see James Douglas, *Parliaments Across Frontiers: A Short History of the Inter-Parliamentary Union* (London, 1976) and Yéfime Zarjevski, *The People Have the Floor: A History of the Inter-Parliamentary Union* (Aldershot, 1989).

[4] IPU, *The Inter-Parliamentary Union: Its Work and Organisation*, third edition (Geneva, 1930), p. 5.

[5] For a comprehensive account of the IPU's work in this field, see William Martin's *Disarmament and the Inter-Parliamentary Union* (Geneva, 1931).

[6] On Christian Lange's work, see Oscar J. Falnes, 'Christian Lange and his Work for Peace,' *American Scandinavian Review*, 57 (1969), pp. 226–74; and S. Sheperd Jones, *The Scandinavian States and the League of Nations* (Princeton, NJ, 1939).

[7] Ceadel, *Semi-Detached Idealists*, p. 430.

organisation, IFoR's role in the disarmament campaign was limited.[8] The World Alliance, on the other hand, was more concerned with practical action. Set up by another English activist, J. Allen Baker, just three days before his country entered the War,[9] the Alliance eventually consisted of national councils in thirty-seven countries. With Willoughby Dickinson as its President, the organisation attempted to intervene practically in the resolution of disputes, especially the problems of religious minorities. Through its work with the national churches, especially those in Britain and the United States, it was also to play an important part in the interwar disarmament campaign.[10]

In addition to the Christian groups, the First World War sparked the creation of the two most significant global women's peace associations of the interwar period: the World Union of Women for International Concord and the Women's International League for Peace and Freedom. The World Union of Women for International Concord was established in Geneva on 9 February 1915 'to spread internationalism by the establishment of a means of communication between the women of the entire world.'[11] Despite having an American president, Clara Guthrie d'Arcis, and despite acquiring a membership spread across 29 countries, the World Union remained a primarily Genevese organisation until its demise in 1958.[12] Its emphasis was upon 'individual effort and intervention by members in their daily life and surroundings' rather than mass campaigns.[13]

The other women's peace organisation to commence its activities during the First World War, the Women's International League for Peace and Freedom (WILPF),[14] took a greater interest in campaigning and therefore played a more visible role in the disarmament movement.[15] Its

---

[8] A brief description of its disarmament work can be found in Jill Wallis, *Valiant For Peace: A History of the Fellowship of Reconciliation, 1914 to 1989* (London, 1991), pp. 77–81.

[9] Ceadel, *Semi-Detached Idealists*, pp. 167–8.

[10] A comprehensive account of the work of the World Alliance is provided in Darrill Hudson's *The Ecumenical Movement in World Affairs* (London, 1969).

[11] World Union of Women for International Concord, *The World Union of Women for International Concord* (Geneva, 1915), p. 3.

[12] A sympathetic account of the history of the World Union is provided in Marguerite Nobs, *Etapes vers la Paix: Un Effort Féminin* (Geneva, 1960).

[13] 'World Union of Women for International Concord, December 1931,' enclosed with Dingman to Drummond, 4 Jan. 1931, dr. 50/33895/31137, R.3604, League of Nations Archives, Geneva.

[14] This name was adopted in May 1919. Its previous name was the International Committee of Women for Permanent Peace.

[15] The most concise account of the Women's International League's interwar activities

interest in campaigning was partly a result of the organisation's origins in the women's suffrage movement. The organisation was dominated by American pacifists from the start, with Jane Addams as the body's first President and Emily Greene Balch its first international secretary. While WILPF never achieved a substantial individual membership, it had ambitious and active national branches. The French branch under Gabrielle Duchêne, for instance, mobilised a successful campaign against the Boncour bill for mobilizing women in wartime, while the British branch organised a massive peace pilgrimage in 1926.[16] This pilgrimage was preceded by the gathering of half a million signatures to a petition promoting arbitration. It was in the gathering of signatures to massive disarmament petitions that was to be the Women's International League's principal contribution to the movement for arms reduction.

The most significant global primary peace organisation of the interwar period, however, was the International Federation of League of Nations Societies (IFLNS). This body was formed in December 1919 to 'unite in co-ordinated action the associations established to promote the principles embodied in the Covenant of the League of Nations and to urge the application of those principles.'[17] To emphasise its unofficial nature and distinctness from the League of Nations, the Federation was based in Brussels. At its peak, the IFLNS could claim to represent a million and a half members in forty countries. Although the British League of Nations Union was by far the most significant national branch of the Federation, the organisation's Secretary-General was a Frenchman, Théodore Ruyssen of the *Association de la Paix par le Droit*. The League of Nations Union's President, Lord Cecil, frequently complained that the IFLNS 'busied itself too much with policy and too little with propaganda.'[18] However, this preoccupation with policy was to prove very useful when the IFLNS formulated the common

---

is provided in its pamphlet, *Women's International League for Peace and Freedom, 1915–1938: A Venture in Internationalism* (Geneva, 1938). For a more detailed account, see Gertrude Bussey and Margaret Tims, *Pioneers for Peace: Women's International League for Peace and Freedom, 1915–1965* (London, 1980).

[16] Bussey and Tims, *Pioneers for Peace*, ch. 4.

[17] Association Française pour la Société des Nations, *Troisième Conférence Interalliée des Associations pour la Société des Nations* (Paris, 1920), p. 26. On the IFLNS in general, see Thomas Richard Davies, *The Possibilities of Transnationalism: The International Federation of League of Nations Societies and the International Peace Campaign, 1919–1939* (MPhil thesis, University of Oxford, 2002), Part One.

[18] Cecil to Drummond, 27 Apr. 1929, Add. MSS. 51111, Cecil of Chelwood papers, British Library, London.

programme for the entire disarmament movement during the World
Disarmament Conference.

*   *   *

The primary peace organisations constituted just one part of the
interwar disarmament movement—a much greater number of 'secondary' organisations also played a vital role. It is possible to distinguish
among the many 'secondary' organisations along the lines of the
Disarmament Committees formed in Geneva in 1931 by groups of
similar type: Christian organisations, student groups, and the women's
movement.

Among the most active of the secondary organisations involved in the
disarmament campaign were the Christian groups. As the previous
chapter has shown, the importance of Christianity in the development
of the movement for arms reduction was considerable. The earliest
national peace societies were Christian in motivation, while at the global
level it was Christian organisations that pioneered the establishment
of international secretariats. The first modern international non-
governmental organisation, the World's Alliance of Young Men's
Christian Associations, was founded in 1855 to 'unite those young men
who, regarding Jesus Christ as their God and Saviour,...desire...to
associate their efforts for the extension of his Kingdom amongst
young men.'[19] It was joined by the World's Young Women's Christian
Association in 1894.[20] From the beginning, YMCA and YWCA
members adopted a wide interpretation of their mission: undoubtedly
the most significant example is the creation of the Red Cross by one
of the World's YMCA founders, Henry Dunant. While the YMCAs
and YWCAs were peripheral to the interwar disarmament campaign,
individual members of their international secretariats were to play
an important role in the international organisation of the campaign:
Mary Dingman was the spirited leader of the Women's Disarmament
Committee, while Joachim Mueller acted as Secretary of the Christian
Disarmament Committee.

---

[19] http://www.ymca.int/mission/parisbasis_en.htm, last accessed on 30 April 2007.
For the history of the World's Alliance of YMCAs, see Clarence Prouty Shedd, *History
of the World's Alliance of Young Men's Christian Associations* (London, 1955).

[20] On the history of the World's YWCA, see Anna Rice, *History of the World's Young
Women's Christian Association* (New York, 1947).

The wider ecumenical movement also played a significant part in the interwar campaign for arms reduction. The World Alliance for Promoting International Friendship through the Churches has already been described. In 1925, it was joined by the Universal Christian Council on Life and Work. This organisation was intended to unite the Anglican, Protestant and Orthodox Churches 'to bring about the application of Christian principles to those problems which confront and challenge the whole of Christendom.'[21] The Roman Catholic Church never participated in this Council. However, the disarmament campaign was not without Catholic participation. The International Union of Catholic Women's Organisations, for example, was a prominent element of the disarmament campaign in continental Europe (although it was not a member of any international co-ordinating body). In addition, *Pax Romana*, the international association of Catholic university students established in Fribourg in 1921, co-operated with the other Christian organisations in the Disarmament Committee of Students' International Organisations.

Like *Pax Romana*, the majority of the students' international organisations were religious in origin. For example, the organisation which created the Disarmament Committee of Students' International Organisations, the International Student Service (ISS), was an outgrowth of the World Student Christian Federation (WSCF). The ISS had been set up in 1920 as European Student Relief, an aid organisation 'for the benefit of starving and destitute students and professors,'[22] but it expanded the range of its activities upon being renamed in 1925. The father of the ISS, the World Student Christian Federation, on the other hand, was founded in 1895 to 'lead students to realise that the principles of Christ should rule in international relationships.'[23] Despite being one of only two organisations to participate in two Disarmament

---

[21] Fund to Continue the International Work of the Churches, *The Churches in Action for World Peace*, (New York, n. d.), p. 1.

[22] Quoted in Lyman Cromwell White and Marie Ragonetti Zocca, *International Non-Governmental Organizations: Their Purposes, Methods and Accomplishments* (New Brunswick, 1951), p. 130.

[23] Tissington Tatlow, *The Story of the Student Christian Movement in Great Britain and Ireland* (London, 1933), pp. 882–7. On the origins of the WSCF, see John R. Mott, *The World Student Christian Federation: Origin, Achievement, Forecast* (London, 1920).

Committees,[24] the WSCF was to play a largely passive role in the disarmament campaign.[25]

The same can be said of many of the other students' organisations, such as the International Federation of University Women (IFUW) and the World Union of Jewish Students.[26] As Michel Poberezski of the International Student Service pointed out, most of the students' associations were not primarily concerned with campaigning and were therefore 'not particularly well adapted for the promotion of disarmament'—in general they could do little more than pass supportive resolutions.[27] Nevertheless some of these organisations could claim to speak on behalf of a large number of people: the International Confederation of Students, for instance, represented nearly a million students in forty-two national student unions.[28]

There were also two small student organisations that *were* primarily concerned with campaigning. One was the International Federation of Socialist Students (IFSS), a body of around eight thousand people founded in Amsterdam in 1926. However, the IFSS played an insignificant role in the socialist youth movement, let alone the campaign for arms reduction.[29] More noteworthy in the disarmament movement was the International Federation of University League of Nations Societies (IFULNS). Established in Prague on 15 April 1924, this Paris-based organisation acquired approximately 20,000 members in 22 countries by 1933.[30] Its location was the same as that of the International Institute of Intellectual Co-operation, with which it co-operated closely. Like the IFLNS, the IFULNS had a tendency to prioritise the formulation

---

[24] It was a member of both the Christian and the Students' Committees. The only other organisation to participate in two Committees was the World's YWCA, a member of the Christian and Women's Committees.

[25] On the WSCF's role in the disarmament campaign, see W. A. Visser 't Hooft, *Students Find the Truth to Serve: The Story of the World's Student Christian Federation, 1930–1935* (Geneva, 1935), pp. 58–9.

[26] On the history of the IFUW, see Edith C. Batho, *A Lamp of Friendship: A Short History of the International Federation of University Women, 1918–1968* (London, 1968).

[27] L'Entr'Aide Universitaire Internationale. *Conférence des représentants des organisations internationales d'étudiants sur une action universitaire internationale en faveur du désarmement* (Geneva, 1931), p. 5.

[28] White, *International Non-Governmental Organizations*, p. 127; Philip G. Altbach, 'The International Student Movement,' *Journal of Contemporary History*, 5/1 (1970), p. 159.

[29] Radomir Luza, *History of the International Socialist Youth Movement* (Leyden, 1970), p. 56. Its one achievement in the disarmament campaign was the publication of a special issue of *L'Etude Socialiste* dedicated to disarmament in Mar. 1931.

[30] George Lutz, *Où en est la Fédération universitaire internationale pour la S.d.N.?* (Paris, 1934), p. 1.

of policy over campaigning, but it would attract influential statesmen such as Joseph Paul-Boncour to its Congresses and it published widely on League of Nations issues.[31]

More numerous than either the Christian or the students' associations were the groups that took part in the Disarmament Committee of Women's International Organisations. Like many of the student organisations, a substantial number of the women's groups that promoted arms reduction were religious. The World's YWCA has already been mentioned. Another prominent Christian women's organisation was the World's Women's Christian Temperance Union, which adopted disarmament as a goal when membership figures began to decline after the introduction of prohibition in the United States.[32] In addition to the Christian groups, two Jewish organisations participated in the Women's Disarmament Committee—the League of Jewish Women and the World Organisation of Jewish Women—although neither was particularly prominent in the movement for arms reduction. The same is true of the two professional women's associations that took part in the Women's Committee: the European Federation of Soroptimist Clubs and the International Federation of Business and Professional Women.[33]

The women's co-operative movement, on the other hand, was much more active in the disarmament campaign. The International Co-operative Women's Guild (ICWG) claimed to represent not only 'the women connected with the co-operative movement,' but 'practically all married working women.'[34] Based in London with Emmy Freundlich as its President, the ICWG saw one of its principal aims as 'to unite the co-operative women of all lands...for international peace.'[35] Questions of peace and disarmament were discussed at every conference of the

---

[31] IFULNS, *Fédération Universitaire Internationale pour la Société des Nations: Principes essentiels des Statuts, Organisation, Activité* (Paris, 1930), pp. 1–3.

[32] See Ian Tyrrell, *Woman's World/Woman's Empire: The Woman's Christian Temperance Union in International Perspective, 1880–1930* (Chapel Hill, NC, 1981).

[33] See the activity summaries of these organisations enclosed with Dingman to Drummond, 4 Jan. 1932, dr. 50/33895/31137, R.3604, League of Nations Archives.

[34] 'The International Co-operative Women's Guild, December 1931,' enclosed with Dingman to Drummond, 4 Jan. 1932, dr. 50/33895/31137, R.3604, League of Nations Archives.

[35] 'The International Co-operative Women's Guild, December 1931,' enclosed with Dingman to Drummond, 4 Jan. 1932, dr. 50/33895/31137, R.3604, League of Nations Archives.

organisation in the interwar years, and the organisation was particularly vocal in its support of proposals for total abolition of armaments, circulating its own declarations and petitions in addition to those of the Women's International League.[36]

Equally important were the global suffragist organisations. It has already been noted that the Women's International League was set up by leaders of the International Alliance of Women for Suffrage and Equal Citizenship (IAW). Established in 1904 'to secure enfranchisement of women of all nations,' the International Alliance represented twelve million women in twenty-six countries.[37] The Alliance was led for most of the interwar period by a British woman, Margery Corbett Ashby, whose active promotion of disarmament was rewarded with her appointment as a member of the British delegation to the World Disarmament Conference. An even larger organisation than the IAW was the International Council of Women (ICW), composed of national councils in forty-one countries with a total membership of forty million women. Although the ICW claimed to 'exclude from its programme political and religious questions of a controversial nature,'[38] it promoted peace and arbitration from its foundation and was vocal in its support for arms limitation throughout the interwar years.[39]

The most notable aspect of the work of the IAW and the ICW was their co-operation to secure common objectives. This was first seen in a joint deputation to the League of Nations Commission in Paris in 1919, at which they both called for disarmament as well as equal rights for women. This co-operation extended much further in the 1920s, when they worked together to create the Joint Standing Committee and Liaison Committee of Women's International Organisations for

---

[36] The International Co-operative Women's Guild was part of the wider international co-operative movement, headed by the International Co-operative Alliance (the largest INGO of the interwar era). The International Co-operative Alliance also promoted disarmament at the World Disarmament Conference, but played a less active role in the interwar disarmament movement than the International Co-operative Women's Guild.

[37] Arnold Whittick, *Woman Into Citizen: The World Movement towards the Emancipation of Women in the Twentieth Century with Accounts of the Contributions of the International Alliance of Women, the League of Nations and the Relevant Agencies of the United Nations, 1902–78* (London, 1979), p. 63.

[38] 'International Council of Women, December 1931,' enclosed with Dingman to Drummond, 4 Jan. 1932, dr. 50/33895/31137, R.3604, League of Nations Archives.

[39] See ICW, *Women in a Changing World: The Dynamic Story of the International Council of Women since 1888* (London, 1966), Part II.

the promotion of equal rights for women at the League of Nations.[40] These Committees set the precedent that made possible the foundation of the Women's Disarmament Committee in 1931.

Three organisations that participated in the disarmament campaign in their own right rather than as a part of a Disarmament Committee also need to be mentioned: the International Federation of Trade Unions (IFTU), the Labour and Socialist International (LSI), and the International Conference of Disabled Soldiers and Ex-Servicemen (CIAMAC).[41]

The role of ex-servicemen's organisations in the disarmament movement is particularly interesting. It must first be noted that a significant number of ex-servicemen's groups made no effort to promote arms limitation, and some extremist organisations—such as the *Croix de Feu* in France—actively attempted to disrupt the disarmament campaign. However, as M. Blondeel of the League of Nations Secretariat noted, the groups that formed CIAMAC in 1925 represented three-quarters of German ex-servicemen and 'the great majority' of those in France.[42] The organisation was founded by René Cassin of the *Union Fédérale des Anciens Combattants*, and its primary purpose was the promotion of Franco-German reconciliation. It also played a far greater role in the campaigns for arbitration and disarmament in continental Europe than the primary peace movement.[43]

The same can be said of the International Federation of Trade Unions, which was reformed in Amsterdam in 1919, and represented approximately twenty million people in twenty-five countries in the interwar years.[44] It was, as one observer remarked, the only global organisation that could 'claim to represent the workers' movement as

---

[40] For a comprehensive account of the work of these bodies, see Carol Ann Miller, *Lobbying the League: Women's International Organizations and the League of Nations* (DPhil thesis, University of Oxford, 1992).

[41] This acronym is derived from the organisation's French name, *Conférence Internationale des Associations de Mutilés de Guerre et Anciens Combattants*.

[42] 'Note sur la Conférence Internationale des Associations de Mutilés et d'Anciens Combattants tenue à Genève le 30 septembre et les 1er et 2 octobre 1926,' dr. 17591, R.1595, League of Nations Archives.

[43] See, for example, Elliott Pennell Fagerberg, *The 'Anciens Combattants' and French Foreign Policy* (Ambilly—Annemasse, 1966) on the role of the movement in France.

[44] White, *International Non-Governmental Organizations*, p. 78.

a whole.'[45] As an organisation dominated by German trade unions,[46] the IFTU saw the promotion of disarmament as the most significant part of its interwar 'campaign against war and fascism.' Its interest in the issue was rewarded in the appointment of three workers' delegates to the League of Nations Temporary Mixed Commission on the Reduction of Armaments.[47] Rather than participating in the International Consultative Group (which all of the other transnational organisations mentioned in this chapter joined), the IFTU chose instead to participate in a separate campaign with the Labour and Socialist International during the World Disarmament Conference.

The Labour and Socialist International, for its part, represented forty-six political parties in thirty-five countries that stood in principle for 'the economic emancipation of the workers from capitalist domination and the establishment of the Socialist Commonwealth.'[48] It was established in Brussels in 1923 as the post-war successor to the Second International and at the time of the World Disarmament Conference its constituent parties had a combined membership of 7,500,000 people.[49] The LSI's French section was to play a particularly important role in the disarmament movement in France.

NATIONAL ORGANISATIONS

Although the focus of this book is on the transnational campaign for disarmament, it is important to be aware of the national branches of the aforementioned global organisations, which usually wielded greater influence over their respective governments than the international secretariats. Since this book focuses on the impact of the disarmament campaign upon the policies of the British, French and American governments, the next few paragraphs will briefly indicate the principal national organisations that promoted disarmament in each of these countries.

---

[45] Alexandre Berenstein, *Les Organisations Ouvrières, Leurs Compétences et Leur Rôle dans la Société des Nations* (Paris, 1936), p. 16.

[46] Richard Hyman, *The International Labour Movement on the Threshold of Two Centuries: Agitation, Organisation, Bureaucracy, Diplomacy* (http://www.arbarkiv.nu/pdf_wrd/Hyman_int.pdf, last accessed on 30 April 2007).

[47] Walther Schevenels, *Forty-Five Years: International Federation of Trade Unions: A Historical Précis* (Brussels, 1945), p. 132.

[48] White, *International Non-Governmental Organizations*, p. 84.

[49] Vox Populi Committee, *Vox Populi* (Geneva, 1932), p. 84.

In the Anglo-Saxon countries (Great Britain and the United States), the most influential organisations in the disarmament campaign tended to be the League of Nations associations, women's groups, and the churches. In Great Britain, the primary peace movement was unusually substantial and was dominated by the League of Nations Union (LNU). Described by Martin Ceadel as 'undoubtedly the most substantial peace association in history,' the LNU had more than four hundred thousand subscribing members in the early 1930s.[50] The Union's President, Lord Cecil, ensured that the organisation spearheaded the disarmament movement in that country from 1927 onwards.[51] Other primary peace organisations, especially the small but ambitious Women's International League, were also to play an important role in Great Britain.[52]

Given the strength and independent-mindedness of the LNU, inter-organisational co-operation was not as substantial in the British disarmament movement as it was elsewhere. However, there were notable exceptions, such as the co-operation of women's organisations in the Women's Peace Crusade, and the co-ordination of peace group activity by the National Peace Council.[53] As for Britain's secondary peace movement, the work of the National Council of Women, the Women's Co-operative Guild, the Trade Union Congress and the churches was particularly notable.

The movement for disarmament in the United States differed from that in Great Britain in two significant ways. First, the campaign was more diffuse than that in Great Britain. The American League of Nations movement, for instance, was split between the Foreign Policy Association (FPA) led by James G. McDonald and the League of Nations Association (LNA), which was ultimately led by the prominent disarmament activist James T. Shotwell. For these organisations, American participation in League of Nations discussions of arms limitation was a useful first

---

[50] Ceadel, *Semi-Detached Idealists*, p. 272.

[51] On the role of the LNU in British politics, see Donald Birn, *The League of Nations Union* (Oxford, 1981), *passim*.

[52] On the work of the British branch of the Women's International League, see Jenny Adams, *Toward Permanent Peace: The Women's International League for Peace and Freedom, 1915–1933* (BA thesis, University of Oxford, n.d.) in Lady Margaret Hall Library, Oxford.

[53] On the disarmament work of the Women's Peace Crusade, see its pamphlet entitled *Women and Disarmament* (London, 1930). On the National Peace Council, see its *Peace Year Books*.

step towards full US involvement in the activities of the Geneva institution.[54]

The second difference between the British and American arms limitation movements was the much greater importance of interorganisational co-operation in the USA. Two of the most prominent examples of this co-operation were the National Council for Prevention of War (NCPW) and the National Committee on the Cause and Cure of War (NCCCW).[55] Frederick Libby's NCPW consisted of over thirty national organisations, including ten peace associations, five educational organisations, four farmers' groups, and eleven women's organisations. Carrie Chapman Catt's NCCCW, on the other hand, united eleven women's organisations, none of which were primarily peace associations. Both interorganisational bodies were dedicated to campaigning for arbitration and disarmament in this period.[56] As in Great Britain, church organisations, especially the Church Peace Union, and WILPF, led in the USA by Dorothy Detzer, also played an important part in the disarmament campaign in the United States.[57]

The movement for arms reduction in France had noticeably different features from that in both Great Britain and the USA. Most importantly, as subsequent chapters will demonstrate, the disarmament campaign in France was considerably less substantial than that in either of the Anglo-Saxon countries. A second difference is that the primary peace movement in France was, as Norman Ingram has pointed out, a much more 'balkanised, splintered movement' than elsewhere.[58]

---

[54] Details of the work of these organisations are provided in Warren Kuehl and Lynne Dunn, *Keeping the Covenant: American Internationalists and the League of Nations, 1920–1939* (Kent, Ohio, 1997) and Frank Winchester Abbot, *From Versailles to Munich: The Foreign Policy Association and American Foreign Policy* (PhD thesis, Texas Tech University, 1972).

[55] The membership of the NCPW and the NCCCW in 1931 is provided in appendix iv.

[56] On the work of the NCPW, see Frederick Libby, *To End War: The Story of the National Council for Prevention of War* (Nyack, NY, 1969). On the NCCCW, see its pamphlet entitled *The National Committee on the Cause and Cure of War: Origins, Aims, Program* (New York, 1931).

[57] For an account of the work of the Church Peace Union, see Charles Stedman MacFarland, *Pioneers for Peace through Religion, Based on the Records of the Church Peace Union (Founded by Andrew Carnegie), 1914–1945* (New York, 1946). On the US branch of WILPF, see Carrie A. Foster, *The Women and the Warriors: The US Section of the Women's International League for Peace and Freedom, 1915–1946* (Syracuse, NY, 1995).

[58] Norman Ingram, *The Politics of Dissent: Pacifism in France, 1919–1939* (Oxford, 1991), p. 2.

Nevertheless, as in Britain and the United States, there were women's peace groups and League of Nations associations in France. The Women's International League, for example, had an active French branch; and an organisation attached to the World Union of Women for International Concord, the *Ligue des Mères et des Educatrices pour la Paix*, was also operational. The League of Nations movement, for its part, was represented by the numerous organisations attached to the *Fédération Française pour la Société des Nations*.[59] One of these, the *Comité d'Action pour la Société des Nations* led by the internationalist Senator Henry de Jouvenel, was particularly significant for the breadth of its membership and its closeness to government members such as Joseph Paul-Boncour.[60] The *Association Française pour la Société des Nations*, on the other hand, drew much of its force from its ties to the left-wing ex-servicemen's movement.

Veterans' organisations such as René Cassin's *Union Fédérale des Anciens Combattants* (which had a membership of nearly a million people), however, were much more influential than the primary peace movement in France.[61] The same applies to the French trade union movement, with the secretary-general of the *Confédération Générale du Travail*, Léon Jouhaux, being an activist of particular renown.[62] As for some of the other groups involved in the promotion of disarmament in France, these included humanitarian organisations such as the *Ligue des Droits de l'Homme*, pacifist bodies such as the *Volonté de Paix*, and Catholic organisations such as the *Union Catholique d'Etudes Internationales*.

* * *

---

[59] At its foundation in 1920, the Federation was composed of: *Association Française pour la Société des Nations, Ligue pour l'Organisation de la Société des Nations, Société de l'Etat-Pax, Conciliation Internationale (Section Française), Bureau Européen de la Dotation Carnegie pour la Paix Internationale, Ligue Internationale de la Paix et de la Liberté, Association de la Paix par le Droit*, and *Association Française d'Arbitrage entre Nations*. The Federation's membership peaked at 17 organisations representing 1.25 million people at the time of the World Disarmament Conference (one million of these people were in the affiliated ex-servicemen's organisations).

[60] This committee was set up in 1924 and consisted of representatives of the wider League of Nations movement in France, including Emile Borel, Pierre Brossolette, René Cassin, Pierre Cot, Léon Jouhaux, Robert Lange, Jules Prudhommeaux, and Louise Weiss.

[61] For an account of the peace work of the ex-servicemen's movement in France, see Fagerberg, *'Anciens Combattants' and French Foreign Policy*.

[62] See his *Le Désarmement* (Paris, 1927). See also Bernard Georges, Denise Tintant and Marie-Anne Renauld, *Léon Jouhaux dans le mouvement syndical français* (Paris, 1979), ch. 2–3.

Now that the principal organisations that participated in the inter-war campaign for disarmament have been described, it is possible to embark upon an outline of the contribution of these organisations to the evolution of the disarmament issue in the years following the First World War.

PART THREE

EVOLUTION OF THE
DISARMAMENT CAMPAIGN

CHAPTER FIVE

THE EMERGENCE OF THE INTERWAR DISARMAMENT MOVEMENT, 1919 TO 1925

The Paris Peace Conference of 1919 was an early opportunity for global campaigning organisations to promote general disarmament as a part of the post-war settlement. However, it was only after the Conference had completed its work that arms reduction became a priority for these groups. Furthermore, the first significant disarmament campaigns were not transnational. They were nationally-based initiatives to promote progress at the Washington Naval Conference, and to promote League of Nations measures intended to provide the foundations for general disarmament, such as the Draft Treaty of Mutual Assistance and the Geneva Protocol. Although there were also a few transnational initiatives for the promotion of disarmament during the five years following the Paris Peace Conference, they were limited, sporadic and uncoordinated.

Disarmament Activism and the Paris Peace Settlement

The Paris Peace Conference was a unique opportunity for global activist organisations: the representatives of many nations were assembled in a single location, and their task was—in the words of US President Woodrow Wilson—to 'create a peace that will win the approval of mankind.'[1] Consequently, groups including the League of Nations associations, the International Council of Women, the International Alliance of Women for Suffrage and Equal Citizenship, and the International Federation of Trade Unions all made use of this chance to express their views as to what form the peace settlement should take.

On the initiative of the French branches of the League of Nations and women's suffrage movements, inter-allied congresses on the peace settlement were held in Paris early in 1919. Representatives from the

---

[1] Quotation from Wilson's 'peace without victory' speech in Arthur Stanley Link (ed.), *The Papers of Woodrow Wilson* (Princeton, NJ, 1966), vol. 40, p. 535.

League of Nations associations of eight countries assembled in 254 Boulevard St. Germain for the last six days of January 1919 for 'a private peace conference parallel to the official one.'[2] It was, according to British delegate Lord Robert Cecil, 'a singularly tiresome entertainment: very hot and very useless.'[3] Women's organisations, on the other hand, participated in a 'Congress of Allied Women' at the Lyceum Club from 10 to 16 February, and managed to persuade Wilson to meet delegates on the opening day.[4]

The resolutions of these conferences were subsequently made known to the delegates on the Commission on the League of Nations. The League of Nations societies presented their peace proposals in a deputation on 1 February 1919,[5] while the International Council of Women and the International Alliance of Women for Suffrage and Equal Citizenship presented theirs in a deputation on 10 April 1919.[6] The International Federation of Trade Unions also met with members of the Commission on the League of Nations on 31 March.[7] During all of these deputations, proposals were presented that included requests for steps towards the general reduction and limitation of armaments.

However, a significant number of activist organisations failed to take up the opportunity offered in Paris in 1919. The Women's International League for Peace and Freedom, for example, failed to hold its second congress in the location of the post-war peace conference as initially intended because the French government refused to allow representatives of the defeated states to enter France.[8] The World Alliance for Promoting International Friendship through the Churches also 'made no organised effort…to act as an effective pressure group in Paris' because of the hesitancy of some of its leading members.[9]

---

[2] *La Paix par le Droit*, Jan. 1919, p. 46.

[3] Diary entry for 26 Jan. 1919, Add. MSS. 51131, Cecil of Chelwood papers, British Library, London.

[4] Arnold Whittick, *Woman Into Citizen: The World Movement towards the Emacipation of Women in the Twentieth Century with Accounts of the Contributions of the International Alliance of Women, the League of Nations and the Relevant Agencies of the United Nations, 1902–78* (London, 1979), p. 70.

[5] *La Paix par le Droit*, Feb.–Mar. 1919, pp. 104–8.

[6] *La Paix par le Droit*, Apr. 1919, pp. 186–90; Deborah Stienstra, *Women's Movements and International Organizations* (Basingstoke, 1994), pp. 55–8.

[7] Diary entry for 31 Mar. 1919, Add. MSS. 51131, Cecil papers.

[8] Gertrude Bussey and Margaret Tims, *Pioneers For Peace: The Women's International League for Peace and Freedom, 1915–1965* (London, 1980), p. 29.

[9] Darril Hudson, *The Ecumenical Movement in World Affairs* (London, 1969), p. 59.

Furthermore, the activities of the organisations that *were* present in Paris in early 1919 failed to match the scale of those undertaken in Geneva at the World Disarmament Conference thirteen years later. The Paris Peace Conference was held too soon after the First World War for mass actions to be viable.

An even more important limitation on the activities of the groups that were present in Paris in 1919 was the low priority that they attached to disarmament. The women's and trade union movements prioritised women's and labour rights respectively, and even the League of Nations associations prioritised the establishment of an international organisation: the British League of Nations Union (LNU), for example, sent a memorandum to the British Prime Minister in January 1919 claiming that no disarmament would be feasible before the establishment of the League of Nations.[10]

The low priority attached to disarmament by activist groups was shared in the official delegations, so disarmament was only partially provided for in the Paris Peace Settlement. Although German armaments were strictly limited in Part V of the Treaty of Versailles, the armaments of the victorious states were left untouched. The only commitment made by the victorious states was contained in the preface to the section on the German restrictions, which stated that these restrictions were undertaken 'in order to render possible the initiation of a general limitation of the armaments of all nations.'[11] The task of putting this commitment into effect was left to the Council of the League of Nations, which, under Article 8 of the League's Covenant, had to devise plans for 'the reduction of national armaments to the lowest point consistent with national safety, and the enforcement by common action of international obligations.'[12]

---

[10] *The Times*, 13 Jan. 1919, cited in David Shorney, *Britain and Disarmament, 1916–1931* (PhD thesis, University of Durham, 1980), p. 84.

[11] John W. Wheeler-Bennett, *Disarmament and Security since Locarno, 1925–1931: Being the Political and Technical Background of the General Disarmament Conference, 1932* (London, 1932), p. 26.

[12] Wheeler-Bennett, *Disarmament and Security since Locarno*, p. 26.

American Activism for Naval Disarmament at the Washington Conference

Although limited, the commitments made by the victorious states in the Versailles Treaty and the Covenant of the League of Nations were important in stimulating the movement for disarmament after the First World War. Another reason why activist groups became increasingly interested in disarmament in the 1920s was that by then many of them had already achieved their primary goals. For example, by 1920, peace groups had secured the creation of a League of Nations, suffragist groups in Britain and the USA had achieved votes for women, and the US temperance movement had secured the Prohibition Act. Multilateral disarmament, on the other hand, was an unfulfilled objective on which all of these organisations could agree.

The first major campaigns in pursuit of the common goal of disarmament were conducted on a national, rather than global, scale. They were of two types. One was the promotion of League of Nations initiatives towards general disarmament, which was a mainly European (and principally British) trend, and will be discussed in the next section. The other was the promotion of naval disarmament, which was a primarily American phenomenon, and is the subject of the rest of this section.

The movement for naval disarmament in the United States emerged in the winter of 1920–21 in response to Senator William Borah's resolution of 14 December 1920 requesting a conference for the reduction and limitation of naval armaments.[13] A particularly notable feature of the US naval disarmament movement was the tendency of many groups with divergent primary goals to unite around the secondary objective of naval disarmament in committees specially created for the purpose. It was a tactic to be mimicked in the promotion of general disarmament at the global level a decade later.

One of the principal American collaborative bodies was the Women's Committee on World Disarmament (the 'Washington Committee'), set up on 15 March 1921 by members of the National Women's Party under the leadership of Miss Emma Wold. Under the Committee's

---

[13] For a thorough assessment of the role of activism in the USA before and during the Washington Conference, see Charles Leonard Hoag, *Preface to Preparedness: The Washington Disarmament Conference and Public Opinion* (Washington, DC, 1941).

direction, groups including the League of Women's Voters, the Women's Christian Temperance Union and the Federation of Women's Clubs promoted a 'National Disarmament Day' on Easter Sunday, when mass meetings were held in sixteen states, and a 'National Disarmament Week' from 22–29 May, observed in 33 states. On 18 April 1921, they sent a deputation to President Harding, who, having taken office on 4 March 1921, had rejected limitation of naval materiel in a speech to Congress on 12 April.[14] Although Harding's position remained officially unchanged after the deputation, he was reported to have said that they 'would not be disappointed.'[15]

In the meantime, church and peace groups in America pursued their own initiatives. In May, for instance, the four largest religious organisations in the USA—the Federal Council of Churches of Christ, the National Catholic Welfare Council, the Central Conference of American Rabbis and the United Synagogue of America—issued a national appeal for a disarmament conference and 100,000 clerics urged their congregations to write to their Congressmen demanding a conference.[16] In May and June the State Department recorded receiving thousands of letters in support of a naval disarmament conference,[17] and on 22 June the campaign culminated in the presentation to Harding of a petition gathered by the Church Peace Union and signed by over 20,000 clergymen of all denominations asking for a disarmament conference as soon as possible. Harding's response to this petition was to say that progress towards a conference was being made.[18] A few days later, on 30 June, Congress adopted Borah's naval conference proposal after Harding had sent a letter indicating that this would be desirable.[19] Just eleven days after this, Harding announced his intention to convene a conference 'to be held in Washington at a time to be mutually agreed upon.'[20]

---

[14] Christopher Hall, *Britain, America and Arms Control, 1921–1937* (London, 1987), p. 25.

[15] Hoag, *Preface to Preparedness*, p. 94.

[16] Adelphia Dane Bowen, *The Disarmament Movement, 1918–1935* (PhD thesis, Columbia University, 1956), pp. 17–18.

[17] Cecelia Lynch, *Beyond Appeasement: Interpreting Interwar Peace Movements in World Politics* (Ithaca, NY, 1999), p. 133.

[18] Hoag, *Preface to Preparedness*, p. 103.

[19] Bowen, *Disarmament Movement*, p. 23.

[20] Quoted in Merze Tate, *The United States and Armaments* (Cambridge, MA, 1948), p. 125.

Few dissent from Robert Gordon Kaufman's conclusion that, despite the President's initial reservations, it was 'domestic pressure [that] had reconciled Harding to calling a naval conference.'[21] However, while the role of activist groups in harnessing public opinion in support of naval disarmament was important, one should note that support for the idea was already widespread, especially among Generals such as Bliss and Pershing. President Harding also had other motives than naval disarmament: he saw the Washington Conference as an opportunity to reach 'a common understanding with respect to principles and policies in the Far East' and to break up the Anglo-Japanese Alliance.[22] As for the timing of Harding's 11 July announcement, it had been necessary to beat the British, who were already considering calling a conference to replace the Anglo-Japanese alliance in response to Dominion pressure.[23]

With official preparations for the Washington Conference under way, further efforts at co-ordination of the American movement for naval disarmament took place. In June, Frederick Libby formed the Friends' International Disarmament Council, and in conjunction with Christina Merriman of the Foreign Policy Association, he arranged for sixteen organisations to meet in Washington on 8 September 1921 to form the National Council for the Limitation of Armaments. This body brought together groups including the Women's Committee on World Disarmament, the Church Peace Union, WILPF, FoR, and the American Farm Bureau Federation 'to unite and make articulate through the member organizations the overwhelming sentiment of the people of the United States in favor of armament reduction.'[24] By 20 October it had a headquarters in Washington and consisted of 21 organisations with a total membership of over six million people, and six months later the totals reached 43 organisations and 10 million members. When attacked by Frederick Wile for not being authorised by the State Department to campaign for the Washington Conference, the National Council secured a statement from Secretary of State Hughes declaring that he welcomed the 'aid of public-spirited citizens.'[25]

---

[21] Robert Gordon Kaufman, *Arms Control during the Pre-Nuclear Era: The United States and Naval Disarmament between the two World Wars* (New York, 1990), p. 32.

[22] Quoted in Tate, *United States and Armaments*, p. 125.

[23] Tate, *United States and Armaments*, pp. 123–4; Kaufman, *Arms Control during the Pre-Nuclear Era*, p. 36.

[24] Hoag, *Preface to Preparedness*, p. 106.

[25] Hoag, *Preface to Preparedness*, p. 108.

The National Council's propaganda work centred on a bi-weekly news bulletin, posters, letters, press releases, articles, 30,000 copies of Will Irwin's pamphlet, *War on War*, and public fora throughout the Conference.[26] Activities by member groups included the gathering of several hundred thousand signatures to farm groups' petitions and the setting aside of Sunday 6 November as a day of prayer for the Conference by the Federal Council of Churches. On Armistice Day, the eve of the opening of the Washington Conference, special services were held by churches throughout the USA and labour organisations hosted pro-disarmament demonstrations in 200 cities.

Although the campaign for naval disarmament at the Washington Conference was most substantial in the United States, a small campaign was also organised in the United Kingdom, after the British government accepted the US government's invitation in the summer of 1921. The British branch of the Women's International League, for instance, declared the seven days before the Conference to be 'International Disarmament Week.'[27] The League of Nations Union, for its part, had set up an Arms Limitation Committee in February 1921, which produced a report urging the British government to commit to reductions at similar levels to those eventually agreed to at Washington.[28]

However, it was in the United States that the naval disarmament campaign had most results. One of the principal activist achievements was the creation by Secretary of State Hughes of an American Advisory Commission to represent US public opinion at the Conference. As Hughes stated, the commission was set up 'to meet the demand of organizations and to supply dignified positions without permitting direct participation in the Conference by membership on the governmental commission.'[29] The official verdict on its reports were that they 'were of the greatest value.'[30] Peace groups were less impressed, however, especially when the Commission produced a report on 1 December opposed to the abolition of submarines despite their 400,000 letters to the Commission in favour of it.[31] In total, activists sent nearly 14 million

---

[26] Charles Chatfield, *For Peace and Justice: Pacifism In America, 1914–1941* (Knoxville, TN, 1971), p. 149.

[27] Lynch, *Beyond Appeasement*, p. 67.

[28] Donald S. Birn, *The League of Nations Union, 1918–1945* (Oxford, 1981), pp. 37–8.

[29] Quoted in Hoag, *Preface to Preparedness*, p. 126

[30] Hoag, *Preface to Preparedness*, p. 127.

[31] Bowen, *Disarmament Movement*, pp. 70–1.

items of correspondence to the Commission, of which ten million were church-inspired,[32] but the Commission's support of the government's position on submarines shows the limits to the body's effectiveness as activism's representative.

As for the US government's policies at the Conference, these were embodied in Secretary's Hughes' plan presented on the opening day, 12 November 1921, which formed the basis of the final settlement. Activism played an indirect role in its formulation, in that the public pressure generated significantly concerned Secretary Hughes about excessive expectations being raised, so a formula that guaranteed success had to be produced.[33] Hughes therefore substantially revised the initial proposal given to him by the General Board,[34] and the final version of the plan advocated a 10-year naval construction holiday and the scrapping of 66 capital ships, 30 of which American.[35] The maximum tonnage of capital ships for Britain and the US was to be 500,000 each, with 300,000 for Japan.

Most of the plan proved to be acceptable to the British delegation, which arrived at the Conference with no plan of its own. In March 1921, Lord Lee had already indicated Britain's abandonment of the two-power naval standard, so the relative capabilities suggested in the Hughes proposal were not challenged. As for Japan, she dropped her demand for a 10:10:7 ratio in exchange for assurances that the UK and US would not construct naval bases closer to Japan than Singapore or Pearl Harbor.

The final Washington Treaty provided for the elimination of about 40% of capital ships in commission or under construction, and no new capital ships were to be built for 10 years. Activists in the USA and Britain were therefore pleased with the outcome of the Washington Conference, with the British LNU being especially glad at the Treaty's resemblance to its own proposals and a Committee for Treaty Ratification being set up in the USA.[36] However, most agreed with the US National Council's conclusion that the reductions did not go far

---

[32] Hoag, *Preface to Preparedness*, pp. 130–1.

[33] Hoag, *Preface to Preparedness*, p. 94; Kaufman, *Arms Control during the Pre-Nuclear Era*, p. 47.

[34] Kaufman, *Arms Control during the Pre-Nuclear Era*, p. 53.

[35] Bowen, *Disarmament Movement*, p. 48.

[36] Hoag, *Preface to Preparedness*, p. 147.

enough and that it was necessary to call for 'other conferences following this to continue what is here begun.'[37]

INITIATIVES FOR DISARMAMENT THROUGH THE LEAGUE OF NATIONS

In the meantime, the primary focus of European activists was on the efforts of the League of Nations towards fulfilment of Article 8 of its Covenant. According to this Article, it was the responsibility of the League Council to draw up plans for the reduction and limitation of armaments. However, it was the first League Assembly that took the initiative, with the secretary-general of the Inter-Parliamentary Union, Christian Lange, putting forward in his capacity as Norwegian delegate a proposal for a 'Permanent Civilian Committee' and a section of the secretariat devoted to the reduction of armaments.[38] The Assembly therefore created a Disarmament Section of the Secretariat and a Temporary Mixed Commission 'to prepare for submission to the Council, in the near future, reports and proposals for the reduction of armaments.'[39] The members of this Commission served in an unofficial capacity, and were therefore able to produce much more radical proposals than the official representatives on the League Council could have.

One of the most prominent of the members of the Temporary Mixed Commission was Lord Robert Cecil, now the leader of the League of Nations Union, whose work in the Third Committee of the second League Assembly in 1921 led to the demand that the Temporary Mixed Commission should create 'a draft treaty or the equally definite plan' for the reduction of armaments to be presented to the Council before the third League Assembly met.[40]

The first such plan—from Lord Esher of Great Britain—was put forward on 20 February 1922, shortly after the success of the Washington Conference, and was heavily influenced by the solutions

---

[37] Lynch, *Beyond Appeasement*, p. 135.

[38] Minutes of the Armaments Sub-Committee of Committee No. 6, 3rd Meeting, 30 Nov. 1920, *Records of the First Assembly: Meetings of the Committees: II*, pp. 286–7.

[39] The text of the Assembly resolution is reproduced in John W. Wheeler-Bennett, *Information on the Reduction of Armaments* (London, 1925).

[40] Minutes of the Third Committee, Annex 21, *Records of the Second Assembly: Minutes of the Committees: I*, p. 404.

to the disarmament problem used in that Conference. Esher proposed that peacetime standing armies should be limited on a numerical basis 'by a ratio following the naval precedent at Washington.'[41] With its lack of accompanying measures for the enhancement of international security, the plan embodied perfectly the direct approach to disarmament favoured by the British government: 'the view that armaments provoked fear and suspicion, and so were themselves a cause of war. Nations should first disarm, and security would then ensue.'[42]

However, any proposal for disarmament taking this direct approach was unacceptable to the French government. The French promoted the opposite—indirect—approach by which armaments are seen to be the product of fear and insecurity and so additional security arrangements are necessary before disarmament is feasible. They argued that the commitment to disarm made in 1919 was contingent upon the commitment made at the same time by Britain and the United States to guarantee French security. However, the Anglo-Saxon countries had reneged on their commitments: the United States had failed to join the League and both countries had rejected the 1919 Anglo-American Treaty of Assistance to France. The French therefore had to rely upon their own armed forces to provide for their security and insisted that they could only agree to a disarmament convention if new security arrangements were made to make up for the absence of the machinery that had been promised in 1919.[43]

The need to bridge the divide between the British and French approaches to disarmament was the principal challenge for the disarmament movement for the next dozen years. The organisation that did most to confront this task was the British League of Nations Union, which began to promote disarmament in December 1920.[44] The Chairman of the Union's Executive Committee, Lord Robert Cecil, co-operated with French members of the Temporary Mixed Commission in ensuring that the Esher Plan was rejected. In its place, he and the other Commission members provided the third League Assembly with a report stating that any disarmament plan would have to be accompanied by a Treaty of

---

[41] Quoted in Carolyn Kitching, *Britain and the Problem of International Disarmament, 1919–1934* (London, 1999), p. 61.

[42] W. M. Jordan, *Great Britain, France and the German Problem* (London, 1943), p. 154.

[43] Lamri Chirouf, *The French Approach to Disarmament between 1920–1930: Policy-Making Process, Principles & Methods* (DPhil thesis, Southampton University, 1988), p. 102.

[44] This was when it called on the British government to respond to appeals for arms limitation issued at the Brussels International Financial Conference.

Mutual Guarantee, under which each signatory, once it had reduced its armaments according to the plan, would, if attacked, be assured of immediate military assistance from the other signatories in the same continent. This, it was hoped, would make up for the lack of explicit enforcement procedures for the guarantee of states' territorial integrity provided in Article 10 of the League's Covenant. The proposal was accepted by the entire Third Assembly, even by the British delegation, and formed the basis of the Assembly's fourteenth Resolution on disarmament. This resolution promoted a 'defensive agreement which should be open to all countries, binding them to provide immediate and effective assistance in accordance with a prearranged plan in the event of one of them being attacked,' in order to make possible 'a general reduction in armaments.'[45]

The Temporary Mixed Commission was given the task of incorporating the proposals contained in Resolution XIV into a draft Treaty. However, the task was in fact first undertaken by the League of Nations Union in Great Britain. Cecil drew up a Draft Treaty of Mutual Assistance (DTMA) and ensured that it received the approval of the Executive Committee of the LNU before he put it to the Temporary Mixed Commission where it was revised for submission for consideration by the fourth League Assembly.[46] With Cecil the official British delegate at this Assembly, the treaty was passed for ratification by both members and non-members of the League.[47]

The USA and USSR were both quick to reject the Draft Treaty. The British and French governments, on the other hand, were non-committal. Campaigns in support of the DTMA were therefore launched by activists in both of these countries. The campaign in France was led by the *Association Française pour la Société des Nations*, the *Union Fédérale des Anciens Combattants*, and the *Ligue des Droits de l'Homme*.[48] In addition to mass meetings, questionnaires were circulated in the run-up to the May 1924 general election asking candidates to reveal their position on France's relationship with the League of Nations.[49] Partly as a result of this campaign, a *Cartel des Gauches* coalition government led by Edouard

---

[45] John W. Wheeler-Bennett, *Information on the Problem of Security, 1917–1926* (London, 1927), pp. 91–4.

[46] Birn, *League of Nations Union*, p. 43.

[47] League of Nations, *Official Journal: Special Supplement 13*, pp. 154–5.

[48] *La Paix par le Droit*, Feb. 1924, pp. 88–91.

[49] *La Paix par le Droit*, Apr.–May 1924, pp. 184–5.

Herriot was brought into power on 11 May and made clear its support for the DTMA.[50]

In Great Britain, however, the campaign in support of the DTMA had less short-term success. The movement there was led by the League of Nations Union, which 'campaigned vigorously for the adoption of the Treaty of Mutual Assistance throughout 1923.'[51] When faced with a new Labour government the following year, the Union attempted to persuade Prime Minister Ramsay MacDonald to set up a Commission of Enquiry into the Treaty. However, the issue was instead dealt with by the Committee of Imperial Defence, which was dominated by the service departments. The LNU was therefore unable to prevent MacDonald's rejection of the Treaty of Mutual Assistance on 19 June 1924.

However, the long-term impact of the LNU's campaign for the DTMA was significant. Rather than giving up its campaign after the British government's rejection of the DTMA, the LNU decided to increase its pressure on the government. In August 1924, the Union circulated a petition that attracted the signature of 124 MPs. The petition expressed anxiety that the British rejection of the Draft Treaty might be interpreted as meaning that the British government had abandoned the attempt to pursue disarmament through the League of Nations and had rejected the link between disarmament and security.[52] In response to this petition, MacDonald spoke in the Commons in support of the principles underlying the Draft Treaty.[53] Furthermore, Foreign Office officials were convinced that the public opinion that had been stirred up by the Union's campaign for the Draft Treaty led to MacDonald going to the fourth Assembly of the League of Nations determined to provide something in its place.[54]

A document drawn up by a committee of American activists and officials organised by Professor James T. Shotwell ('the American

---

[50] John L. Hogge II, *Arbitrage, Sécurité, Désarmement: French Security and the League of Nations, 1920–1925* (DPhil thesis, New York University, 1994), ch. 6. See also Crewe to Chamberlain, 27 Feb. 1928, FO 371/13372, Foreign Office General Correspondence, National Archives, London.

[51] Birn, *League of Nations Union*, p. 44.

[52] See MacDonald to Sir Ellis Hume-Williams, 11 Aug. 1924, PRO 30/69/183, Ramsay MacDonald papers, National Archives, London.

[53] Birn, *League of Nations Union*, p. 57.

[54] Memorandum entitled 'The Geneva Protocol,' p. 1, PRO 30/69/1273, MacDonald papers.

Committee on Disarmament and Security')[55] provided MacDonald with the basis for a replacement for the DTMA. The document was called the 'Draft Treaty of Disarmament and Security,' and had been sent by Shotwell to the Secretary General of the League of Nations on 10 June 1924.[56] In an unprecedented action, the League Council agreed to distribute the document to member states on 16 June, before they had even received the final version. Despite the opinion of British Foreign Office officials that the proposal was 'typically American…It approaches the difficulties only to recede away from them,'[57] the central proposal of this plan, compulsory arbitration, was adopted by MacDonald as an alternative to the multilateral security guarantees of the Draft Treaty.[58] The outcome was the 'Protocol for the Pacific Settlement of International Disputes' (or 'Geneva Protocol'), that was adopted unanimously by the fifth League Assembly on 2 October 1924. It provided for compulsory arbitration through signatories' adherence to the Optional Clause of the Statute of the Permanent Court of International Justice for juridical disputes, and arbitration by Council-appointed arbitrators in the case of political disputes on which the Council could not reach a unanimous verdict (a clause which had been inserted in order to fill the 'gap' in the Covenant left by Articles 12 and 15). Most importantly, the Protocol was designed in order to make possible a general disarmament conference to be convened by the Council in Geneva on 15 June 1925 to which all countries would be invited, whether League members or not.

---

[55] This committee was set up by Professor James T. Shotwell in January 1924. Its members were Dr. James T. Shotwell (Professor of History at Columbia University), General Tasker H. Bliss (American representative at the Supreme War Council), Dr. Isaiah Bowman (executive head of the technical experts of the US delegation at the Paris Peace Conference), Dr. Joseph P. Chamberlain (Professor of Public Law at Columbia University), Professor John Bates Clark (former director of the Division of Economics and History of the Carnegie Endowment for International Peace), Dr. Stephen P. Duggan (Director of the Institute for International Education of the Carnegie Foundation), General James G. Harbord (former Chief of Staff of the US Army), Frederick P. Keppel (former Assistant Secretary of War), David Hunter Miller (legal advisor to the US delegation to the Paris Peace Conference), and Dr. Henry S. Pritchett (President of the Carnegie Foundation).

[56] Shotwell to Drummond, 10 Jun. 1924, R. 224, League of Nations Archives, Geneva.

[57] 'Draft Treaty of Disarmament and Security prepared by an American Group,' FO 371/10569/W6242/134/98, Foreign Office General Correspondence.

[58] Carl Bouchard, 'Le "Plan Américain" Shotwell-Bliss de 1924: une initiative méconnue pour le renforcement de la paix,' *Guerres mondiales et conflits contemporains*, 202–203 (2002), p. 222.

With the conciliatory Herriot still Prime Minister in France, the Geneva Protocol was immediately ratified by that country. The British government failed to do the same, so British activists once more had the task of persuading their government to follow the French example. Although Cecil believed that the Geneva Protocol was greatly inferior to the DTMA,[59] the League of Nations Union took the lead in promoting the Protocol in Britain and made it the subject of two parts of a questionnaire circulated to all candidates in the October 1924 General Election. However, the Conservative Party which won the election campaigned on a platform opposed to the Protocol. Although on 29 December 1924 the League of Nations Union managed to persuade the new Prime Minister, Stanley Baldwin, to issue invitations to the Dominions for an Imperial Conference to be held in March to discuss the Protocol,[60] the plan was shelved due to the negative replies received and on 12 March 1925 Foreign Secretary Austen Chamberlain told the League Council that his government would not sign the Protocol. The planned disarmament conference for June 1925 therefore never took place.

Despite their disappointment, groups such as the League of Nations Union continued to promote the principles of 'arbitration, security and disarmament' embodied in the Geneva Protocol. Mass meetings were held and petitions gathered in support of a revised protocol throughout the early summer of 1925. They were enough to cause the British Foreign Secretary to become 'seriously concerned.'[61] However, by the time of the sixth League Assembly the following autumn, activists had new plans in mind. It was felt that the discussions that were taking place outside of the League between Stresemann, Briand and Chamberlain on the matter of international security arrangements offered a new opportunity for discussions on disarmament to be launched.

Christian Lange of the Inter-Parliamentary Union and James Shotwell of the Carnegie Endowment for International Peace were two prominent activists who held this view. They both went to Geneva during the sixth League Assembly and persuaded the Spanish delegation

---

[59] Cecil thought that the arbitration proposals contained in the Geneva Protocol were 'very complicated indeed and...lend themselves to every kind of misrepresentation' (Cecil to Murray, 25 Sep. 1924, Add. MSS. 51132, Cecil papers). As Cecil pointed out, the Protocol's complexity made it difficult for campaigners to promote.

[60] See Birn, *League of Nations Union*, p. 59.

[61] Chamberlain to Cecil, 19 Jun. 1925, Add. MSS. 51078, Cecil papers.

to put forward a Resolution on 12 September 1925 requesting that the Council prepare for a Conference for the Reduction and Limitation of Armaments as soon as security arrangements permitted.[62] An amended Resolution to this effect was adopted on 25 September. Due to fears of Council procrastination on the disarmament issue, the Resolution was accompanied by a memorandum stating that 'any inactivity of the Council in this respect would fail to meet the ideas of the Sixth Assembly.'[63] The next day, therefore, the Council requested a Committee of Enquiry chaired by the internationalist French delegate Joseph Paul-Boncour to submit to it proposals for the establishment of an organ entrusted with the task of preparation for a disarmament conference. This idea of first establishing a preparatory committee 'to study the ways and means' of disarmament before the actual conference met had been taken from a memorandum of 5 September 1925 by Shotwell, which was circulated among Assembly delegates and is said to have 'strongly influenced' Paul-Boncour.[64]

At the first meeting of this Committee on 3 December 1925, therefore, Paul-Boncour emphasised the need to avoid 'seriously disappointing' public opinion.[65] However, it was Cecil—serving as a British delegate—who pushed the pace along; and the Committee completed its business on 5 December 1925 with a proposal along the lines envisaged in Shotwell's plan for the establishment of a 'Preparatory Commission' to lay the foundations for a global Conference on the Reduction and Limitation of Armaments. A week later, the League Council adopted the proposal, and invitations to participate in the Commission were sent to members and non-members of the League alike. In the meantime, Cecil had also ensured that the covering protocol of the Locarno Treaties contained a commitment on the part of the Contracting Parties 'to give their sincere co-operation in the work relating to disarmament

---

[62] Wheeler-Bennett, *Disarmament and Security since Locarno*, pp. 44–5.

[63] Wheeler-Bennett, *Disarmament and Security since Locarno*, p. 46.

[64] Harold Josephson, *James T. Shotwell and the Rise of Internationalism in America* (Rutherford, 1975), p. 149. Paul-Boncour privately told Herriot that he supported the establishment of a preparatory commission because he felt it was important not to disappoint those who placed their faith in the League of Nations and because he wanted to thwart suspected US attempts to convene a disarmament conference outside the League framework (Paul-Boncour to Briand, 16 Sep. 1925, cote 831, série SDN, French Foreign Ministry Archives, Paris).

[65] *League of Nations—Committee of the Council—Second Session—Provisional Minutes (CDC/2nd Session/PV1–5)*, p. 1.

already undertaken by the League of Nations and to seek the realization thereof in a general agreement.'[66]

Early Transnational Promotion of Disarmament

In the period leading up to the establishment of the Preparatory Commission, it has been shown that the disarmament campaign was principally conducted by British and American activists and groups. During this period, transnational organisations were able to play only a minor role, doing little more than passing resolutions on disarmament and forwarding them to the Secretariat of the League of Nations.

The main global primary peace associations, including the International Federation of League of Nations Societies and the Women's International League for Peace and Freedom, regularly passed resolutions in support of disarmament at their annual or biennial conferences.[67] This was also true of a few secondary peace organisations, such as the International Co-operative Women's Guild.[68] Most secondary peace organisations, on the other hand, tended to pass resolutions in favour of disarmament less frequently, and often only at special conferences dedicated to peace. Examples of these special conferences include the Hague Peace Conference convened by the International Federation of Trade Unions in 1922 and the Wembley Conference on the Prevention of the Causes of War held by the International Council of Women in 1924.[69]

After passing their resolutions on disarmament, most organisations tended to send copies to the Secretariat of the League of Nations, which in turn forwarded them to the members of the Temporary

---

[66] Wheeler-Bennett, *Disarmament and Security since Locarno*, p. 40.

[67] The resolutions of the International Federation of League of Nations Societies are contained in the annual supplements to its *Bulletin*; the resolutions of the Women's International League for Peace and Freedom are printed in its journal *Pax International*.

[68] The disarmament resolutions passed at the conferences of the International Co-operative Women's Guild are contained in file DCX/8/1 of the International Co-operative Women's Guild archives, Brynmor Jones Library, Hull.

[69] Details of the Hague Peace Conference can be found in files 109–119, International Federation of Trade Unions archives, International Institute of Social History, Amsterdam; an account of the Wembley Conference is provided in International Council of Women, *The Prevention of the Causes of War: Addresses delivered at the Conference held at the British Empire Exhibition, Wembley, May 2nd to 8th, 1924* (London, 1924).

Mixed Commission.[70] One organisation, the International Federation of League of Nations Societies, also managed to get its annual resolutions published in the Journal of the annual League Assemblies.[71]

However, the number of pro-disarmament resolutions sent to the League before the establishment of the Preparatory Commission should not be exaggerated. For example, as of 1923, the League Secretariat compiled lists of all resolutions received that were intended for the attention of the Council. Not until 2 June 1928 was a resolution sent to the Council that dealt exclusively with the promotion of disarmament.[72]

Furthermore, most members of the Secretariat of the League of Nations felt that the global organisations that were sending them their resolutions were choosing the wrong target and that 'communications to the League itself should be discouraged.'[73] They agreed with Cecil's statement to the Council of December 1923, in which he claimed that 'influence could never be usefully exerted on the League as a corporate body, but only on the governments which composed it.'[74]

Nevertheless, because the Secretariat felt that transnational organisations could serve a useful purpose in stimulating the actions of their national branches, in January 1922 it drew up 'a list of the various peace associations to which the Commission might think it desirable to communicate documents concerning disarmament' in order to help them 'spread the idea of disarmament' through their national sections.[75]

---

[70] See, for instance, the correspondence contained in R. 189, R. 209 and R. 226, League of Nations Archives.

[71] F. P. Walters to Eugène Baie, 21 Dec. 1920, R. 1333, League of Nations Archives.

[72] The lists are contained in boxes R. 1598 and R. 3568 in the League of Nations Archives.

[73] Drummond to Cecil, 27 Apr. 1927, Add. MSS. 51111, Cecil papers. See also the correspondence in box R. 1598 in the League of Nations Archives.

[74] Speech to 27th Council meeting, 10 Dec. 1923, R. 1598, League of Nations Archives.

[75] C.T.A. 52, Geneva, 15 Feb. 1922: 'TMC for the Reduction of Armaments: Propaganda for the Reduction of Armaments,' R. 217, League of Nations Archives; and Note by Aghnides, 30 Jan. 1922, R. 1595, League of Nations Archives.

CHAPTER SIX

THE PREPARATORY COMMISSION AND THE DEVELOPMENT OF DISARMAMENT ACTIVISM, 1926 TO 1930

The establishment of the Preparatory Commission in 1926 was eventually to provide transnational bodies with a focus for their activities. However, during the first year and a half of the Preparatory Commission's existence, the campaign was muted. It was only after the resignations of two key European activists—Viscount Cecil in Great Britain and Henry de Jouvenel in France—that the campaign took off in Europe. Three years later, the movement was further stimulated by the success of the London Naval Conference of 1930. Both the Preparatory Commission and the London Naval Conference provided activists with opportunities to experiment with campaigning techniques that were later adopted on a much greater scale at the World Disarmament Conference of 1932–34.

THE INITIAL DISCUSSIONS OF THE PREPARATORY COMMISSION

Disarmament campaigners had grounds for optimism at the beginning of 1926. The Locarno treaties had partially allayed French security concerns, and had made possible that country's agreement to participate in a Preparatory Commission for an eventual World Disarmament Conference. Cecil therefore felt that 'the attitude of [Aristide] Briand and Austen [Chamberlain] is all that we could wish.'[1]

Furthermore, due to his concern about domestic pressure for arms reduction, the President of the United States—Calvin Coolidge—agreed to participate in the work of the Preparatory Commission and to appoint James T. Shotwell's American Committee on Disarmament as an advisory committee to the State Department on disarmament matters.[2]

---

[1] Cecil to Drummond, 14 Oct. 1925, Add. MSS. 51110, Cecil of Chelwood papers, British Library, London.

[2] Cecelia Lynch, *Beyond Appeasement: Interpreting Interwar Peace Movements in World Politics* (Ithaca, NY, 1999), p. 140; Charles DeBenedetti, *Origins of the Modern American Peace Movement, 1915–1929* (Millwood, NY, 1978), p. 155.

However, the movement for arms reduction made little progress during the first year and a half of the Preparatory Commission's existence. There were a few national initiatives in 1926: in Britain, for instance, the League of Nations Union set up a reduction of armaments committee[3] and women's organisations staged a peace pilgrimage in Hyde Park.[4] There were also a number of small developments at the international level, such as the establishment of a commission of the Labour and Socialist International to study the disarmament problem[5] and the issuing of a memorandum by the International Co-operative Women's Guild to the members of the Preparatory Commission demanding steps towards total disarmament.[6] However, the Secretariat of the League of Nations continued to receive only a trickle of disarmament resolutions[7] and no significant global campaigns for disarmament were launched.

The work of the Preparatory Commission was equally lacklustre. Its first meeting was moved from February to May 1926 and quickly got mired in discussions of how to define armaments, how to compare them, how to distinguish between offensive and defensive weapons, what form arms limitation might take, whether total war strength or merely peace establishments should be limited, how geography, population and resources can be taken into account, whether disarmament should be global or regional, and whether or not international supervision would be necessary.[8]

Nevertheless, by the time of the Preparatory Commission's third session in March 1927, the British and French delegations were concerned about growing public dissatisfaction at their lack of progress. As the French delegate, Joseph Paul-Boncour, pointed out, there would

---

[3] Lorna Lloyd, *Peace through Law: Britain and the International Court in the 1920s* (Woodbridge, Suffolk, 1997), p. 68.

[4] Jill Liddington, *The Long Road to Greenham: Feminism and Anti-Militarism in Britain since 1820* (London, 1989), pp. 144–7.

[5] Adler to the national secretaries of the Labour and Socialist International, 26 Jul. 1926, file 758, Labour and Socialist International (LSI) archives, International Institute of Social History, Amsterdam.

[6] 'Memorandum on Disarmament,' file DCX/8/1, International Co-operative Women's Guild (ICWG) archives, Brynmor Jones Library, Hull.

[7] See the resolutions in boxes R. 182–3, League of Nations Archives, Geneva.

[8] John W. Wheeler-Bennett, *Disarmament and Security since Locarno, 1925–1931: Being the Political and Technical Background of the General Disarmament Conference, 1932* (London, 1932), pp. 49–58.

be 'great disappointment to public opinion' if the Commission failed to complete its task at that session.[9]

Consequently, both the British and the French delegations put forward separate draft conventions intended to form the basis of discussion at the planned World Disarmament Conference. The internationalist members of the British and French committees that had drafted these conventions, Cecil and Paul-Boncour, had ensured that both conventions contained genuine proposals for disarmament. Paul-Boncour had managed to overcome the French army's opposition to the incorporation of budgetary limitation of materiel in the French draft,[10] while Cecil had managed to persuade the British army to provide for limitation of all types of effectives in the British draft.[11]

However, in order to gain concessions by the armed services, Cecil had failed to ensure provision for budgetary limitation of materiel in the British plan, and Paul-Boncour had failed to secure limitation of all types of effectives in the French plan.[12] The two conventions also clashed on whether or not to provide for international supervision of states' arms reduction and whether to limit naval armaments by classes of ship or by total tonnage for all classes of ship.

So, although a single draft convention was agreed upon at the Preparatory Commission on 26 April 1927, there was deadlock between the Anglo-Saxon and French positions on all of these issues. Discussion of these problems was postponed until November, and it was hoped that the naval disarmament issue could be resolved at the Geneva Naval Conference held between June and August 1927.

---

[9] League of Nations, *Documents of the Preparatory Commission for the Disarmament Conference*, series 4, p. 13.

[10] Minutes of the 1 Feb. 1926 meeting of the *Conseil Supérieur de la Défense Nationale*, folder 2, file 7N 3535, Service Historique de l'Armée de Terre, Vincennes. See also Lamri Chirouf, *The French Approach to Disarmament between 1920–1930: Policy-Making Process, Principles & Methods* (DPhil thesis, Southampton University, 1988), pp. 148–60.

[11] Minutes of meeting 222 of the Committee of Imperial Defence, CAB 2/5, National Archives, London. See also David Shorney, *Britain and Disarmament, 1916–1931* (PhD thesis, University of Durham, 1980), pp. 300–01.

[12] Dick Richardson, *The Evolution of British Disarmament Policy in the 1920s* (London, 1989), p. 88.

1927—A Turning Point in Europe

The Geneva Naval Conference failed to live up to expectations and collapsed in August 1927 because of the refusal of the British and American governments to abandon their original positions.[13] However, its failure was one of the most significant stimuli for the mobilisation of disarmament activism in Europe. The 'determined and ingenious' opposition of members of the British Cabinet to compromise at the Geneva Naval Conference caused Cecil to resign his position as Chancellor of the Duchy of Lancaster on 9 August 1927.[14] No longer tied by the requirements of Cabinet collective responsibility, Cecil felt that he now had 'full freedom to advocate disarmament.'[15] His organisation, the League of Nations Union, launched a reinvigorated disarmament campaign shortly afterwards with a letter by its Chairman to the *Times* on 2 September 1927.[16] Will Arnold-Forster of the National Peace Council (which also decided to circulate a 'General Disarmament' petition) was poached for the LNU's campaign and was provided with separate funding and office-space to conduct it.[17] By the end of the year six hundred disarmament meetings had been held by the LNU, making the 1927 disarmament campaign the largest Union initiative so far.[18] As for the women's peace movement in Britain, a 'Women's Peace Crusade' representing two million Britons in 28 organisations was launched, forming the nucleus of an international movement.[19]

Another resignation that took place in 1927 was to have a similar impact on the disarmament movement in France as Cecil's resignation had had in Great Britain. On 24 July 1927, Henry de Jouvenel—a prominent senator and activist in the *Comité d'Action pour la Société des Nations*—wrote to Aristide Briand to tell him that he could no longer

---

[13] Richardson, *Evolution of British Disarmament Policy*, p. 139.

[14] A frank account of Cecil's reasons for resigning is provided in Cecil to Chamberlain, 16 Aug. 1927, Add. MSS. 51079, Cecil papers. Cecil placed much of the blame on Winston Churchill, of whom Cecil said in this letter: 'war is the only thing that really interests him in politics.'

[15] Cecil to Murray, 2 Sep. 1927, Add. MSS. 51132, Cecil papers.

[16] Donald S. Birn, *The League of Nations Union, 1918–1945* (Oxford, 1981), pp. 68–9.

[17] Martin Ceadel, *Semi-Detached Idealists: The British Peace Movement and International Relations, 1854–1945* (Oxford, 2000), p. 275. Details of this campaign can be found in Lloyd, *Peace through Law*, pp. 67–70.

[18] Shorney, *Britain and Disarmament*, p. 98.

[19] Lynch, *Beyond Appeasement*, p. 98.

act as a French delegate to the League of Nations because his government was undertaking a 'policy of adjournment' on matters before
the League including disarmament.[20] Just as Cecil used his position of
leadership in the League of Nations Union in Great Britain, Jouvenel
used his leadership of the *Comité d'Action* to launch a campaign in France
for progress towards 'arbitration, security and disarmament' through
the League of Nations. The following year, the diverse French League
of Nations societies were stimulated into circulating questionnaires to
all candidates in the general election, and the year after that Jouvenel
launched an arbitration campaign that was to form the backbone of
French activism for the World Disarmament Conference from 1931
onwards.[21]

ACTIVISM AND THE SOVIET UNION'S PROPOSALS AT THE PREPARATORY COMMISSION

According to a British campaigner present at the eighth League
Assembly in September 1927, Philip Noel Baker, the resignations had
a 'profound and very beneficial impact... [and] made disarmament the
most important issue in the development of the League.'[22]

The subsequent meeting of the Preparatory Commission in November
1927 was further boosted by the presence for the first time of a Soviet
delegation. It brought with it a utopian proposal for immediate, complete and universal disarmament with no strings attached, which was
seen by the other delegates as little more than a publicity stunt.[23]

However, many fellow-travelling and pacifist organisations welcomed
the Soviet proposals, and activism was further stimulated. For the
first time, the Secretariat of the League of Nations received a considerable stream of disarmament resolutions from non-governmental
organisations.[24]

The most substantial initiative in support of the Soviet proposals
was by the International Co-operative Women's Guild, which had

---

[20] The text of the letter is reproduced in *La Paix par le Droit*, Oct. 1927, p. 354.

[21] See the issues of *La Paix par le Droit* for Jan. 1928 and Apr.–May 1929, and
Jouvenel to Cecil, 11 Mar. 1931, Add. MSS. 51100, Cecil papers.

[22] Noel Baker to Cecil, 17 Sep. 1927, Add. MSS. 51106, Cecil papers.

[23] Wheeler-Bennett, *Disarmament and Security since Locarno*, pp. 234–9.

[24] These resolutions are contained in file R. 2380 in the League of Nations
Archives.

been promoting total disarmament since its foundation in 1921.[25] It circulated a declaration 'gratefully welcoming the courageous proposals of the Soviet Government for complete and universal disarmament,' which acquired the signatures of 34 national organisations and 4 international organisations including the Women's International League for Peace and Freedom, the War Resisters' International, the Fellowship of Reconciliation, the US Women's Peace Committee, the British Friends' Peace Committee, and the British Standing Joint Committee of Industrial Women's Organisations.[26]

The declaration was sent to all of the delegations to the Preparatory Commission, and the Soviet delegation ensured the publication of the declaration in the records of the Preparatory Commission.[27] The Soviet delegate, Litvinoff, wrote to the Secretary of the International Co-operative Women's Guild, Honora Enfield, to tell her that he found the declarations he had received 'of such importance that I quoted them bodily in my speech at the Preparatory Disarmament Commission' in March 1928.[28]

However, with all of the other countries on the Preparatory Commission united in opposition to the Soviet proposals, the Commission's President—Jonkheer Loudon—concluded the fifth session of the Preparatory Commission by rejecting the Soviet plan and demanding that Litvinoff approach 'our next and any ensuing meetings in a constructive spirit and not with the idea of destroying the work we have already done.'[29] The Preparatory Commission was again postponed until the following year.

---

[25] 'Co-operative Women and their Work for Peace, 1921–1933,' file DCX/8/1, ICWG archives.

[26] Special report on the disarmament declaration campaign enclosed with Honora Enfield's circular letter to the members of the ICWG, 1 May 1928, file DCX/8/1, ICWG archives. Enfield said in this letter that 'I feel that this campaign cannot be regarded as a success' because of the small number of local organisations worldwide that had been persuaded to sign the declaration (just 89). The fact that the declaration was in support of proposals emanating from the Soviet Union proved to be an obstacle to the signature of many organisations.

[27] *Documents of the Preparatory Commission for the Disarmament Conference*, series 6, annex 3.

[28] The text is reproduced in the special report on the disarmament declaration campaign enclosed with Honora Enfield's circular letter to the members of the ICWG, 1 May 1928, file DCX/8/1, ICWG archives.

[29] Quoted in Wheeler-Bennett, *Disarmament and Security since Locarno*, p. 238.

Activism and the Conclusion of the Preparatory Commission's Work

With the Preparatory Commission having failed to make any progress for three years, the frustration of those who supported disarmament became increasingly pronounced. Noel Baker and members of the League Secretariat including Eric Drummond, Arthur Salter, Arthur Sweetser, Henri Bonnet and Konni Zilliacus agreed that the Preparatory Commission had become 'a complete and possibly a disastrous fiasco...the only good thing about the Preparatory Commission was that it had now furnished a fine opportunity for an outburst of popular indignation.'[30]

The disarmament campaign was further spurred by the signing of the Kellogg-Briand pact for the renunciation of war in August 1928. American activist James Shotwell played a central role in negotiating this agreement, which was substantially based on his March 1927 'Notes for a Suggested Statement on Franco-American Policies' submitted to French Foreign Minister Aristide Briand.[31] Many organisations, such as the branches of the Women's International League for Peace and Freedom (WILPF), consequently passed resolutions in the summer of 1928 demanding that governments 'give effective expression to the policy of renunciation of war by instituting measures for speedy disarmament.'[32]

The national disarmament campaigns increased in scale, and that in Great Britain became of particular concern to its government. In May 1928, the new British representative on the Preparatory Commission—Lord Cushendun—became worried about being 'severely blamed' by 'a large body of opinion in this country' if disarmament negotiations were to break down altogether; while in January 1929 the War Office permanent under-secretary complained that the armed services

---

[30] Noel Baker to Cecil, 2 Apr. 1928 Add. MSS. 51107, Cecil papers.

[31] These notes are contained in box 2 of the James T. Shotwell papers, Columbia University, New York. For accounts of Shotwell's role in the negotiation of the Kellogg-Briand Pact, see James T. Shotwell, *The Autobiography of James T. Shotwell* (Indianapolis, 1961), ch. 12; and Harold Josephson, *James T. Shotwell and the Rise of Internationalism in America* (Rutherford, NJ, 1975), ch. 9.

[32] Ann Flynn, 'World-wide campaign for renunciation of war and for disarmament,' 30 Jul. 1928, reel 98, Women's International League for Peace and Freedom archives on UMI microfilm.

had 'no obvious means of dealing with...[the League of Nations Union's]...unfair propaganda.'[33]

At the global level, resolutions were sent to the League Secretariat at such a rate that they could no longer be filed individually.[34] The Disarmament Commission of the Labour and Socialist International embarked on a particularly substantial campaign to secure the signatures of representatives of national and local labour organisations worldwide to a resolution dated 13 February 1929 demanding that the Preparatory Commission 'complete its work as soon as possible.'[35]

The strength of the disarmament campaign was particularly noticeable at the ninth League Assembly at which the Women's International League for Peace and Freedom was allowed a deputation on disarmament to the League Secretariat on 11 September 1928.[36] In response to this pressure, a French delegate at the Assembly—Joseph Paul-Boncour—demanded that the next meeting of the Preparatory Commission 'must be held soon, but it was still more important that it should be the last, so as not to place a further strain upon public opinion.'[37]

By the time the Preparatory Commission reconvened in April 1929, the number of activist communications sent to the League Secretariat was considerable enough to be highlighted by the President of the Commission in his opening comments:

> Public opinion is growing impatient, and rightly so. I have had a striking proof of this in the very large number of letters which, as President of this Commission, I have received during the last few weeks....These letters have been classified and are on view. They express the opinion that the Preparatory Commission should complete its work as soon as possible, in order that a General Convention may be concluded, thus fulfilling the solemn promises of disarmament made to all the nations

---

[33] Quoted in Lynch, *Beyond Appeasement*, p. 80; and Ceadel, *Semi-Detached Idealists*, p. 278 respectively.

[34] They are contained in file R. 2380 in the League of Nations Archives.

[35] An account of this campaign is contained in pp. 65–71 of Labour and Socialist International, *Reports and Proceedings of the Fourth Congress of the Labour and Socialist International, Vienna, 25th July to 1st August 1931* (London, 1932). The records of the campaign are contained in file 1178 of the LSI archives.

[36] 'The WIL Deputation on Disarmament,' *Pax International*, Oct. 1928, p. 4. The transcript of the deputation is contained in file R. 2380 in the League of Nations Archives and in reel 98 of the Women's International League for Peace and Freedom archives on UMI microfilm.

[37] *Official Journal*, special supplement 67, 'Records of the Ninth Ordinary Session of the Assembly: Minutes of the Third Committee,' p. 58.

> of the world…I venture to hope that… it will bring increasing pressure upon governments, whose action in this field more than in any other depends on the will of the people.[38]

The communications put on view included over 14,000 letters in support of the disarmament resolution of the Labour and Socialist International, 177 letters in support of a disarmament resolution of the International Order of Good Templars, and letters promoting resolutions from the Universal Christian Conference on Life and Work, the Women's International League for Peace and Freedom, the International Federation of Trade Unions, the International Federation of Officials, and the International Co-operative Women's Guild.[39]

The value attached by members of the Preparatory Commission to these private communications was not universally as high as that of the Commission's President. For example, when Loudon read out a letter promoting disarmament sent to him by the President of the International League of Aviators, the British representative—Lord Cushendun—reacted angrily: 'I consider it very improper that an outside individual, probably having no authority whatsoever, should attempt to influence the opinion of this Commission…on no occasion should we give publicity, by reading them here, to unsolicited letters received from external sources the value of which nobody knows.'[40]

In a move that foreshadowed the responses of governments to the greater activism at the World Disarmament Conference three years later, the members of the Preparatory Commission reacted to activist pressure in 1929 by moving towards agreement, but not towards disarmament: each party simply showed willingness not to press for disarmament measures that any of the others might refuse to accept. As regards trained reserves, for instance, both Britain and America were willing to accept the French position that these should be exempt from limitation. In return, the French accepted the Anglo-American position that limitation of materiel should be by publicity rather than budgetary limitation: a proposal that effectively abandoned the principle of limitation of materiel. This was a disappointment to the German member of the Commission, Count Bernstorff, and to activists such

---

[38] *Documents of the Preparatory Commission for the Disarmament Conference*, series 8, p. 7.

[39] *Documents of the Preparatory Commission for the Disarmament Conference*, series 8, annex 10.

[40] *Documents of the Preparatory Commission for the Disarmament Conference*, series 8, p. 11.

as Cecil, who at the subsequent League Assembly remarked that 'it is easy to agree to nothing.'[41]

What made genuine progress at the Preparatory Commission possible was a change of government in both Great Britain and the United States in 1929. In the USA, a man of Quaker parentage—Herbert Hoover—became President, while in Great Britain the Labour Party returned to government following the general election in May. One of the principal reasons cited for the Labour Party's success is the vigour of the League of Nations Union's campaign in opposition to the disarmament policy of the incumbent Conservative government.[42] The new British Prime Minister, Ramsay MacDonald, therefore reappointed Cecil as British representative on the Preparatory Commission, even though he was a member of the defeated Conservative Party. When this Commission met for the last time in November 1930, it was Cecil who pushed through agreement to renegotiate the settlement reached at the 1929 meeting. After that, concessions on the part of both Britain and the United States made possible the final agreement upon a Draft Disarmament Convention: both countries allowed incorporation of budgetary limitation and supervision of disarmament in the Convention.[43] On 9 December 1930, therefore, the Commission finally approved a Draft Disarmament Convention, which left blank the figures for arms reduction and limitation that were to be decided upon at the World Disarmament Conference. The date for this Conference was subsequently set for 2 February 1932 at the January 1931 meeting of the Council of the League of Nations.

The London Naval Conference

In addition to facilitating progress in the Preparatory Commission, the new governments in Britain and the United States convened a third naval conference in London in 1930. National activist groups played an important role in promoting this Conference, particularly in the United States where the disarmament campaign was boosted by the

---

[41] Wheeler-Bennett, *Disarmament and Security since Locarno*, pp. 73–5.

[42] Shorney, *Britain and Disarmament*, pp. 116–7. Lorna Lloyd, on the other hand, argues that 'In fact, the campaigning of the LNU left no mark on the 1929 election' (*Peace through Law*, p. 86).

[43] Shorney, *Britain and Disarmament*, pp. 331–4.

revelation that naval arms interests had sponsored lobbyist William Shearer to wreck the Geneva Naval Conference.[44] In addition to highlighting this, American activists participated in a mass letter-writing campaign initiated by WILPF leader Dorothy Detzer. So many letters were sent that one State Department official exclaimed: 'The State Department is flooded…We are having to commandeer every typist in the stenographic pool to handle the letters.'[45] Detzer's initiative even caused President Hoover to summon her to his office at the end of the Conference to show her the constraints on how far he had been able to go, in the hope that the flood of letters would stop.[46]

Faced with this pressure, it was the US government that made the vital concession at the London Naval Conference by agreeing that 18 (instead of 21) 8-inch-gun cruisers would be adequate in its plan of 5 February that formed the basis of the final settlement of 22 April 1930.[47] Even so, this settlement was a disappointment to disarmament activists in that it provided only for limitation and not for reduction of auxiliary vessels.[48]

However, the London Naval Conference boosted the disarmament movement in three ways. First, because activists played a useful role in securing ratification of the final settlement in the United States, the President was left with a debt of gratitude. For example, an umbrella-group of American organisations that campaigned for ratification led by James G. McDonald of the Foreign Policy Association was rewarded for its efforts in 1931 with two deputations promoting the World Disarmament Conference.[49]

Secondly, the relative success of the London Naval Conference, at least compared to the previous naval conference in Geneva, boosted

---

[44] Richard W. Fanning, *Peace and Disarmament: Naval Rivalry & Arms Control, 1922–33* (Lexington, KY, 1995), pp. 118–9.

[45] Quoted in Fanning, *Peace and Disarmament*, p. 119.

[46] Dorothy Detzer, *Appointment on the Hill* (New York, 1948), pp. 86–99.

[47] Robert Gordon Kaufman, *Arms Control During the Pre-Nuclear Era: The United States and Naval Limitation between the Two World Wars* (New York, 1990), p. 129.

[48] Charles Chatfield, *For Peace and Justice: Pacifism in America, 1914–1941* (Knoxville, TN, 1971), p. 160; Fanning, *Peace and Disarmament*, p. 129.

[49] The group became the Interorganization Council on Disarmament. See Stephen P. Waring, *Herbert Hoover and the Promotion of Disarmament, 1929–1932* (MA thesis, University of Iowa, 1985), p. 23; McDonald to Hoover, 26 June 1930, Pres. F. A. 1000, Herbert Hoover papers, Herbert Hoover Presidential Library, West Branch, IA.

the disarmament movement's confidence that real achievements could be produced at the World Disarmament Conference two years later.[50]

And finally, the London Naval Conference is particularly significant for having provided an early opportunity for transnational co-operation between previously nationally-based disarmament campaigns. The most notable example was the co-operation of the British Women's Peace Crusade and the American Committee on the Cause and Cure of War in gathering signatures to a mass petition. The petition was presented in a joint deputation to British Prime Minister Ramsay MacDonald and US Secretary of State Henry Stimson in London on 6 February 1930, after British Cabinet Secretary Maurice Hankey had warned MacDonald that their demands could not be ignored.[51] The presentation of this petition to the London Conference delegates provided an important precedent that helped make possible the presentation of a much larger women's petition to the delegates at the World Disarmament Conference in February 1932.

---

[50] Richard W. Fanning, 'Peace Groups and the Campaign for Naval Disarmament, 1927–1936,' *Peace & Change*, 15/1 (1990), p. 39.

[51] Fanning, *Peace and Disarmament*, p. 119; Lynch, *Beyond Appeasement*, p. 98. A full account of the deputation is given in the pamphlet by the Women's Peace Crusade entitled *Women and Disarmament: The Deputation of American, British, French and Japanese Women received by the Chairman of the London Naval Conference at St. James' Palace on February 6th 1930* (London, 1930).

PART FOUR

THE WORLD DISARMAMENT CONFERENCE

CHAPTER SEVEN

PREPARATIONS FOR THE WORLD DISARMAMENT CONFERENCE, 1931

> *If the people want disarmament, they can have it. If they will exert their will, they can compel results... I hope you will show the Governments that however far they may be ready to go their people will be behind them.*[1]
> Arthur Henderson, *Future President of the World Disarmament Conference, 9 February 1931*

Intergovernmental agreement upon a Draft Disarmament Convention in December 1930 and the setting of a date for the Conference for the Reduction and Limitation of Armaments in January 1931 accelerated the global non-governmental disarmament campaign. During the period between December 1930 and February 1932, the transnational dimension of the movement became especially prominent, with the establishment of *super*-international non-governmental organisations to co-ordinate the disarmament campaign, the staging of a massive unofficial World Disarmament Conference in Paris, and the circulation of arguably the largest petition in history.[2] However, the impact of all this activity on government policy before the opening of the World Disarmament Conference was limited.

DEVELOPMENT OF THE TRANSNATIONAL CAMPAIGN

At the last session of the Preparatory Commission, Viscount Cecil concluded his final speech by saying: 'the last word is with the peoples of the world. We have given them in this Convention a great opportunity... The world can be disarmed if the peoples wish... it will be part of the duty

---

[1] Quoted in Martin Ceadel, *Semi-Detached Idealists: The British Peace Movement and International Relations, 1854–1945* (Oxford, 2000), p. 279 and in *Headway*, Mar. 1931, supplement, p. i.

[2] The women's disarmament petition (details of which are provided in appendix v) remains the largest international petition ever to have been circulated in terms of the proportion of the population of the world that signed it. See page 160, footnote 22.

of every one of us to assist in that solution.'[3] No single individual did
more to stimulate the transnational disarmament campaign during
the year preceding the World Disarmament Conference than Cecil.
Nearly all of the principal transnational activities for the promotion
of disarmament that took place during 1931 were initiated in response
to Cecil's action.

During a sequence of 'disarmament lunches' that took place in the
winter of 1930–1, Cecil and other British activists including Philip Noel
Baker, Kathleen Courtney and Sir Norman Angell discussed proposals
for the global mobilisation of public opinion in support of the goals
of the forthcoming World Disarmament Conference.[4] Their proposals
included 'special conferences' by organisations such as the International
Federation of League of Nations Societies, the Labour and Socialist
International, the World Alliance for Promoting International Friendship
through the Churches, and the international ex-servicemen's movement,
as well as a 'special conference of all peace societies of every kind' to
take place in November 1931.[5]

In order to stimulate the transnational campaign, Cecil arranged
meetings in Geneva and Paris between 2 and 8 February 1931 with
the principal French and international non-governmental organisations
with a direct or indirect interest in disarmament. At each meeting he
secured acceptance of a programme outlining his principal objectives.[6]
In this programme, Cecil called for 'all organisations working directly or
indirectly for peace... [to]... concentrate during 1931 upon obtaining
successful issue to the [World Disarmament] Conference....[and]...they
should make a 25% all round reduction of total military budgets their
first objective.'[7]

---

[3] League of Nations, *Documents of the Preparatory Commission for the Disarmament Conference, Series X: Minutes of the Sixth Session (Second Part) of the Preparatory Commission for the
Disarmament Conference* (Geneva, 1931), p. 408.

[4] Noel Baker to Angell, 15 Jul. 1931, box 5/146, Philip Noel Baker papers, Churchill
Archives Centre, Cambridge.

[5] 'Preliminary Suggestions for the Disarmament Campaign,' box 5/144, Noel
Baker papers.

[6] The complete text of his programme is contained in 'Action en vue de la première
Conférence Générale pour la Réduction et la Limitation des Armements, 1932,' box
209, Gilbert Murray papers, Bodleian Library, Oxford.

[7] 'International Organisations and the Disarmament Conference, 1932. Report of
the Negotiations in Geneva and Paris, February 2nd–8th, 1931,' box 209, Murray
papers.

At the meeting held in the Hôtel Richemond in Geneva on 5 February 1931, Cecil assembled representatives of all of the principal international peace societies, including the League of Nations associations, the Women's International League for Peace and Freedom (WILPF), the International Peace Bureau, the Inter-Parliamentary Union, the Catholic Union for International Studies, the Geneva Research Information Bureau, and the International Conference of Disabled Soldiers and Ex-Servicemen (CIAMAC).[8] One of the principal outcomes of this meeting was agreement to co-operate in the publication in Geneva of 'a monthly bulletin reviewing the acts of governments and parliaments, and the trends of public and press opinion in different countries on the subject of disarmament.'[9] A 'Disarmament Information Committee' was set up in Geneva for this purpose under the Presidency of Christian Lange, Secretary-General of the Inter-Parliamentary Union. The Committee published the first issue of its bulletin, simply entitled *Disarmament*, in June 1931. Its front page declared that the journal's goal was 'to give as true an impression as possible of the movements of opinion, official and unofficial, in the different countries concerning the prospects of disarmament.'[10] The periodical continued to be published at least monthly until May 1933, when it was replaced by a journal entitled *Recovery*, which focused on the World Economic Conference as well as disarmament.

The meeting held in the International Christian Study Centre in Geneva on 6 February 1931 secured support for Cecil's disarmament campaign from the principal international religious and student organisations, including the Universal Christian Council on Life and Work, the World Alliance for Promoting International Friendship through the Churches, the Society of Friends, the International Missionary Council, the World's Alliances of YMCAs and YWCAs, the World Student Christian Federation and the International Student Service.[11]

---

[8] 'L'Opinion Publique et le Désarmement. Résumé de l'échange de vues qui a eu lieu à l'Hôtel Richemond, à Genève, le 5 février 1931,' frames 0299–0311, reel 99, Women's International League for Peace and Freedom (WILPF) papers (UMI microfilm edition).

[9] 'L'Opinion Publique et le Désarmement. Résumé de l'échange de vues qui a eu lieu à l'Hôtel Richemond, à Genève, le 5 février 1931,' frame 0309, reel 99, WILPF papers.

[10] *Disarmament*, Jun. 1931, p. 1.

[11] 'Report of Conference with the Rt. Hon. the Viscount Cecil, K.C., Friday, February 6th, 1931,' file 213.10.42, World Student Christian Federation (WSCF) papers, World Council of Churches Library, Geneva.

These organisations requested that Cecil write an open letter to each of them, 'officially inviting their co-operation.'[12]

On 5 March 1931, this letter was sent, telling each organisation: 'nothing has encouraged me more than the sympathy with which you received my suggestion that your great organisation might devote special attention during the current year to preparing the success of the first World Disarmament Conference...I believe it to be possible and desirable to arrive at an all-round reduction in the total sums provided in national budgets for military purposes by 25%...Those of us who believe in the vital importance of saving the Conference from failure must unite our efforts and must work hard.'[13] In response to this appeal, three committees for the co-ordination of the disarmament efforts of these organisations were established: the Disarmament Committee of Christian International Organisations (DCCIO), the Disarmament Committee of Women's International Organisations (DCWIO), and the Disarmament Committee of Students' International Organisations (DCSIO).

The Disarmament Committee of Students' International Organisations was the first to be created, on 12 July 1931 at a meeting in Geneva convened by Michel Poberezski, secretary-general of the International Student Service.[14] The meeting was attended by representatives of the World Student Christian Federation, the World's Alliances of YMCAs and YWCAs, the International Federation of University Women, the International Confederation of Students, the International Federation of University League of Nations Societies, *Pax Romana*, the World Union of Jewish Students and the International Federation of Socialist Students. They agreed 'to unite in a common effort in favour of the Disarmament Conference' and jointly to organise public lectures on disarmament in university towns, to promote disarmament on university campuses, and to pass resolutions on the subject at their annual congresses.[15]

---

[12] 'Report of Conference with the Rt. Hon. the Viscount Cecil, K.C., Friday, February 6th, 1931,' p. 6, file 213.10.42, WSCF papers.

[13] Cecil to Miss Charlotte T. Niven [of the World's Alliance of YWCAs], 5 Mar. 1931, frame 1893, reel 98, WILPF papers; Cecil to Dr. W. A. Visser 't Hooft [of the World Student Christian Federation], 5 Mar. 1931, file 213.10.42, WSCF papers.

[14] Poberezski to de la Grandière, 7 Jul. 1931, R. 2381, League of Nations Archives, Geneva.

[15] 'Students and Disarmament,' file 213.10.42, WSCF papers.

Unlike the Students' Committee, the Disarmament Committee of Women's International Organisations had deeper origins than Cecil's proposals. The DCWIO was an offshoot of the Liaison Committee of Women's International Organisations, which had been established in September 1930 to co-ordinate the activities of eight women's organisations 'when matters of international importance arise.'[16] The first action of this committee was to launch an 'Appeal of Women to the Statesmen of the World' in September 1930 demanding that statesmen 'make the whole-hearted observance of the Kellogg-Briand Pact the supreme charge of national honour and the safeguard of humanity.'[17] By 12 February 1931, the organisation had received several proposals for co-operation to promote the success of the World Disarmament Conference.[18] One of these came from Carrie Chapman Catt of the US National Committee on the Cause and Cure of War, who proposed that the international women's organisations arrange a mass demonstration in Geneva at the time of the World Disarmament Conference.[19] A second proposal from the International Co-operative Women's Guild promoted the same idea. A third proposal, from Mary Dingman (an American industrial secretary of the World's Alliance of YWCAs) who had attended Cecil's Geneva meeting of 6 February 1931, suggested that the international women's organisations create 'a co-ordinating committee' for the promotion of disarmament by the international women's organisations.[20]

The Liaison Committee of Women's International Organisations therefore created an 'Ad Hoc Disarmament Conference Committee'

---

[16] Minutes of the first meeting of the Temporary Liaison Committee of the International Women's Organisations, 4 Nov. 1930, file 1, Liaison Committee of Women's International Organisations (LCWIO) archives, International Institute of Social History, Amsterdam. The eight organisations that participated in this committee were the International Council of Women, the International Alliance of Women for Suffrage and Equal Citizenship, the World's Young Women's Christian Association, the International Federation of University Women, the World's Women's Christian Temperance Union, the Women's International League for Peace and Freedom, the International Council of Nurses, and the World Union of Women for International Concord.

[17] Minutes of the Temporary Co-operation Committee, Geneva, 12 Sep. 1930, file 1, LCWIO archives.

[18] Minutes of the meeting of the Liaison Committee of Women's International Organisations of 12 Feb. 1931, file 1, LCWIO archives.

[19] 'Disarmament. Liaison Committee of Women's International Organisations. Suggestions for Collaboration, 19 February 1931' and Clara Guthrie d'Arcis to E. M. Zimmern, 10 Mar. 1931, frames 1840–4, reel 98, WILPF papers.

[20] 'Suggestions,' frame 1888, reel 98, WILPF papers.

under the chairmanship of Margery Corbett Ashby (President of the International Alliance of Women).[21] It met for the first time in Crosby Hall in London on 9 June 1931 and was attended by representatives of the World's Alliance of YWCAs, the International Alliance of Women, the World Union of Women for International Concord, the International Federation of University Women, the International Council of Women and WILPF.[22] By 5 September 1931, the permanent 'Disarmament Committee of Women's International Organisations' had been set up to promote disarmament, starting with a co-ordinated campaign during the twelfth League Assembly.[23] Since she had proposed the creation of this committee in February, Mary Dingman was made the Chairwoman of the DCWIO, which was to become, in its own words, 'the greatest concerted action that women have ever undertaken.'[24]

As well as chairing the DCWIO, Mary Dingman played a crucial role in the establishment of the Disarmament Committee of Christian International Organisations in October 1931. She convened the first meeting of the organisations that were to form the DCCIO on 13 October 1931 in the offices of the World's Alliance of YWCAs in Geneva.[25] The purpose of the committee was 'the co-ordinating and strengthening of the work of each organisation in preparation for the [World Disarmament] Conference.'[26] The founding organisations were the World's Alliances of YMCAs and YWCAs, the World Student Christian Federation, the Universal Christian Council on Life and Work, the International Missionary Council and the World Alliance for Promoting International Friendship through the Churches.[27] By

---

[21] Minutes of the meeting of the Liaison Committee of Women's International Organisations of 9 Jun. 1931, file 1, LCWIO archives.

[22] Minutes of the 'Ad Hoc Committee on the Disarmament Conference,' 9 Jun. 1931, frame 0605, reel 99, WILPF papers.

[23] Minutes of the meeting of the Disarmament Committee of Women's International Organisations of 5 Sep. 1931, frame 2361, reel 98, WILPF papers.

[24] Memorandum by the Disarmament Committee of Women's International Organisations, frame 0679, WILPF papers.

[25] Joachim Mueller to Bertram Pickard, 7 Oct. 1931, box 1, International Consultative Group (ICG) papers, League of Nations Archives, Geneva.

[26] 'Disarmament Committee of the Joint Christian Centre. First Session on Wednesday 21st October, 1931,' file 212.013, World Alliance for Promoting International Friendship through the Churches papers, World Council of Churches Library, Geneva.

[27] 'Circular to the National Councils on the Disarmament Conference by H. L. Henriod,' 29 Feb. 1932, file 212.013, World Alliance for Promoting International Friendship through the Churches papers.

the end of November 1931, the DCCIO had decided that its main roles during the Disarmament Conference would be the provision of a Christian press service and daily commentaries on the progress of the Conference.[28]

A fourth disarmament committee was also set up by the principal international peace organisation of the interwar years, the International Federation of League of Nations Societies (IFLNS). Again, the stimulus came from Cecil. In his capacity as President of this organisation, Cecil ensured that the 16 February 1931 meeting of the Federation's Executive Committee in Brussels passed a resolution calling 'upon all the affiliated societies to do all in their power during the coming year to awaken public opinion in their respective countries to the urgent need of concentrated national effort so as to ensure that the first Disarmament Conference shall result in immediate and substantial reduction of the armies, navies and air forces of the world.'[29] Cecil also secured agreement upon the establishment of a disarmament committee, the principal purpose of which was to produce a resolution outlining the common objectives of the Federation's disarmament campaign.

This resolution was drawn up at the IFLNS Disarmament Committee meeting held in Paris on 21 and 22 March 1931. The resolution's essential elements were put forward by Cecil and the Belgian activist Henri Rolin, who argued that existing security arrangements were adequate to make possible a 25% cut in global arms expenditure and that the equal rights of the defeated powers could be recognised by universally abolishing the 'aggressive weapons' denied to Germany, such as bombing aircraft, tanks, submarines, large war vessels and heavy artillery. Upon the insistence of the French delegate, the ex-servicemen's leader René Cassin, a clause was also inserted outlining the various multilateral security guarantees that could make possible further disarmament.[30]

---

[28] 'The Joint Disarmament Committee of the Christian International Organisations established at Geneva. Statement of aims and policy made by the Chairman, Mr. Bertram Pickard, at a meeting held at the American Church House in Paris, on Friday, November 27th, to which were convened representatives of Christian organisations attending the International Disarmament Conference,' file 212.013, World Alliance for Promoting International Friendship through the Churches papers.

[29] International Federation of League of Nations Societies, *Bulletin*, 1931, no. 2, p. 71.

[30] Records of the Paris meeting of the Disarmament Committee of the International Federation of League of Nations Societies, 21–22 Mar. 1931, file 1, box P.97, International Federation of League of Nations Societies (IFLNS) papers, League of Nations Archives, Geneva.

Two months after the Paris meeting, the annual congress of the International Federation of League of Nations Societies held in Budapest in May 1931 voted unanimously in support of the resolution.[31] As Cecil told League of Nations Secretary-General Eric Drummond, he felt that this resolution indicated the possibility of real agreement at the coming World Disarmament Conference because 'in view of the close relations between the Societies on the Continent and their Governments I cannot but believe that the Governments were fully aware of the Budapest resolution before it was passed, and if they or any of them had strongly disapproved of it they would have instructed their delegations to oppose it.'[32] After approval at the IFLNS Congress, the 'Budapest resolution' was promoted as the common platform not only of each of the national League of Nations societies, but also of the global disarmament movement as a whole.[33]

In addition to spearheading the creation of the *Disarmament* periodical and the four international disarmament committees, and as well as drawing up the common programme of the international disarmament movement, Cecil also pioneered the most substantial global disarmament rally to be held in the fourteen months preceding the World Disarmament Conference: the 'International Disarmament Demonstration' held at the Trocadéro in Paris in November 1931.[34]

Although the idea of a global non-governmental disarmament conference was put forward at the disarmament lunches that took place during the winter of 1930–1, it was not until May 1931 that the idea began to be transformed into a practical proposal, when Cecil persuaded Rotary International to act as an interim secretariat and John D. Rockefeller, Jr., to provide funding for such a conference.[35] By July 1931, a permanent secretariat had been found in the form of the offices of the All People's Association in London.[36] Later that month, at a meeting held in Paris

---

[31] For the text, see International Federation of League of Nations Societies, *XV Plenary Congress, Budapest, 1931* (Brussels, 1931), pp. 156–60. It is reproduced in appendix vi of this book.

[32] Cecil to Drummond, 19 Jun. 1931, Add. MSS. 51112, Cecil of Chelwood papers, British Library, London.

[33] For evidence of this, see page 100.

[34] The most complete account of the Trocadéro Conference is contained in the French periodical *L'Europe Nouvelle*, 5 Dec. 1931.

[35] Noel Baker to Courtney, 4 May 1931, and Blair-Fish to Noel Baker, 14 May 1931, file 5/146, Noel Baker papers; Cecil to Fosdick, 8 May 1931, and Fosdick to Cecil, 18 Jun. 1931, file 5/144, Noel Baker papers.

[36] Blair-Fish to Noel Baker, 6 Jul. 1931, file 5/146, Noel Baker papers. The All

and attended by representatives of fifty international organisations, including Cecil, Henry de Jouvenel, Mary Dingman and Baron von Bodman, an organising committee was established to invite INGOs to send representatives to attend the conference, and to ask prominent speakers to address the conference.[37] Paris was chosen as the location for the event not only because of its historic importance and influx of foreign visitors, but primarily because the French population was the one most in need of convincing of the urgent need to disarm.[38]

It was hoped that the Trocadéro Conference, which took place between 25 and 27 November 1931, would 'bring together the leaders of a more representative gathering of the great political, social, religious and cultural organisations of many nations than has ever taken part in any international meeting in the past… [and] would show the governments, as they can be shown perhaps in no other way, that the peoples will support any proposals for peace and disarmament, however bold, which their leaders may put before them.'[39] As the Head of the Disarmament Section of the League of Nations, Thanassis Aghnides, commented at the time, the event was 'likely to give an insight into the possibilities of disarmament at the February Conference.'[40]

In certain respects, the Trocadéro Conference lived up to the high expectations placed upon it. More than one thousand representatives of no fewer than 395 national and international non-governmental organisations attended the 'plenary sessions' held on the first two days at which the purposes and methods of disarmament were discussed. The organisations represented varied from the International Council of Women to the International Accountants Corporation, and from the British Headmasters' Conference to the Lithuanian Chamber of

---

People's Association described itself as 'a society of men and women, belonging to all nations, which seeks to remove prejudice and misunderstanding between the peoples of the world.' Its Chairman was John Evelyn Wrench and its Honorary Secretary was E. D. W. Chaplin. See Chaplin to Noel Baker, 17 Jul. 1931, file 5/144, Noel Baker papers.

[37] 'International Conference on Disarmament. Draft Minutes, Organising Committee Meeting, Paris, 25 July 1931,' file 5/144, Noel Baker papers, and file 1, box P.97, IFLNS papers.

[38] Minutes of the preparatory meeting for the Trocadéro Conference, 25 Jul. 1931, file 1, box P.97, IFLNS papers.

[39] Untitled, undated, anonymous memorandum contained in files 5/144 and 5/146 of the Noel Baker papers.

[40] Aghnides to Pierre de Lanux, 23 Nov. 1931, R. 2410, League of Nations Archives.

Commerce.[41] At the public demonstration held on the evening of the last day, many high calibre speakers addressed the audience of 4000, including Baron von Rheinbaben from Germany, Edouard Herriot and Joseph Paul-Boncour from France, and Cecil and Senator Borah from the Anglo-Saxon countries.

However, the International Disarmament Demonstration is better-known for its setbacks. Even the initial 'plenary sessions' of NGO representatives were discordant. As the observer for the League of Nations, Francis Colt de Wolf, noted: 'the speakers either engaged in generalities on the horrors of war and the desirability of obtaining disarmament, or sustained the particular theses of their own countries.'[42] Paul Painlevé's speech, which took the 'security first' line, was met with jeers and protests from many of the French women delegates, and Gabrielle Duchêne of the French branch of WILPF demanded that the account of the Conference contain an official protest by the women's organisations against the 'dangerous' influences of the pro-security speakers.[43]

Far worse occurred during the mass public demonstration that took place on the final night. The audience contained 700 members of the nationalistic French ex-servicemen's group, the *Croix de Feu*, who shouted down the speakers, started fights with the pacifist delegates 'in almost every section of the great auditorium,' raided the platform, assaulted all the foreign dignitaries sat upon it, and forced an early closure.[44] The police refused to intervene until the very end: as the leader of the *Croix de Feu*, Colonel de la Rocque, later remarked: 'when we took one step forward, the police took two steps back.'[45] Since the tumult had been broadcast internationally and involved the physical assault of many foreign dignitaries, the French government was forced to defend the police's handling of the event in a debate held in the Chamber of Deputies on 8 December, which the government made a matter of confidence and won by a narrow majority. Prime Minister Laval refused to apologise for the conduct of the police, for which he as Minister

---

[41] A complete list of the organisations that attended is provided in *L'Europe Nouvelle*, 5 Dec. 1931, pp. 1617–21. It is reproduced in appendix iii of this book.

[42] Colt de Wolf to Aghnides, 1 Dec. 1931, R. 2410, League of Nations Archives.

[43] *New York Herald* (Paris), 27 Nov. 1931; F Δ Rés 235/3/8, Gabrielle Duchêne papers, Library of Contemporary International Documentation, Nanterre.

[44] *New York Herald* (Paris), 28 Nov. 1931.

[45] Quoted in Paul Chopine, *Six Ans chez les Croix de Feu* (Paris, 1935), p. 71.

of Interior was responsible, and stated that the organisers should have expected what was coming.[46]

*   *   *

A number of other initiatives to promote disarmament in 1931 are also worth noting. The Inter-Parliamentary Union, for example, passed a resolution in April 1931 encouraging member Parliamentarians to pressurise their governments to limit their arms expenditure and to arrange 'Inter-Parliamentary Contacts' between the groups from 'countries whose military policies may have repercussions upon one another.'[47]

Furthermore, although many of the principal elements of the transnational disarmament movement were spearheaded by Cecil, a significant number of important campaigns were of independent origin. For instance, the two principal international women's organisations, the International Alliance of Women and the International Council of Women, spent the year before the World Disarmament Conference promoting the appointment of women to official delegations to the Conference.[48] As for the ex-servicemen's movement, René Cassin ensured that his organisation, CIAMAC, passed a resolution at its seventh general meeting in Prague in July 1931 requesting that its member organisations 'take a really energetic action' to promote disarmament.[49]

Some of the most notable disarmament initiatives took place as a result of collaboration between the two principal international labour organisations of the interwar years: the Labour and Socialist International (LSI) and the International Federation of Trade Unions (IFTU).[50] These organisations were wary of co-operating with bourgeois organisations to promote disarmament, and their international

---

[46] On the debate, see 'A Debate on a Tumult: French Chamber and Trocadero Meeting', *Headway*, Jan. 1932, pp. 13–14.

[47] *Disarmament*, Jun. 1931, p. 17, and Jul. 1931, p. 18. See also William Martin, *Disarmament and the Inter-Parliamentary Union* (Lausanne, 1931), p. 43.

[48] Arnold Whittick, *Woman Into Citizen: The World Movement towards the Emancipation of Women in the Twentieth Century with Accounts of the Contributions of the International Alliance of Women, the League of Nations and the Relevant Agencies of the United Nations, 1902–78* (London, 1979), p. 109.

[49] *Disarmament*, Aug.-Sep. 1931, p. 19.

[50] *The International Trade Union Movement*, 1931, p. 49.

secretariats refused to participate in the Trocadéro Conference for this reason.[51] Nevertheless, the LSI and IFTU made substantial efforts to co-ordinate the disarmament campaigns of the labour movement, and established a Joint Disarmament Commission for this purpose on 10 April 1931.[52] It was set up on the initiative of the International Federation of Trade Unions[53] and was chaired by Léon Jouhaux, the French trade union leader, and Johan Willem Albarda, who had been President of the Disarmament Commission of the Labour and Socialist International since its foundation in 1926.[54]

At its meeting of 21 June 1931, the Joint Disarmament Commission agreed upon a common programme for the promotion of disarmament by the labour movement. This included using the Second Workers' Olympiad held in Vienna in July 1931 to demonstrate for disarmament, passing resolutions in support of disarmament at the congresses of the LSI and IFTU, organising 'frontier demonstrations by Parties and Trade Unions in countries adjacent to one another,' applying parliamentary pressure upon governments in support of disarmament, convening 'large public meetings in the most important European cities' to promote disarmament, and distributing pamphlets, posters and press releases.[55] The main joint activity of the LSI and IFTU to promote disarmament was a common petition which was circulated amongst their constituent branches for signatures. The original intention was to gather individual signatures from the general public, but the recalcitrance of member organisations ensured that only the signatures of the leaders of the constituent local branches of the LSI and IFTU were collected.[56]

Much more significant than the labour movement's disarmament petition was the petition circulated by the members of the Disarmament

---

[51] Adler to Noel Baker, 25 Nov. 1931, file 4480, Labour and Socialist International (LSI) archives, International Institute of Social History, Amsterdam.

[52] Adler to the members of the Joint Disarmament Commission of the LSI and the IFTU, 17 Mar. 1931, file 775, LSI archives.

[53] 'Protokoll-Auszug der Vorstandsitzung am 23 und 24 Januar 1931 in Zurich,' file 99, International Federation of Trade Union (IFTU) archives, International Institute of Social History, Amsterdam; Schevenels to Albarda, 9 Feb. 1931, file 384, LSI archives.

[54] Albarda, Jouhaux, Adler and Schevenels to the national centres affiliated to the IFTU and the LSI, 18 May 1932, file 777, LSI archives.

[55] Labour and Socialist International, *Fourth Congress of the Labour and Socialist International, Vienna, 25th July to 1st August, 1931: Reports and Proceedings* (Zurich, 1932), pp. 63–4. Albarda's original draft of these proposals is contained in file 776, LSI archives.

[56] Albarda's original aim to collect individual signatures is contained in his memorandum of 23 Mar. 1931 in file 775 of the LSI archives. The change of plan occurred in response to the replies of the national branches contained in file 777 of the LSI archives.

Committee of Women's International Organisations during the year preceding the World Disarmament Conference. The intention in this case *was* to collect individual signatures, and it was the world's largest petition to date, the scale of which surpasses even the recent Jubilee 2000 and Global Call to Action Against Poverty petitions in terms of the proportion of the world's population that signed it.[57]

The petition's origins lie in a suggestion of Frida Perlen of the German branch of the Women's International League for Peace and Freedom that WILPF should gather a 'polyglot petition for universal disarmament;' and the idea was formally adopted by WILPF's International Executive Committee shortly after its 1929 Congress.[58] The English text of WILPF's petition stated:

> The undersigned men and women, irrespective of party, *stand for world disarmament*. They are convinced that competition in armaments is leading all countries to ruin without bringing them security, that this policy renders further wars inevitable, that wars in future will be wars of indiscriminate destruction of human life, and that the Governments' assurances of peaceful policy will be valueless as long as those measures of disarmament are delayed that should be the first result of the Pact for the Renunciation of War.[59]

WILPF launched its petition simultaneously in forty countries on 30 May 1930. By that time the signatures of prominent individuals, including Albert Einstein and Bertrand Russell, had already been secured. With its inoffensive declaration that the undersigned simply 'stand for world disarmament,' the English text of WILPF's petition also rapidly gained the support of numerous organisations in addition to the national branches of the Women's International League. In 1931, the promotion of this text became the principal goal of all of the members of the Disarmament Committee of Women's International Organisations, and the DCWIO gave itself the task of collating the signatures for presentation to government delegates at the World Disarmament Conference in February 1932.[60]

---

[57] See page 160, footnote 22.

[58] *Pax International*, Sep. 1929, p. 2; Edith Zangwill, *The Story of the Disarmament Declaration* (London, 1932), p. 2.

[59] Press release of 30 May 1930, frame 1786, reel 98, WILPF papers. The text highlighted in italics appeared in large print in the original petition.

[60] Minutes of the 9 Jun. 1931 meeting of the 'Ad Hoc Committee on the Disarmament Conference,' frame 0605, reel 99, WILPF papers (also located in file 1 of the LCWIO papers).

THE NATIONAL CAMPAIGNS

Throughout the 1920s, transnational disarmament initiatives had tended to be less substantial than—and were sometimes simply by-products of—nationally-based disarmament campaigns. During the year preceding the opening of the World Disarmament Conference, however, the national disarmament campaigns were subjected to transnational co-ordination to an unprecedented degree.

The simultaneous collection of signatures to the women's movement's disarmament petition in forty countries during the two years preceding the World Disarmament Conference was one of the most prominent examples of this phenomenon. In Britain, for instance, sixty-five organisations co-operated in the collection of signatures, including a national newspaper, the *News Chronicle*, and the Labour and Liberal Parties. As a result, ten thousand British signatures per day were being collected by the end of 1931. In France, over 500,000 signatures were gathered by the end of that year, including the signature of Edouard Herriot. In Germany and the United States, meanwhile, the total number of signatories exceeded a million.[61]

Another example of transnational co-ordination was the worldwide agreement to support the disarmament programme embodied in the 'Budapest resolution' of the International Federation of League of Nations Societies. In Britain, for instance, the leading activist Will Arnold-Forster noted that the Budapest policy was endorsed by 'practically the whole of the peace movement in this country.'[62] In France, meanwhile, activist and Deputy Pierre Cot ensured that the policy was formally incorporated into the political platform of the Radical Socialist Party.[63]

However, the extent of transnational agreement upon common objectives was less substantial than activists portrayed. For example, the women's disarmament petition consisted of four different texts. The original petition of the Women's International League had a different meaning in its French and German forms from the English version: in the continental European texts, the undersigned stood not for '*world* dis-

---

[61] 'Rapport de la Secretaire Camille Drevet, 20 août 1931,' frames 2109–26, reel 98, WILPF papers.

[62] Will Arnold-Forster, *The Disarmament Conference* (London, 1931), p. 48.

[63] Adelphia Dane Bowen, *The Disarmament Movement, 1918–1935* (DPhil thesis, Columbia University, 1956), p. 221; *Disarmament*, Dec. 1931, p. 5.

armament' (as in the English version) but for '*total and universal* disarmament.'[64] As Quaker activist Bertram Pickard pointed out, 'considerable embarrassment…is being created by the important difference between the English text of the Women's International League on the one hand and the French and German texts on the other, which no one believes to be practical politics so far as the 1932 Conference is concerned.'[65] The Disarmament Committee of Women's International Organisations also circulated two further texts, written by the International Alliance of Women for Suffrage and Equal Citizenship and the US National Committee on the Cause and Cure of War. Because of the problems with the continental version of WILPF's text, these often acquired more signatures in continental Europe than WILPF's text.[66]

The promotion of the Budapest resolution suffered from similar problems. Since the Budapest programme contained many different elements, those elements that were most appealing to public opinion in each country were emphasised, while those that were unappealing were dropped. In Britain and the United States, for instance, no reference was made to the need for further security guarantees before greater disarmament could take place.[67] The propaganda of the American League of Nations Association was so cautious that its call for a 25% cut was restricted to naval armaments.[68] The French League of Nations movement, on the other hand, emphasised the security guarantees that the Anglo-Saxon organisations failed to promote.[69] Rather than following Henderson's advice that they must 'show the Governments that however far they may be ready to go their people will be behind them,' activists took the easy option and simply promoted the aspects of the Budapest resolution that were most appealing in their respective national contexts.

---

[64] Both the continental and the British texts of WILPF's 'International Disarmament Declaration' are provided in appendix v of this book.

[65] 'Extract from the Minutes of the Centre Committee held at Taconnerie 5, on Monday, 13 April 1931,' frame 0124, reel 99, WILPF papers.

[66] All four texts circulated by the Disarmament Committee of Women's International Organisations are provided in appendix v, together with a breakdown by country of the number of signatures to each text.

[67] See, for example, the description of the Budapest resolution in the 1932 LNU report in *The Peace Year Book, 1933* (London, 1933), p. 129.

[68] See the US League of Nations Association's Apr. 1931 pamphlet, *Disarmament*, point 26.

[69] See the above comments on the Trocadéro Conference (page 96).

It should also be noted that many important nationally-based disarmament initiatives were of indigenous rather than transnational origin. In France, the national disarmament campaign in 1931 began with the publication of a manifesto by the chief federation of French trade unions, the *Confédération Générale du Travail* (CGT), which stated: 'It is now for the public opinion of the world, and in particular for the proletarian organisations, to force on the Governments concerned...the achievement of general, simulataneous, controlled disarmament.'[70] By February, this manifesto had gained the approval of all of the principal centre-left parties in France: the Socialist Party, the Radical Party, and the Republican Socialist Party.[71] In addition to this, fifteen of the principal French Catholic associations, including the Frenchwomen's Catholic League and the Catholic Association of Young Frenchmen, jointly published a manifesto in support of disarmament on 9 April 1931 under the auspices of the *Comité d'Action Catholique pour la Paix*.[72] A month later, at its annual meeting, the principal ex-servicemen's organisation in France, the *Union Fédérale des Anciens Combattants*, passed a similar resolution.[73] The participation of this organisation was highly significiant, for, as John Eppstein of the British League of Nations Union noted, it was 'the only popular organisation which *could* carry effective propaganda into the provinces' in France.[74]

A number of other national initiatives in France are also noteworthy, such as the petition in support of the goals of the Disarmament Conference that was circulated by the League for the Rights of Man and which acquired over 200,000 signatures. Henry de Jouvenel, for his part, ensured that his Action Committee for the League of Nations (which was composed of the main French League of Nations associations, as well as ex-servicemen's, religious and student groups), 'after having succeeded in its campaign for ratification of the Act of Arbitration, made its primary goal that of mobilising French public opinion in support of the reduction of armaments.'[75] The French League of Nations

---

[70] *Disarmament*, Jun. 1931, p. 5.
[71] 'Note upon the Prospects of the Disarmament Movement in France,' 28 Feb. 1931, file 209, Murray papers.
[72] *Disarmament*, Jun. 1931, p. 6.
[73] *La Paix par le Droit*, Jul. 1931, pp. 341–2; *Disarmament*, Jun. 1931, pp. 5–6.
[74] 'Note upon the Prospects of the Disarmament Movement in France,' 28 Feb. 1931, file 209, Murray papers.
[75] Jouvenel to Cecil, 11 Mar. 1931, Add. MSS. 51100, Cecil papers. See also *La Paix par le Droit*, Feb. 1931, pp. 120–2.

associations therefore organised disarmament manifestations across the country and established 180 peace cartels nationwide to co-ordinate disarmament activism provincially.

The campaign in France reached a climax on 18 December 1931 with a demonstration of ten thousand activists in the *Salle Japy* in Paris.[76] This demonstration was organised by the CGT, the Radical and Socialist Parties, the French League of Nations associations and the French pacifist groups. It was intended 'as a reply to those demonstrators who had caused a disturbance at the Trocadéro meeting,' and the organisers believed it to have been 'completely successful.'[77]

Although it began later, the disarmament campaign in the United States was larger than that which took place in France. The principal American peace organisation, the National Council for Prevention of War, waited until after its World Court Campaign had come to an end before moving on to the promotion of the World Disarmament Conference.[78] When the campaign started, the US branch of the Women's International League took the lead, organising a much-publicised 'Peace Caravan' of 150 cars that departed from Los Angeles on 21 June 1931 and made front-page news in the 125 cities at which it stopped on the way to Washington, DC. When it arrived there on 10 October, WILPF's demands were presented in a deputation to the President, Herbert Hoover. In addition to the caravan, the Women's International League collected signatures to its disarmament petition, which had to compete with three other petitions organised by the National Committee on the Cause and Cure of War, the Federal Council of Churches of Christ and the National Student Federation respectively.[79] As for other US organisations, the League of Nations Association set up Disarmament Institutes throughout the country and the American Friends' Service Committee sent its own peace caravans around the rural states.[80]

---

[76] Bowen, *Disarmament Movement*, p. 224.

[77] *Disarmament*, 15 Jan. 1932, p. 5.

[78] Laura Puffer Morgan to Philip Noel Baker, 21 Feb. 1931, file 5/146, Noel Baker papers.

[79] Laura Puffer Morgan, 'National Organisations to Lead Peace Sentiment,' *The Peace Review*, May–Jun. 1931; *Disarmament*, Jul. 1931, p. 17.

[80] Details of these activities can be found in Charles Chatfield, *For Peace and Justice: Pacifism in America, 1914–1941* (Knoxville, TN, 1971), pp. 160–3; Arnold J. Toynbee, *Survey of International Affairs, 1931* (London, 1932), pp. 290–1; and 'Organisations throughout the country are planning intensive disarmament campaign,' *National Council for Prevention of War News Bulletin*, 1931, no. 6, p. 2.

The most impressive feature of the disarmament campaign in the United States, however, was the extent of co-operation between different national organisations, which was greater than in any other country and which was later emulated at the global level. On 13 April 1931, representatives of twenty-eight national organisations met in New York to discuss how to co-ordinate action to 'give effect to Stimson's statement that public opinion must be educated if the Disarmament Conference is to succeed.'[81] The meeting was convened by the Chairman of the Foreign Policy Association, James G. McDonald, who had also led the US disarmament campaign during the London Naval Conference. The organisations present agreed 'to study and recommend or encourage new and more fruitful methods of education for use by the organisations in connection with the Disarmament Conference;' and, 'without binding any of these organisations, to determine what they should stand for in connection with the Disarmament Conference.'[82] These objectives were later to form a model for the goals of the International Consultative Group for Peace and Disarmament.

The organisations present at the April 1931 meeting created the Interorganization Council on Disarmament (ICD),[83] an umbrella body that acquired an affiliated membership of ten million people in thirty-eight organisations including the Federal Council of Churches, the Foreign Policy Association, the League of Nations Association, the National Council for Prevention of War, and the Women's International League.[84] The ICD's common programme was outlined in a manifesto distributed on 8 June 1931, which urged that 'the United States government exert every influence at its command to ensure the success of the Disarmament Conference' by promoting budgetary limitation by 10% per annum over five years and a 'treaty agreement for conference with the other Powers' in the event of a threatened violation of the Kellogg Pact.[85] As well as deputations to President Herbert Hoover in April and July 1931, co-ordinated demonstrations in favour of these

---

[81] 'Condensed minutes of a meeting of persons connected with various national organisations, held at 99 Park Avenue, New York City, April 13, 1931', Interorganization Council on Disarmament (ICD) papers, Swarthmore College Peace Collection, Swarthmore, PA.

[82] *Disarmament*, Jun. 1931, p. 15.

[83] The name 'Interorganization Council on Disarmament' was adopted on 29 Sep. 1931.

[84] The complete list of member organisations on 29 Sep. 1931 is provided in appendix iv.

[85] 'Statement of Objectives and Program, 8 June 1931,' ICD papers.

objectives took place on 'World Goodwill Day' (18 May 1931), the anniversary of the Kellogg Pact (27 August 1931), Armistice Day (11 November 1931) and the opening day of the Disarmament Conference (2 February 1932).

Although less co-ordinated than activism in the United States, the British disarmament campaign was even larger in scale. It began on 9 February 1931 with a gathering of British activists in London's Queen's Hall arranged by the British branch of the Women's International League and at which Foreign Secretary Arthur Henderson delivered a speech containing the quotation that opens this chapter. In the year that followed Henderson's speech, hundreds of provincial 'Joint Disarmament Committees' were created throughout Britain and over 4,000 disarmament demonstrations took place across the country. The demonstrations were organised, often conjointly, by educational establishments, trades unions, co-operative societies, chambers of commerce, women's groups and the peace movement. At one of the meetings, the Archbishop of York and other Christian leaders spoke to an overcrowded Westminster Hall on 15 June 1931 to demonstrate the churches' support for disarmament. This was followed on Armistice Eve by the 'United Churches Disarmament Declaration', with an audience of 6,000 in the Albert Hall.[86]

On 11 July, twice as many people packed this hall for an event billed by the *Daily Herald* as 'History's Greatest Disarmament Meeting,' at which all three of the country's principal party leaders had been persuaded to speak on a common platform.[87] It was organised by Britain's leading pro-disarmament organisation, the League of Nations Union (LNU), and was preceded by a pageant organised by the Women's International League. Even the Conservative leader, Stanley Baldwin, attended, albeit reluctantly: he had been threatened by the LNU that the event would be cancelled if any one of the three leaders refused to go, and had been warned by the Permanent Under-Secretary to the Foreign Office, Robert Vansittart, of the political risk of appearing less in favour of the League and peace than the other parties.[88] The audience was the largest that the Hall had ever contained, with a further 30,000

---

[86] Details of these events can be found in the 1931 issues of the journal of the League of Nations Union, *Headway*.

[87] *Towards Disarmament*, no. 2, 12 Jun. 1931, p. 13.

[88] Geoffrey Fry to Stanley Baldwin, 4 Apr. 1931, file 133, Stanley Baldwin papers, Cambridge University Library, Cambridge; see also Ceadel, *Semi-Detached Idealists*, p. 279.

in the street outside, and verbatim reports of the speeches appeared in the international as well as British press, with the New York Times devoting an entire page to the demonstration.[89] However, the verdict of the hosts was mixed. One attendee, Monica Glasebrook, described it as 'a magnificent opportunity wasted. Audience splendid, speeches deplorable,' because of the speakers' focus upon the foreigners' turn to disarm.[90] Nevertheless, LNU President Viscount Cecil thought that 'the meeting in the Albert Hall was really a very remarkable success…I think all the three speakers were a good deal impressed which, after all, is one of our main objects.'[91] Although Baldwin has been quoted as privately describing the demonstration as 'rather pathetic,'[92] it did leave a lasting impression on the party leaders, for the resolution passed at the meeting was later endorsed in the government's draft statement of disarmament policy of October 1931.[93]

IMPACT OF THE CAMPAIGNS

Given the scale of the campaigns that took place during the year preceding the opening of the World Disarmament Conference, it is unsurprising that national governments took activist proposals into account in their preparations for the Conference. In the USA, for example, President Hoover was particularly impressed by the deputations he received and took up the idea promoted by groups such as the League of Nations Association of an across-the-board percentage cut in naval expenditure. While this was not initially incorporated into US policy at the Conference, it was ultimately to form one of the central tenets of the Hoover Plan of June 1932.[94]

Furthermore, two of the policies that were advocated by pro-disarmament groups were formally accepted by the Anglo-Saxon governments before the end of 1931. One of these was the demand that

---

[89] W. Arnold-Forster, '1931—A Review,' *The Peace Year Book*, 1932, p. 11.

[90] Murray to Cecil, 15 Jul. 1931, Add. MSS. 51132, Cecil papers.

[91] Cecil to Murray, 16 Jul. 1931, file 210, Murray papers.

[92] Ceadel, *Semi-Detached Idealists*, p. 279.

[93] PRO 30/69/485, Ramsay MacDonald papers, National Archives, London. The resolution stated: 'That this meeting warmly welcomes the forthcoming Disarmament Conference and urges the Government to do all in its power to bring about a real reduction in the Armies, Navies and Air Forces of the world.'

[94] See, for instance, the entries for 1 May and 30 Sep. 1931 in the Henry L. Stimson diary, Vere Harmsworth Library, Oxford.

the Disarmament Conference should not be postponed. As Professor Arnold Toynbee noted at the time: 'Proposals for adjournment were strenuously resisted by the organisations and the individual men and women of various nationalities who were concentrating their efforts on preparations for the Conference.'[95] In Great Britain, therefore, Cabinet members observed: 'we must be extremely careful to avoid being accused by public opinion of deliberately trying to hold up the disarmament discussions,'[96] although the main reason for pressing ahead with the Conference was concern about 'Germany and the possible reactions on her domestic political situation.'[97] As for the USA, its chief delegate to the Disarmament Conference Hugh Gibson noted that he could not 'put himself in the position of affronting the popular demand for a measure of disarmament by demanding postponement...popular insistence in America is more and more clamorous, not only for the calling of the conference, but for the achievement of very tangible results.'[98]

The other activist demand which bore fruit was the appeal for the appointment of women to national delegations to the Conference.[99] To the United States delegation was appointed the university president and peace advocate Mary Emma Woolley,[100] who was thought to be 'of genuine value to the delegation since she was respected by the women's clubs of this country.'[101] This appointment was made in response to pressure from Dorothy Detzer and the American women's movement,[102] despite the Secretary of State's concern that Woolley was 'a woman of 69 years of age, and knows nothing of the subject.'[103] As for the British delegation, Margery Corbett Ashby was appointed as a substitute delegate in response to pressure from Lady Astor and the British women's movement.[104]

---

[95] Arnold Toynbee, *Survey of International Affairs, 1931* (London, 1932), p. 287.

[96] Thomas' contribution to the third meeting of the Cabinet Committee on Preparations for the Disarmament Conference, CAB 27/476, National Archives, London.

[97] Summary of disarmament discussions of 8 Dec. 1931, FO 800/285, Sir John Simon papers, National Archives, London.

[98] 'Impressions on Disarmament (First week of Council and Assembly),' 7 Sep. 1931, box 105, Hugh Gibson papers, Hoover Institution Archives, Stanford, CA.

[99] See minutes of 22 Jun. 1931 meeting, ICD papers.

[100] Entry of 13 Dec. 1931, Stimson diary.

[101] Hugh R. Wilson, *Diplomat Between Wars* (New York, 1941), p. 271.

[102] Dorothy Detzer, *Appointment on the Hill* (New York, 1948), pp. 104–8.

[103] Cited in Robert H. Ferrell, *American Diplomacy in the Great Depression: Hoover-Stimson Foreign Policy, 1929–1933* (New Haven, CT, 1979), p. 206.

[104] Corbett Ashby to Simon, 17 Dec. 1932, FO 800/285, Simon papers.

Activism in Great Britain was so substantial that the Foreign Secretary, Sir John Simon, was also keen to appoint Viscount Cecil as a principal delegate. Simon was even prepared to offer him the post of alternate delegate to the Foreign Secretary for the purposes of the Conference, despite Cecil's insistence that his acceptance of the appointment would be conditional upon his having an entirely free hand in decision-making.[105] However, although he thought that failure to appoint Cecil would 'have a very bad effect and will be used not only to the detriment of the government but of the country,' the Prime Minister was unwilling to allow Cecil the independence on which he insisted.[106] Consequently, Cecil refused to be a delegate, stating: 'I hope to be able to do something outside the Delegation to help us on the cause we both have at heart. It happens that this year I am the President of the International Federation of League of Nations Societies which if not an important position at any rate gives one a certain platform.'[107]

*   *   *

Although it helped to prevent postponement of the World Disarmament Conference and although it contributed towards the decision to appoint activists to national delegations, activism failed to persuade any major government to make substantial policy concessions to facilitate agreement at the opening of the Conference.

In Great Britain, for instance, activist demands for a bold proposal to open the Conference caused members of Cabinet privately to admit that they were 'very much afraid that the government would put themselves in the wrong, especially vis-à-vis public opinion, if they could not make some bold declaration that, for example, undersea warfare and military aircraft should be abolished,' for 'there was a tremendous amount of propaganda taking place at present in regard to this matter.'[108] However, no such declaration was approved because Cabinet Secretary Maurice Hankey convinced most Cabinet members that the

---

[105] Simon to MacDonald, 1 Dec. 1931, FO 800/285, Simon papers.

[106] MacDonald to Cecil, 22 Jan. 1932, Add. MSS. 51081, Cecil papers.

[107] Cecil to MacDonald, 22 Jan. 1932, PRO 30/69/678, MacDonald papers. MacDonald highlighted this part of Cecil's letter with crayon. Cecil often agreed to lead the British delegation at the League Assembly, but did not represent Britain officially at the Disarmament Conference. Cecelia Lynch's book, *Beyond Appeasement: Interpreting Interwar Peace Movements in World Politics* (Ithaca, NY, 1999), confuses these two appointments on page 104.

[108] Fourth meeting of the Cabinet Committee on Preparations for the Disarmament Conference, CAB 27/476, National Archives, London.

government's majority was so large that they could afford to ignore this propaganda.[109] Britain's delegation therefore went to the World Disarmament Conference with an unhelpful policy. On the eve of the Conference, the British government stated that it was 'unable to offer further reductions;'[110] and Prime Minister Ramsay MacDonald told his delegates that they 'ought to emphasise the fact that we had not waited for the Disarmament Conference to begin disarming, and to describe the situation which had been reached as a result of our efforts. In this respect we had a magnificent case. Whether other nations believed us or not was not very material, provided that the whole case were put and reached our own public.'[111] Hoover's advice to the US delegation was virtually identical: 'Our role at the forthcoming conference would naturally have to be an inactive one, since the Navy, which was our principal arm, was already strictly limited and our Army was on the lowest possible terms, even for the maintenance of internal order.'[112]

In the case of the French government, it sought to present itself as supporting activism: the French Foreign Ministry, for instance, sponsored a 400-page booklet describing the aims, activities and details of all the peace groups in France[113] and to the consternation of many of the groups included, War Minister André Tardieu's photograph was inserted as the frontispiece.[114] However, France went to the World Disarmament Conference with a policy as unhelpful as that of the Anglo-Saxon powers. This was outlined in a memorandum released in July 1931 that declared that French armaments were at 'the lowest point consistent with her national security' and could be reduced only if new security guarantees were forthcoming from the Anglo-Saxons.[115]

---

[109] Letter by Hankey dated 12 Jan. 1932, PRO 30/69/483, MacDonald papers.

[110] Quoted in Lynch, *Beyond Appeasement*, p. 101.

[111] Quoted in Carolyn Kitching, *Britain and the Geneva Disarmament Conference: A Study in International History* (Basingstoke, 2002), pp. 139–40.

[112] 'Memorandum of a conversation at the White House, 5 January 1932,' container 20, Norman Davis papers, Library of Congress, Washington, DC.

[113] *Nous voulons la paix: concentration des efforts universels des forces pacifistes sous le haut patronage du Ministère des Affaires Étrangères. 1932* (Paris, 1932).

[114] Henry Obry to Gabrielle Duchêne, 16 Apr. 1932, F Δ Rés 273, Duchêne papers.

[115] Maurice Vaïsse, *Sécurité d'abord: la politique française en matière de désarmement, 9 décembre 1930–17 avril 1934* (Paris, 1981), p. 133. For the text of the memorandum, see L'Europe Nouvelle, *Comment et pourquoi désarmer? avec le texte intégral du mémorandum français sur le désarmement* (Paris, 1931).

CHAPTER EIGHT

THE WORLD DISARMAMENT CONFERENCE: THE FIRST SIX MONTHS, FEBRUARY TO JULY 1932

> *The Rt. Hon. Arthur Henderson, President of the Disarmament Conference, appealed both before and at the opening of the Disarmament Conference for the active interest and support of public opinion. The response to that appeal, if it ever comes to be related, provides material for a moving story.*
> Bertram Pickard, 18 October 1932[1]

The global disarmament campaign reached its peak at the time of the opening of the World Disarmament Conference in Geneva in February 1932. The special session of the Conference held on 6 February 1932 was an unprecedented opportunity for activists directly to present their objectives to nearly all of the national governments of the world. During the first six months of the Conference, the governments of both France and the United States responded to the activists' appeals by putting forward comprehensive plans to the Conference. However, the Conference made little substantive progress and had to be suspended in July 1932, after the German delegation temporarily walked out because of the failure to reach agreement.

THE DISARMAMENT COMMITTEES IN GENEVA

By January 1932, the transnational disarmament committees representing the world's principal Christian, women's, students' and peace organisations had established themselves in Geneva.[2] The members of all of these committees wanted to be present at the opening of the World Disarmament Conference to present the results of their activities over the previous year. The Disarmament Committee of Women's

---

[1] 'The Disarmament Work of Unofficial Organisations at Geneva (February–October 1932),' Note prepared by Bertram Pickard, 18 Oct. 1932, box 1, International Consultative Group (ICG) papers, League of Nations Archives, Geneva.

[2] The Disarmament Committee of the International Federation of League of Nations Societies (IFLNS) was initially based in Brussels (the headquarters of the IFLNS), but moved to Geneva in Jan. 1932. The Christian, students' and women's committees were in Geneva from the time of their foundation.

International Organisations, for example, was there to present to the official delegates the enormous disarmament petition that its member groups had circulated during 1931,[3] while the Disarmament Committee of the International Federation of League of Nations Societies (IFLNS) moved to Geneva in January 1932 to promote its 'Budapest' resolution on disarmament.[4]

Together, these committees co-operated with the Geneva Federation of Private International Organisations, an umbrella-group of all permanently Geneva-based INGOs, to persuade the League Secretariat to ensure that their demands would be heard at the Conference.[5] As well as pushing for the presentation of the women's disarmament petition and the IFLNS Budapest resolution on disarmament, they asked for 'special facilities' during the Conference, such as guaranteed seats for observers and Conference documentation.

They had little trouble securing these facilities from the Disarmament Section of the League Secretariat, which 'recognised that in view of the fact that various international organisations as well as several national organisations have been doing a considerable amount of propaganda work in preparation for the Conference, and that their services in this connection will also be very useful during the Conference itself, the Secretariat should facilitate the work of these organisations as much as possible.'[6]

As well as granting these organisations the special facilities, the League Secretariat published every resolution it received from an INGO in the Conference Journal throughout the two years that the Conference lasted. Furthermore, Conference President Arthur Henderson needed little persuasion to invite these organisations to present their petitions and goals at an Extraordinary Session in the opening stages of the Conference.[7]

---

[3] Memorandum submitted by the Disarmament Committee of Women's International Organisations: 'Collaboration of Women in the Organisation of Peace,' 1 Jan. 1932, R. 2448, League of Nations Archives, Geneva.

[4] See Eppstein to Aghnides, 20 Jan. 1932, and Ruyssen to Henderson, 31 Jan. 1932, R. 2455, League of Nations Archives.

[5] See E. J. Phelan and Bertram Pickard to Eric Drummond, 1 Dec. 1931, R. 2455, League of Nations Archives.

[6] 'Relations between the Secretariat and Private International Organisations during the Disarmament Conference. Report to the Secretary-General, 29 December 1931,' R. 2444, League of Nations Archives.

[7] See Noel Baker to Drummond, 9 Dec. 1931, R. 2442, League of Nations Archives.

THE OPENING OF THE WORLD DISARMAMENT CONFERENCE

The Conference that the four Disarmament Committees had worked so hard to promote opened at 16:30 on 2 February 1932. It had been arranged for an hour earlier, but had to be postponed to allow for an emergency meeting of the members of the League Council. They had been summoned to discuss their response to the Japanese bombardment of Shanghai that had begun earlier that day. To some, the timing of Japan's actions was no mere coincidence.[8] Nevertheless, the Japanese delegation was present alongside the representatives of fifty-eight other countries in the *Bâtiment Electoral* for the largest international gathering in history to that time. Only the Dominican Republic, Ecuador, Nicaragua, Paraguay and Salvador had no delegates to hear Henderson's opening speech.[9] He had been appointed to the Conference Presidency in a personal capacity in May 1931 when still Foreign Minister in a British Labour government, but he was now merely a member of the minuscule Opposition to Ramsay MacDonald's National Government.

Henderson presented the Conference with its principal objective: 'to arrive at a collective agreement on an effective programme of practical proposals speedily to secure a substantial reduction and limitation of all national armaments.'[10] He also proposed the establishment of three committees to lay the foundations for the plenary sessions which would begin on 8 February.

The first of these committees examined the credentials of the delegates, while the second drew up the Conference's procedures. The Bureau of the Conference was elected under Henderson's chairmanship, with representatives from the USA, the Soviet Union, Britain, France, Germany, Italy, Japan, Argentina, Spain, Belgium, Czechoslovakia, Poland, Sweden and Austria, while the General Commission was established with one delegate from each state.

The third committee examined the non-governmental petitions and established the procedure for their presentation to delegates. The Extraordinary Session of the Disarmament Conference at which the petitions would be presented was set for 6 February. This followed

---

[8] See Noel Baker's comments in *Recovery*, 10 Nov. 1933, p. 12.

[9] The Dominican Republic subsequently participated in the Conference, making the total attendance sixty countries.

[10] John W. Wheeler-Bennett, *The Disarmament Deadlock* (London, 1934), p. 14.

the precedent set at the Hague Peace Congresses of 1899 and 1907.[11] One representative of each of the four disarmament committees in Geneva, as well as a representative of the labour movement, was invited to speak. Upon French insistence, speeches made by these representatives required advance approval by the Committee.[12] According to an American peace activist, Laura Puffer Morgan (who was in Geneva to follow proceedings on behalf of the US National Council for Prevention of War), it was Mary Woolley's participation in the petitions committee that...

> ... was of unusual importance.... At first she found all the other members of the committee of five opposed to a public hearing, but little by little, through the exercise of the tact and patience for which she is known, she was able to win them to her point of view. It was a great victory for the forces of peace and forced the delegates at the outset of the Conference to pause and listen to the voices of the people who told them not to leave Geneva until their task was accomplished.[13]

When it took place two days after the petitions committee had finished its deliberations, the Extraordinary Session was attended by delegates from all but three of the countries represented and was addressed by many more speakers than initially intended, representing a total of over 200 million people.[14] It had two main purposes. One was the presentation of the global petitions, including the petition gathered by the Disarmament Committee of Women's International Organisations, which had by then acquired eight million signatures worldwide (which grew to 12 million at the final count)[15] making it one of the largest petitions in history.[16] Henderson introduced the presentation of these

---

[11] Note entitled 'Précédents relatifs à la Présentation des Pétitions, Genève, le 3 février 1932,' cote 867, série SDN, French Foreign Ministry Archives, Paris.

[12] 'Report of the Petitions Committee,' 4 Feb. 1932, R. 2458, League of Nations Archives.

[13] Report of 6 Feb. 1932, box LON 28, Laura Puffer Morgan papers, League of Nations Archives, Geneva.

[14] The full text of the speeches is presented in Vox Populi Committee, *Vox Populi* (Geneva, 1932). The co-operation between the four disarmament committees and CIAMAC in the production of this pamphlet eventually resulted in the formation of the International Consultative Group.

[15] 'Report from September 1931 to June 1933 of the Disarmament Committee of the Women's International Organisations,' reel 99, Women's International League for Peace and Freedom archives on UMI microfilm.

[16] In terms of numbers, the largest are the Jubilee 2000 debt relief petition which acquired 24 million signatures, and the petition of the Global Call to Action Against Poverty and Live 8 which has acquired even more names. The women's disarmament petition, on the other hand, represented a significantly larger proportion of the world's population at the time it was collected.

petitions by telling delegates that the petitions gave 'very striking evidence...of the universal desire of the peoples of the world that our work shall succeed.'[17] There was some truth in this statement: the women's petition, for example, was truly global in that it had signatures from fifty-six countries. However, it manifested an imbalance between the number of signatures from each of the four major powers: over two million came from Great Britain, alongside a million each from Germany and the USA, but only half a million came from France.[18] This imbalance was also displayed in the other petitions presented that day: whereas a Dutch petition had received the signatures of a third of its 6 million population, the petition of the French League for the Rights of Man acquired just a fifth of its intended million signatures; and while the labour movement's disarmament petition acquired the approval of 2,991 sections of the British trade union movement with a membership of 3,881,900, it secured the support of only 1,554 branches of the French trade union movement with a membership of 885,707.[19]

The other main purpose of the Extraordinary Session was to hear the speech by Viscount Cecil on behalf of the pre-eminent international peace organisation of the interwar period, the International Federation of League of Nations Societies.[20] He presented the Federation's Budapest resolution on disarmament which had become the common platform of the majority of the pro-disarmament movement world-wide.[21] Cecil told delegates that the resolution contained 'a concrete plan...[which] if it were adopted...would make a genuine first step

---

[17] League of Nations, *Records of the Conference for the Reduction and Limitation of Armaments, Series A, Verbatim Records of Plenary Meetings, Vol. 1, February 2nd–July 23rd 1932* (Geneva, 1932), p. 187.

[18] For a complete breakdown of the petition statistics, see Disarmament Committee of the Women's International Organisations, *Official Record of the Declarations and Petitions presented by the Disarmament Committee of the Women's International Organisations to the Disarmament Conference, Geneva, February 6th, 1932* (Geneva, 1932), pp. 16–19. This information is also provided in appendix v of this book.

[19] William Gillies to Friedrich Adler, 29 Jan. 1932; Jouhaux to Adler, 2 Feb. 1932; and handwritten table of petitions received: all contained in file 4481, Labour and Socialist International archives, International Institute of Social History, Amsterdam.

[20] On the history and significance of the International Federation of League of Nations Societies, see Thomas Richard Davies, *The Possibilities of Transnationalism: the International Federation of League of Nations Societies and the International Peace Campaign, 1919–1939* (MPhil thesis, University of Oxford, 2002), Part One.

[21] For the text of the Budapest Resolution, see International Federation of League of Nations Societies, *XV Plenary Congress, Budapest, 1931* (Brussels, 1931), pp. 156–60. It is reproduced in appendix vi of this book.

towards disarmament.'[22] The plan was intended to demonstrate how the different national approaches to disarmament could be reconciled, and it contained elements of all of these approaches. In line with the Anglo-American position, it argued that existing provisions for security were sufficient for a 25% decrease in arms expenditure worldwide. In accordance with the French position, it argued that further security provisions (such as an international air force and mutual assistance treaties) would make possible further disarmament. Thirdly, in agreement with the German position, it argued that Germany's right to equality of status should be recognised and that the production of 'offensive' weapons denied to Germany should be prohibited to all (later termed 'qualitative disarmament'). According to Laura Puffer Morgan, Cecil's speech was received with 'a tremendous ovation...in which his own delegation was conspicuously silent.'[23]

In addition to Cecil's oration, speeches were given by Mary Dingman and Petronille Steenberghe-Engeringh on behalf of the women's movement, Paul Dupuy on behalf of the League for the Rights of Man, Joachim Mueller on behalf of the ecumenical movement, Jean Dupuy and James Green on behalf of students' organisations, and Émile Vandervelde and Léon Jouhaux on behalf of the labour and trade union movements. As well as those who spoke, there were seven hundred representatives from global non-governmental organisations present at this Extraordinary Session of the Disarmament Conference. The activists who participated believed that at this meeting 'the "public opinion of the world" so often rightly or wrongly invoked was in evidence... [and]...had taken a concrete shape' for the first time in history.[24] One later wrote: 'Never before have the governments of the world been so sure of the united support of unofficial opinion.'[25]

There was one significant absentee at the Extraordinary Session: owing to a bureaucratic error, the representatives of the ex-servicemen of the world were unable to attend the meeting of 6 February, and instead presented their request for disarmament in a deputation

---

[22] League of Nations, *Records of the Conference for the Reduction and Limitation of Armaments, Series A, Verbatim Records of Plenary Meetings, Vol. 1, February 2nd–July 23rd 1932* (Geneva, 1932), pp. 196–8.

[23] Report of 6 Feb. 1932, box LON 28, Morgan papers.

[24] *Disarmament*, 15 Feb. 1932, p. 6.

[25] 'Memorandum from Leslie Adie to Dame Adelaide Livingstone,' box 6, ICG papers.

to Henderson the following day.[26] One of the main ex-servicemen's organisations, CIAMAC, was to become a leading participant in the International Consultative Group for Peace and Disarmament, alongside the Christian, women's, students' and League of Nations societies' disarmament committees that had been represented on 6 February.

The Extraordinary Session made a significant impression on both the delegates and the press at the time, and nearly all of the Conference delegates referred back to it in their subsequent opening speeches. British Foreign Secretary Sir John Simon, for instance, claimed the speeches had 'gripped one's heart,' while the German Chancellor and Foreign Minister, Heinrich Bruening, declared it a 'remarkable manifestation.'[27]

On the day itself, the principal US delegate, Hugh Gibson, privately described the meeting as 'impressive' and the speeches by Cecil and Vandervelde as 'outstanding.'[28] As for the French delegation, it had a mixed assessment of the event: of Cecil's programme, René Massigli said 'in its reference to the need for equality of armaments between victor and vanquished states, he promoted a policy we cannot allow, but it must also be pointed out that some of his suggestions, such as internationalisation of civil aviation, can be found in our proposals.'[29]

The proposals to which Massigli was referring were contained in a new disarmament plan brought to the attention of delegates by the right-wing French War Minister André Tardieu the day before the Extraordinary Session. This was intended to scupper the original plan at the Conference of adopting the Preparatory Commission's Draft Convention as the basis for discussion, which the British Foreign Secretary planned to do when the first plenary session of the Conference began on 8 February 1932.

---

[26] There was confusion over dates: see J. Ch. de Watteville to Aghnides, 13 Jan. 1932, R. 2455, League of Nations Archives. For an account of the deputation, see Vox Populi Committee, *Vox Populi*, pp. 67–70.

[27] League of Nations, *Records of the Conference for the Reduction and Limitation of Armaments, Series A, Verbatim Records of Plenary Meetings, Vol. 1, February 2nd–July 23rd 1932* (Geneva, 1932), pp. 56, 68.

[28] Gibson to Stimson (telegram), 6 Feb. 1932, box 120, Hugh Gibson papers, Hoover Institution Archives, Stanford, CA.

[29] Massigli's report of 6 Feb. 1932, cote 867, série SDN, French Foreign Ministry Archives.

THE TARDIEU PLAN

André Tardieu's proposal was based on the traditional French demand that greater security provisions precede disarmament. It insisted upon a clear definition of aggression, breaches of which would be enforceable by an international police force. All the heaviest weapons (such as heavy guns, battleships and bombing aircraft) were to be reserved for use only under the orders of the League or in self-defence. The plan's immediate origins lie in Colonel Fabry's 23 December 1931 suggestion that France should present a plan right at the start of the Conference in order to give France 'considerable moral authority.'[30] Prime Minister Pierre Laval supported Fabry's idea as this would make it difficult to blame France for the Conference's failure.[31] And Tardieu set about producing the plan, asking for the help of Generals Weygand, Gamelin and Réquin as well as Louis Aubert in its preparation.

The fact that activist organisations supported the idea of an international force contributed towards the inclusion of the proposal in Tardieu's plan. He collected many INGO resolutions in favour of the idea,[32] tried to get Cecil's approval of the project, and stated in a radio address to the American people on 7 February 1932 that the plan 'contains ideas which do not belong to any party in particular, as is clear from the way it has been received by the French public. It contains ideas which have been well received by men and associations in other countries which are devoting their energies to the organisation of peace, ideas which we find in the paper read yesterday by Lord Cecil on behalf of the International Federation of League of Nations Societies.'[33] As Aubert had pointed out, the idea also 'cut the ground from beneath the feet of the left' before the elections.[34]

---

[30] 11th séance of Special Commission, 23 Dec. 1931, cote 726, série SDN, French Foreign Ministry Archives.

[31] CSDN meeting of 8 Jan. 1932, cote 726, série SDN, French Foreign Ministry Archives.

[32] ff. 201–254, cote 498, André Tardieu papers, French Foreign Ministry Archives, Paris. This contains the resolutions of the Radical Socialist congress, Catholic organisations, women's suffrage groups, CIAMAC, and the International Peace Bureau (IPB), as well as the 'Manifeste du Comité international de cooperation des forces pacifiques' containing CIAMAC, the IFLNS, the IPB, the World Alliance for Promoting International Friendship through the Churches, the International Council of Women, and many other women's, students' and Christian organisations.

[33] Message for broadcast over US radio, 7 Feb. 1932, cote 504, Tardieu papers.

[34] Maurice Vaïsse, *Sécurité d'abord: la politique française en matière de désarmement, 9 décembre 1930–17 avril 1934* (Paris, 1981), p. 199.

As for the plan's long-term origins, these lie in the parameters set in the discussions of the members of the *Conseil Supérieur de la Défense Nationale* (CSDN) in the meetings of a Special Commission from 27 October 1931 onwards. At these meetings, the War and Navy Ministries both refused to envisage reductions and even succeeded in getting military expenditure increased, to the dismay of the more moderate members of the Committee, Joseph Paul-Boncour and René Massigli from the French Foreign Ministry.[35] As the historian Maurice Vaïsse notes, the generals were able to have their way at a time when politicians' positions were not at risk.[36]

As a precondition for any agreement by France to disarm, the War Ministry insisted upon a clear definition of aggression and mutual assistance treaties. Paul-Boncour proposed in addition both an international army and an international air force, which the Foreign Ministry and French League of Nations societies (both of which were dominated by Paul-Boncour) had been promoting throughout 1931. Although Generals Gamelin and Réquin thought the international army idea 'utopian in the current world situation,' Weygand did not object, thinking that 'it is necessary to take a generous attitude on this question for the sake of public opinion.'[37] In any case, Louis Aubert pointed out that although these ideas were 'irréelle' they were 'réelle comme tactique,' and 'the reality of the Conference is not everyday reality, but a demagogic and theatrical reality, determined by manoeuvres made in view of captivating universal public opinion with simple ideas.'[38]

THE FIRST SESSION OF THE DISARMAMENT CONFERENCE

Aubert's judgement proved to be sound: for instance, the British Liberal newspaper, *The News Chronicle*, thought that 'there is no ground whatever for doubting the sincerity of the proposals.'[39] Furthermore, many members of the disarmament movement greeted the Tardieu proposal with enthusiasm. In France, all but the extreme left-wing

---

[35] See the minutes of CSDN special committee meetings in cote 726, série SDN, French Foreign Ministry Archives; and Vaïsse, *Sécurité d'abord*, pp. 138–48.

[36] Vaïsse, *Sécurité d'abord*, p. 146.

[37] 'Note pour le ministre' (Laval), 8 Jan. 1932, cote 726, série SDN, French Foreign Ministry Archives.

[38] 'Note de M. Aubert remise au Président du Conseil le 6 janvier 1932: Observations à soumettre au CSDN (8 janvier),' cote 498, Tardieu papers.

[39] Quoted in *Disarmament*, vol. 2, no. 4, 15 Feb. 1932.

groups welcomed his 'profoundly satisfactory' ideas,[40] while Cecil wrote to Tardieu upon receiving an advance copy to tell him that 'as far as they deal with disarmament, they seem to proceed on the same lines as those which I am about to present the Conference.'[41]

However, the official representatives of the Anglo-Saxon countries vehemently objected to the increased security commitments entailed by Tardieu's proposal. When Sir John Simon opened the main debate on 8 February, he ignored the French plan and presented in its place the Draft Convention that had been drawn up by the Preparatory Commission as the basis for discussion. Beyond this, the highlight of his speech was the proposal that a distinction be made between offensive and defensive armaments. This went far beyond his brief, for the Cabinet Committee on Preparations for the Conference had concluded: 'we should not support any proposal for the abolition of offensive weapons on the grounds that such distinctions do not appear to be possible.'[42] Although there is a lack of documentary evidence to back his claim, the personal assistant to the President of the Conference, Philip Noel Baker, was convinced that Simon had been 'deeply impressed by Cecil's speech' two days before, which had also emphasised the need for abolition of offensive weapons.[43] However, apart from this departure, Simon's speech was essentially based upon Prime Minister MacDonald's recommendation that 'the Delegation ought to emphasise the fact that we had not waited for the Disarmament Conference to begin disarming, and to describe the situation which had been reached as a result of our efforts.'[44]

As for the other opening speeches, Hugh Gibson's on behalf of the American delegation was almost identical to Sir John Simon's: it too promoted the offensive/defensive distinction, with particular emphasis upon the offensive nature of submarines, but like the British Prime Minister, the American President at the time, the Republican Herbert Hoover, felt that his country's role at the Disarmament Conference

---

[40] *La Paix par le Droit*, vol. 42, nos. 2–3, Feb.–Mar. 1932, p. 123; Resolution of the French Federation of League of Nations Societies, F Δ Rés 718, Jules Prudhommeaux papers, Library of Contemporary International Documentation, Nanterre.

[41] Cecil to Tardieu, 6 Feb. 1932, cote 504, Tardieu papers.

[42] Report of the Cabinet Committee on Preparations for the Disarmament Conference, p.17, CP 5(32), CAB 24/227, National Archives, London.

[43] Philip Noel-Baker, *The First World Disarmament Conference, 1932–1934, and Why It Failed* (Oxford, 1979), p. 77. Simon kept a copy of Cecil's speech in his papers (file 71, Sir John Simon papers, Bodleian Library, Oxford).

[44] Quoted in Carolyn Kitching, *Britain and the Problem of International Disarmament, 1919–1934* (London, 1999), pp. 139–40.

should be 'an inactive one.'[45] Immediately after Gibson, Dr. Bruening spoke on behalf of the German government. He accepted the Draft Convention as a 'point of departure,' despite his huge reservations regarding Article LIII, and appealed for a solution of the problem of general disarmament 'on the basis of equal rights and equal security for all peoples,' a solution that had deliberately not been proposed in the Tardieu Plan.[46]

The Italian speaker, Grandi, proceeded to agree with the German position and bluntly to reject the French proposals for greater security. Matsudaira declared the Japanese desire for 'a fair and equitable limitation and reduction of armaments compatible with national safety,' while Litvinoff outlined the Soviet case for total disarmament ('the only infallible remedy') or, failing that, the abolition of aggressive weaponry.[47] As for the other nations, France's allies spoke in favour of the Tardieu proposals, while the remaining smaller states tended to emphasise the proposals for the abolition of aggressive weaponry.

The opening speeches finished on 25 February. Although most states had paid lip-service to the Draft Convention as the basis for discussion, the tendency simply to present their own particular proposals for the resolution of the disarmament issue was already evident, and on 23 February the Bureau of the Conference decided that the General Commission would have to study all fifty speeches to reconcile them with the Draft Convention. Nevertheless, as League of Nations historian F. P. Walters points out: 'Contrary to expectation, the technical arguments and squabbles over matters of detail, which had almost paralysed the Preparatory Commission, had not been revived.'[48] Agreement appeared to be a real possibility, especially in regard to the control of offensive weaponry, so long as the Anglo-American and French conceptions of the necessary prior security arrangements could be reconciled. Furthermore, disarmament activists were pleased that 'scarcely a delegate failed to refer to the impression made on him by the spokesmen of the private international organisations at the public hearing accorded them

---

[45] 'Memorandum of a conversation at the White House, 5 January 1932,' container 20, Norman Davis papers, Library of Congress, Washington, DC.

[46] Quoted in Arnold Toynbee, *Survey of International Affairs, 1932* (London, 1933), p. 204.

[47] Quoted in Wheeler-Bennett, *Disarmament Deadlock*, p. 21.

[48] F. P. Walters, *A History of the League of Nations* (London, 1960), p. 504.

throughout the Extraordinary Session of February 6th.'[49] Henderson's summative speech therefore reflected this widely-held optimism.

However, progress was interrupted by a Special Assembly on the Sino-Japanese dispute in early March, and the Conference did not reassemble until 11 April. During the recess, most of the delegates departed Geneva, while five 'technical commissions' were left to discuss land, air and naval armaments, budgetary control, and (on the insistence of the French) political matters. Little progress was made in any of these commissions, and agreement as to what counted as offensive weapons proved to be elusive. In the naval commission, for instance, the Anglo-American position was that submarines were offensive, while the French insisted that they were defensive. The Disarmament Conference was thus starting to suffer from the lengthy disputes over technicalities typical of the Preparatory Commission. In the meantime, as the contemporary observer John Wheeler-Bennett noted: 'While the Committees and Sub-Committees disputed amicably together the grains were running out in the German hourglass.'[50] It took more than one round of voting in the German Presidential election before Hitler was finally defeated by Hindenburg on the day before the Conference reconvened.

THE SECOND SESSION

Gibson made the first speech of the second session on 11 April 1932, and outlined a precise plan for the abolition of offensive weaponry—such as tanks, gases and mobile guns over 155mm calibre—that proved to be acceptable to the British, German and Italian delegations.[51] However, Tardieu, who was concerned that his plan was still being ignored, insisted that he could not comply without further security guarantees. The USA's concrete proposals were therefore brushed aside and the Conference instead spent the subsequent week discussing vague 'general principles.' Nevertheless, one important resolution was adopted on

---

[49] Will Arnold-Forster, 'The Budapest Resolution and the Proposals before the Disarmament Conference,' file 4, box P.97, International Federation of League of Nations Societies (IFLNS) papers, League of Nations Archives, Geneva.

[50] Wheeler-Bennett, *Disarmament Deadlock*, p. 24.

[51] Gibson's proposal originated at a meeting of State and War Department officials in Washington on 30 Mar. 1932 at which Norman Davis emphasised that a proposal was needed because of 'economic necessity, the state of public opinion at home, the fear of social disorders and the like.' See 'Memorandum of Conversation in the Office of Assistant Secretary of State Rogers,' 30 Mar. 1932, box 121, Gibson papers.

22 April as a result of Sir John Simon's efforts: it approved 'the principle of qualitative disarmament in the selection of certain classes of weapons, the possession or use of which should be absolutely prohibited to all states or internationalised by means of a general convention.'[52] Since this accorded with the demands of the IFLNS' Budapest programme, this resolution was broadly welcomed by most disarmament activists.[53]

In the meantime, Bruening had decided that the Disarmament Conference provided an opportunity for securing his position at home and stemming the rise of Nazi electoral support, which had sharply increased in the 1930 Reichstag election and further doubled by the time of the 1932 Presidential election.[54] He hoped to gain international support at Geneva for a plan that would recognise his interpretation of German equality of status, and he timed its presentation to coincide with arrival of the highest-level delegates from Britain and America: Prime Minister Ramsay MacDonald and Secretary of State Henry L. Stimson. On 26 April, he presented these two men with his proposals, which he insisted should legally replace Part V of the Versailles Treaty. The proposals included halving the period of Reichswehr service, doubling the number of Reichswehr or militia troops to 200,000, and sticking to the Versailles restrictions on offensive weapons if all other countries did likewise. Both MacDonald and Stimson agreed that the proposals could form the basis of a settlement, a position shared by the Italians.

It was hoped that the proposals would be discussed with Tardieu at a subsequent meeting on 29 April. However, Tardieu never attended, supposedly because of an attack of laryngitis. Wheeler-Bennett has claimed that one reason for Tardieu's non-appearance was that General von Schleicher had disingenuously told the French Ambassador to Berlin that Bruening was about to fall and that his successor would be more amenable to French concerns. As a result, it has been argued that 'had Mr. MacDonald, in the face of M. Tardieu's refusal to return to Geneva and discuss the German proposals, persuaded his colleagues to make public the nature of Dr. Bruening's offer, together with the fact that his contention was considered justified and reasonable by the British,

---

[52] Quoted in Wheeler-Bennett, *Disarmament Deadlock*, p. 30.

[53] See, for instance, Cecil to Simon, 16 Jun. 1932, Add. MSS. 51082, Cecil of Chelwood papers, British Library, London.

[54] See Christoph M. Kimmich, *Germany and the League of Nations* (Chicago, 1976), pp. 162–3.

American, and Italian delegations, the French government would have been placed in an untenable position by reason of the very fairness of the German proposals.'[55] Tardieu would therefore have had to go to Geneva and accept Bruening's proposals as the basis of a settlement.

Wheeler-Bennett's proposition has been accepted by both traditionalist and revisionist British historians alike.[56] There is good reason, however, to doubt the viability of the Bruening proposals as the basis of a settlement. There is little evidence that the British or Americans were willing to extend more than good-will towards the proposals. Furthermore, Bruening's proposals were hardly very fair from a French perspective: Germany would have doubled her army's strength while France would have had to lose all of her 'offensive' weapons. The proposals therefore fell by the wayside. Both Tardieu and Bruening proceeded to lose their posts shortly afterwards: Tardieu was eventually replaced by the more conciliatory Herriot in June; and Bruening, having returned to Berlin empty-handed, was replaced by the much more militaristic von Papen on 30 May. In the meantime, the General Commission suspended its work on 26 April until the reports of the technical commissions had been received, and progress was put back once more.

Over the subsequent couple of months each of the technical committees attempted in vain to define the distinction between offensive and defensive weapons. As one activist observing proceedings remarked, the delegates on these commissions simply behaved 'like children trying to take away each others' toys.'[57] Only the committee set up to examine chemical and bacteriological warfare produced a unanimous report, which advocated the abolition of both. The Commissions on Naval, Air and Land Armaments, on the other hand, all failed to produce unanimous agreement. The Naval Commission reached deadlock between the German argument that battleships were offensive and submarines defensive, the Anglo-American argument that submarines were offensive and battleships defensive, and the French argument that

---

[55] Wheeler-Bennett, *Disarmament Deadlock*, pp. 33–4.

[56] See F. S. Northedge, *The League of Nations: Its Life and Times, 1920–1946* (Leicester, 1986), p. 124, and Dick Richardson, 'The Geneva Disarmament Conference, 1932–34' in Dick Richardson and Glyn Stone (eds.), *Decisions and Diplomacy: Essays in Twentieth Century International History: In Memory of George Grun and Esmonde Robertson* (London, 1995), p. 71.

[57] Honora Enfield's 'Secretary's Geneva Report,' 26 Jun. 1932, file DCX/8/1, International Co-operative Women's Guild (ICWG) archives, Brynmor Jones Library, Hull.

both were defensive. The Land Commission reached deadlock over the exact calibre of guns that should be abolished and the definition of a tank, although it was eventually agreed that artillery over 220mm and mechanically-propelled vehicles cver 70 tons should be abolished. The Air Commission produced the blandest report possible, offering no recommendations and concluding merely that 'all aircraft…may constitute a danger to civilians.'[58] A further Committee set up to define 'effectives' also reached no conclusion. The Bureau met on 14 June to examine these futile efforts, and the German delegate called once more in vain for the distinctions used in the Versailles Treaty to form the offensive-defensive distinction.

The Hoover Plan

In the meantime, activists had started to express their frustration at the lack of progress. At the international level, several disarmament demonstrations were organised. The Labour and Socialist International and the International Federation of Trade Unions, for instance, held their first ever joint conference in May 1932 at which the 'profoundly disappointing' progress of the World Disarmament Conference was denounced.[59] That month, the Disarmament Committee of Women's International Organisations and the Women's International League for Peace and Freedom also held conferences urging swifter progress at the World Disarmament Conference.[60]

However, it was activism at the national level, and in particular in the United States, that was to have the greatest impact. By May 1932, American delegates had been sent over two thousand resolutions expressing the disappointment of pro-disarmament groups throughout the United States at the slowness of progress at the World Disarmament

---

[58] Wheeler-Bennett, *Disarmament Deadlock*, p. 37.

[59] 'Resolution A. Second text proposed by the Joint Disarmament Commission of the LSI and the IFTU for the Joint Disarmament Conference of the LSI and the IFTU, Zurich, May 22nd and 23rd, 1932,' file 4482, Labour and Socialist International archives, International Institute of Social History, Amsterdam.

[60] Minutes of the meeting of the Liaison Committee of Women's International Organisations of 4 May 1932, file 1, Liaison Committee of Women's International Organisations archives, International Institute of Social History, Amsterdam; Women's International League for Peace and Freedom, *Women's International League for Peace and Freedom, 1915–1938: A Venture in Internationalism* (Geneva, 1938), pp. 25–6.

Conference.[61] At the same time, the Interorganization Council in New York, a collaborative body consisting of more than thirty American pro-disarmament organisations, decided to hold a substantial conference in Chicago on the occasion of the party conventions in June to persuade both parties to take a more pro-active stand on disarmament and consultation.[62] President Hoover thus began to feel that he should 'seek an early opportunity to say something on the disarmament question for the effect of opinion at home as well as abroad.'[63]

By May 1932, the principal members of the American delegation in Geneva had also decided that they needed to play a more positive role, under pressure from the Geneva-based American activists who had set up a parallel 'Interorganization Council in Geneva' in February. On 26 May, Gibson wrote to Stimson to inform him: 'One of the more responsible representatives of American peace organizations in Geneva tells me that regardless of their views as to what ought to be accomplished by this conference they are unanimous in disapproving the present attitude of our government.'[64] Two days later, he wrote an extensive telegram to Stimson informing him that 'the situation in Geneva has touched bottom' and that 'according to the indications we receive here, [peace organisations] are thoroughly discontented with the situation and intend to express their dissatisfaction with the policy very vigorously at Chicago.' Although he denied 'advocating any specific plan of a comprehensive nature,' he urged Stimson to consider 'what real concessions the United States might be willing to share with other countries' because 'something substantial and effective must be done.'[65]

On 7 June, Stimson replied with scepticism: 'The real strength of America's position in the movement for peace today does not depend on her taking the initiative in the Conference.... Nor do I think there

---

[61] See the representative selection sent by Mary Woolley to President Hoover on 6 May 1932, 500. A 15 A 4 /1113, container 2390, Department of State Decimal File, 1930–9, National Archives 2, College Park, MD.

[62] Meeting of 21 Apr. 1932, Interorganization Council on Disarmament (ICD) papers, Swarthmore College Peace Collection, Swarthmore, PA.

[63] Davis to Gibson (telegram), 31 Mar. 1932, 500. A15 A 4 / 953, container 2390, Department of State Decimal File, 1930–9, National Archives 2.

[64] Gibson to Stimson (telegram), 26 May 1932, 500. A 15 A 4 / 1074, container 2390, Department of State Decimal File, 1930–9, National Archives 2.

[65] Gibson to Stimson (telegram), 28 May 1932, *Papers Relating to the Foreign Relations of the United States (FRUS)*, 1932, vol. 1, pp. 145–50.

is reason to anticipate alarming dissatisfaction from peace groups at Chicago.'[66] President Hoover, on the other hand, had had similar thoughts to those of his delegation, and on 24 May he outlined to his Cabinet a radical plan to reduce battleships, destroyers, cruisers and the defence components of all armies by a third as well as the complete abolition of all tanks, military aircraft, heavy guns, aircraft carriers and submarines. In the face of the European 'divisions and dissensions' at the Conference and the 'continued economic degeneration of the world,' he hoped this plan would provide 'some lift in spirit.'[67] It was also calculated to win him support in the November elections, as he hoped the reduced European defence expenditures resulting from the plan would enable repayment of war debts upon expiry of his moratorium.[68] Foreign diplomats in Washington were convinced that the proposal was 'designed for home consumption first and foremost.'[69] The plan greatly frustrated Stimson, whose attempts to block the proposal in Cabinet failed. In his diary, Stimson described the proposal as

> a mistake and a proposition that cut pretty deep. Unfortunately it reaches down to the President's Quaker nature.... But really so far as a practical proposition is concerned, to me it is just a proposal from Alice in Wonderland. It is no reality, but is just as bad as it can be in its practical effect. It will appeal to a small element in this country, the pacifist element; it will not appeal to the large sensible element.[70]

When Hoover's plan was presented simultaneously in Washington and Geneva on 22 June 1932, it was lauded by disarmament activists throughout the world. In the United States, a resolution supported by over sixty national organisations in Chicago 'rejoiced' in Hoover's action, and the Interorganization Council in Geneva proudly communicated the thanks of the American disarmament movement to the US delegation.[71] In the days following the presentation of the Hoover Plan, the President

---

[66] Stimson to Gibson (telegram), 7 Jun. 1932, *FRUS*, 1932, vol. 1, pp. 153–7.

[67] Memorandum of 24 May 1932, *FRUS*, 1932, vol. 1, pp. 180–3.

[68] See B. J. C. McKercher, 'Of Horns and Teeth: The Preparatory Commission and the World Disarmament Conference, 1926–1934' in his edited volume, *Arms Limitation and Disarmament: Restraints on War, 1899–1939* (Westport, CT, 1992), pp. 185–6.

[69] Memorandum by A. F. H. Wigram, 22 Jun. 1932, FO 371/16462, Foreign Office General Correspondence, National Archives, London.

[70] Entry for 24 May 1932, Henry L. Stimson diary, Vere Harmsworth Library, Oxford.

[71] See Morgan to Henderson, 25 Jun. 1932, R. 2452, League of Nations Archives.

of the Disarmament Conference received over 180 resolutions a day from organisations supporting the proposal.[72]

In the Conference Chamber, the German, Soviet and Italian delegations all accepted Hoover's proposals with little hesitation. Most of the representatives of the smaller states did likewise. However, the proposals were greeted with far less enthusiam by the British and French delegates, who opened the discussion. Simon spoke of the additional need to reduce the 'monstrous size' of capital ships and the need to abolish submarines, while Paul-Boncour repeated the French demand for greater security commitments before any reductions could take place. The Japanese also made clear their hostility. A subsequent 'Statement of Views' announced in the House of Commons on 7 July by the British Foreign Secretary made especially clear Britain's opposition to most of Hoover's proposals, particularly the abolition of tanks and bombing aircraft, which were considered by the service departments to be necessary for imperial policing. This statement, as Noel Baker was to claim, effectively 'killed the Hoover plan.'[73]

Rather than adopting the American proposal, on 5 July the Bureau gave itself the task of drawing up a resolution setting out the points on which all states could agree before the Conference adjourned for the summer. Having received innumerable petitions and resolutions on disarmament throughout the first six months of the Conference,[74] Henderson wrote to the rapporteur, Edvard Beneš, on 12 July to recommend that he try to get delegates to incorporate into the resolution the common goals of the pro-disarmament organisations, such as abolition of aerial bombardment, tanks, large mobile artillery, biological and chemical warfare, and submarines.[75] Four days later, on the initiative of British disarmament campaigner Will Arnold-Forster, all the most prominent activists in Geneva at the time presented the Bureau with a Joint Memorial on Disarmament promoting much the same ideas.[76]

After another week of debate, the 'Beneš resolution' was passed on 23 July by 41 votes to 2, with 8 abstentions. It affirmed that a 'substantial reduction' of world armaments should be effected, that 'a

---

[72] See the document 'sent to Mr. Jenkins, 19 February 1933,' p. 10, box S. 475, Arthur Henderson papers, League of Nations Archives, Geneva.

[73] Noel-Baker, *First World Disarmament Conference*, p. 110.

[74] See boxes R. 2448–57, League of Nations Archives.

[75] Henderson to Beneš, 12 Jul. 1932, box S. 475, Henderson papers.

[76] 'Memorial from members of organisations in Geneva to the President of the Conference and heads of delegations,' box 5, ICG papers.

primary objective shall be to reduce the means of attack,' that guns and tanks should be forbidden above undefined limits, and that aerial bombardment should be abolished except for policing purposes. The disarmament movement's proposals had therefore been incorporated to some degree.[77]

However, the resolution was far more notable for what it omitted than for what it contained: there was not one concrete proposal for reduction; there were no additional security arrangements; and there was no mention of equal rights for Germany. As the observer for the International Co-operative Women's Guild noted, the resolution was 'a profound disappointment… utterly inadequate both in the general principles it laid down, from which some important principles are excluded, and still more in its few and feeble attempts at concrete and positive decisions.'[78]

Even by the states that accepted it, the resolution was regarded as an admission of the Conference's failure. As for Russia and Germany, which voted against it, the resolution was seen as an affront. Litvinoff declared: 'I vote for disarmament, but against the resolution.'[79] Since this reflected the opinion of many of the activists watching the proceedings, as Dorothy Detzer noted in her diary, 'the gallery, packed with bourgeois women, was swept into such spontaneous, riotous applause for the Soviet delegate that the guards couldn't get order and cleared most of us out.'[80] Nadolny, the German representative, not only rejected the resolution, but insisted that Germany could no longer participate in the Conference until her equality of status was recognised. Until she could be persuaded to return, the Disarmament Conference had to be suspended.

---

[77] An assessment by the Geneva-based activists of progress to this point in time can be found in Will Arnold-Forster et al., *The First Stage in Disarmament: A Commentary on the Continuing Programme of the Conference* (Geneva, 1932).

[78] 'Secretary's Report on the Final Resolution and General Position of the Disarmament Conference, August 1932,' file DCX/8/1, ICWG archives.

[79] Quoted in Walters, *History of the League of Nations*, p. 512.

[80] Dorothy Detzer, *Appointment on the Hill* (New York, 1948), p. 113.

CHAPTER NINE

THE INTERNATIONAL CONSULTATIVE GROUP AND THE COLLAPSE OF THE WORLD DISARMAMENT CONFERENCE, JULY 1932 TO OCTOBER 1933

> *The work of the International Consultative Group for Disarmament represents the largest and most effective effort to mobilize public peace opinion yet attempted in the realm of peace organisation Never before has there been an international co-ordinated effort on so wide and effective a scale.*
>
> Bertram Pickard, 18 November 1933[1]

Faced with the lack of substantial progress at the World Disarmament Conference by July 1932, activists decided to step up their campaign. In Geneva, a transnational collaborative body, the International Consultative Group for Peace and Disarmament (ICG), was set up by representatives of all of the principal international non-governmental organisations in the city. The British and French governments responded to the heightened activism by making efforts to bring Germany back to the Disarmament Conference and by proposing two new disarmament schemes. When progress had still not been made in the summer of 1933, the ICG organised a last-ditch global campaign to rescue the Conference. However, these efforts came to nought when in October 1933 Adolf Hitler withdrew Germany from both the World Disarmament Conference and the League of Nations.

FORMATION OF THE INTERNATIONAL CONSULTATIVE GROUP

When the final version of the Beneš resolution made clear the meagre results of the first six months of the Disarmament Conference, members of the women's, students,' Christian and IFLNS Disarmament Committees, CIAMAC, and the American and British Interorganization Councils in Geneva met on 23 and 26 July 1932 'to create a simple

---

[1] 'Memorandum concerning future development' by Mr. and Mrs. Pickard, 18 Nov. 1933, box 2, International Consultative Group (ICG) papers, League of Nations Archives, Geneva.

Council, with Mr. Malcolm Davis as convenor, the function of which will be to help the various Disarmament Committees concerned to co-ordinate, where necessary and desirable, their programmes and policies, in order that the action of public opinion during the second phase of the Conference may be more effective than it has been during the first.'[2] By 26 September, these organisations (which had a combined membership of over a hundred million people) had agreed to the name 'International Consultative Group for Peace and Disarmament,'[3] and two days later they issued a Joint Statement outlining their common goals, placing special emphasis on qualitative disarmament, abolition of bombing and the establishment of a permanent disarmament commission.[4]

The purposes of the group were: '1) to consult regularly concerning all questions concerning disarmament and peace; 2) to supply relevant information to the associated organisations; 3) to make reports on special aspects of disarmament and peace issues; 4) to promote co-ordinated policies and programmes of work among the associated organisations; and 5) to make private and public representations to delegates and official bodies meeting in Geneva.'[5]

From the beginning, the organisation realised its limitations. It was never intended to be an 'Executive Committee' but, as its name suggested, it was primarily a 'consultative group to keep organisations here in touch with each other.'[6] At the global level, it could only influence the League of Nations and delegates at the Disarmament Conference when in session. As has been demonstrated in the development of the Tardieu and Hoover Plans, it was the national-level activities of the ICG's member groups that had been having the greatest impact. With Germany abstaining from the Conference proceedings for the rest of the year and attention moving away from Geneva, this trend continued for the remainder of 1932.

---

[2] Pickard to the members of the Disarmament Committee of the Christian International Organisations, 30 Jul. 1932, box 1, ICG papers.

[3] Sixth meeting of 26 Sep. 1932, box 2, ICG papers.

[4] Draft Joint Statement on Disarmament, box 5, ICG papers.

[5] International Consultative Group for Peace and Disarmament, *The International Consultative Group (for Peace and Disarmament): Its Origins, Aims and Development* (Geneva, 1937), pp. 7–8.

[6] Comment by Malcolm Davis at the meeting of 19 Oct. 1932, box 2, ICG papers.

Summer Activism and American Consultation

During the summer of 1932, significant activist campaigns were directed at national governments, especially in the Anglo-Saxon countries. In Great Britain, attention was focused upon condemning the government's 'deeply disappointing,' 'unintelligent' and 'obstructive' response to the Hoover Plan; and 'all constitutional means' were used to pressurise the government.[7] Numerous resolutions condemning the British government's Statement of Views of 7 July were received by the Foreign Office,[8] and Prime Minister Ramsay MacDonald wrote to Foreign Secretary Sir John Simon shortly after the Conference adjourned to warn him that 'we shall have to face a pretty steady propaganda...We must defend ourselves and show the others that they will attack at their own peril.'[9]

In the United States, meanwhile, activists saw that this country would need to play a more active role in European security affairs than had been allowed for in the Hoover Plan. As a result, one of the primary purposes of the peace rallies held during the party conventions at Chicago was to secure in the electoral platforms of both political parties an agreement to consult with European states in the event of a violation of the Kellogg-Briand Pact.[10] Activists had little trouble securing the inclusion of a commitment to consult in the platform of the Republican Party because Secretary of State Henry Stimson agreed that such a commitment was vital. In fact, he had already advocated an announcement 'in respect to the Kellogg Pact and our action in case of a struggle between a combined Europe and an aggressor nation' instead of the Hoover Plan.[11] When the Democrat Convention took place two weeks

---

[7] Women's International League Executive Committee Minutes, 19 Jul. 1932, file 1/8, British Women's International League for Peace and Freedom (UKWILPF) papers, British Library of Political and Economic Science, London; Murray to W. H., 8 Jul. 1932, file 213, Gilbert Murray papers, Bodleian Library, Oxford; *Headway*, Sep. 1932, p. 178.

[8] See the file containing them in FO 371/16451, Foreign Office General Correspondence, National Archives, London.

[9] MacDonald to Simon, 25 Jul. 1932, file 72, Sir John Simon papers, Bodleian Library, Oxford.

[10] This idea was present in both the left and right wing platforms of the peace advocates at Chicago. The platforms are printed and discussed in *League of Nations Chronicle*, vol. 5, Jun. 1932.

[11] Memorandum by the Secretary of State, 25 May 1932, *Papers Relating to the Foreign Relations of the United States (FRUS)*, 1932, vol. 1, pp. 182–4.

later the party was split on the issue, but prominent activists worked with Cordell Hull and other members of the Resolutions Committee to draw up a platform which also included 'provisions for consultation and conference in case of threatened violation of treaties.'[12] With the peace movement having helped to make consultation a matter of cross-party agreement, Stimson publicly announced in an address to the Council on Foreign Relations on 8 August 1932 that 'consultation between the signatories of the Pact when faced with the threat of its violation becomes inevitable.'[13]

Paul-Boncour's 'Constructive Plan'

Stimson's announcement had a significant impact in Europe, and particularly inspired Joseph Paul-Boncour in France. He had become War Minister in the new left-wing government of Edouard Herriot and he became concerned at the unpopularity of France amongst the public in the Anglo-Saxon countries after the new government had rejected the Hoover Plan.[14] Rather than the disaffection of French disarmament activist organisations (which in the case of the French League of Nations societies tended simply to promote whatever Paul-Boncour told them to), it was the concern of activists in Anglo-Saxon countries that appears to have been a greater concern to him, as revealed in Herriot's diaries of the time.[15]

By October 1932, therefore, Paul-Boncour thought it was time for a new French 'Constructive Plan.' Its contents were first indicated in a polemical note of 4 October 1932, which stated: 'If we do not provide a plan for progressive and controlled disarmament, international public opinion will hold us responsible for the failure of the Conference. If the French plan does not appear to be easily realisable, if it subordinates disarmament to other problems that are difficult to resolve, we will be accused of wanting to hide our refusal to disarm.'[16] The note also

---

[12] Russell M. Cooper, *American Consultation in World Affairs for the Preservation of Peace* (New York, 1934), p. 58.

[13] Henry L. Stimson, *The Pact of Paris: Three Years of Development [Department of State Publication No. 357]* (Washington, DC, 1932), pp. 11–12.

[14] See, for example, 'Conversation avec Sir Austen Chamberlain,' 8 Oct. 1932, cote 5, Joseph Paul-Boncour papers, French Foreign Ministry Archives, Paris.

[15] f. 215, cote 29, Edouard Herriot papers, French Foreign Ministry Archives, Paris; see also Tyrrell to Simon (telegram), 18 Oct. 1932, FO 371/16465, Foreign Office General Correspondence.

[16] 'Note sur l'Egalité des Droits, la Sécurité et le Désarmement, Genève, le 4

displayed Paul-Boncour's concern that France could be held responsible by international public opinion for Germany's temporary departure from the Conference over the failure to grant her equal rights, and the fact that the International Federation of League of Nations Societies was in favour of recognition of German equality of status was cited as evidence for this.

The new plan incorporated Stimson's commitment to consult in its provision for a global consultative pact. This became the sole security commitment demanded of Britain and the USA in exchange for French commitment to disarm—a fundamental retreat from the Tardieu policy. Demands for a security pact enforceable by an international army were now limited to continental Europe. Under the new scheme, European armies would be surrendered to an international army and continental states would be left only with militias, thus implicitly granting equal rights to Germany. This idea caused substantial controversy when the plan was discussed in the meetings of the *Conseil Supérieur de la Défense Nationale* (CSDN). General Weygand, in particular, was entirely opposed as it would leave the Maginot Line vulnerable to attack, yet Paul-Boncour pressed ahead despite Weygand's opposition.[17] This also marked a significant break from previous French disarmament policy in that the politicians rather than the generals had for the first time had their way. And this was at a time when the French government was in a precarious condition: the need to keep the socialists in the ruling coalition was evident, for the 'Constructive Plan' had partly been introduced in response to socialist leader Léon Blum's call for a bold new initiative.[18]

However, when the 'Constructive Plan' was presented on 14 November 1932, it failed to have its intended impact. The Bureau of the Disarmament Conference had decided on 21 September that the full Conference could not reassemble until Germany had been persuaded to return. Despite Paul-Boncour's efforts towards satisfying German demands for equality in his plan, Kurt von Schleicher, the German

---

Octobre 1932,' cote 872, série SDN, French Foreign Ministry Archives, Paris. For the importance of this note, see Maurice Vaïsse, *Sécurité d'abord: la politique française en matière de désarmement, 9 décembre 1930–17 avril 1934* (Paris, 1981), p. 299.

[17] See Vaïsse, *Sécurité d'abord*, pp. 302–23 and *Documents Diplomatiques Français* (*DDF*), vol. 1, documents 250, 255, 260, 266, 268, 272–3 and 286 for the details of the CSDN discussions of the 'Constructive Plan.'

[18] See *DDF*, vol. 1, document 244, p. 439, footnote 3.

War Minister who had been responsible for the July withdrawal, made it clear that they were not adequate.[19]

BRITISH EFFORTS FOR GERMAN RETURN TO THE CONFERENCE

In Great Britain, on the other hand, more productive steps were taken to bring Germany back to the Conference. Domestic activist pressure for this goal was felt particularly strongly here. On 30 September 1932, Cabinet Secretary Maurice Hankey noted in his diary that the British Cabinet 'decided to summon a Conference in London to consider how to bring Germany back to the Disarmament Conference. I doubt if the French will come...But our government has "got the wind up" badly owing to the threats of the pacifists, Bishops and Free Churches, etc. over the coming failure of the Disarmament Conference, which has been certain from the first.'[20] Hankey correctly predicted the French response, so the Cabinet instead agreed to organise a four-power conference in Geneva preceded by a British initiative to bring about a compromise formula. Simon thought this necessary because 'If the disarmament propagandists in this country were told of the German intentions, their reply would be "Can you be surprised at Germany's attitude, when she has been refused all reasonable treatment?".'[21]

At the same time, Ramsay MacDonald hoped to arrange a deputation of prominent disarmament activists such as Maxwell Garnett (Secretary of the League of Nations Union), Gerald Bailey (Secretary of the National Peace Council) and Will Arnold-Forster 'whose eminence and distinction would enable the Prime Minister to explain to his Cabinet colleagues that he could not avoid answering their questions.'[22] Disarmers in the churches and the League of Nations Union were also appealing to be allowed deputations, and they were allowed one each on 20 October, because 'for the Prime Minister to refuse such a deputation would surely be regarded as a proof that Her Majesty's Government were not serious in their enthusiasm for disarmament.'[23]

---

[19] Christoph Kimmich, *Germany and the League of Nations* (Chicago, 1976), p. 169.

[20] Quoted in Stephen Roskill, *Hankey: Man of Secrets, Volume III: 1931–1963* (London, 1974), p. 60.

[21] Cabinet meeting 50 of 11 Oct. 1932, CAB 23/72, National Archives, London.

[22] Garnett to Cecil, 3 Oct. 1932, Add. MSS. 51136, Cecil of Chelwood papers, British Library, London.

[23] Leeper note of 28 Sep. 1932, FO 371/16439, Foreign Office General Correspondence.

At the Cabinet meeting of 19 October, MacDonald brought up these deputations to back his case that action had to be taken:

> A position was being created that would overwhelm the government if it was not met. On the following day he had to meet several Deputations on the subject, and a few days ago he had received an impressively sound Address, appended to which were the names of leaders in many branches of our national life. A position had been reached where the Government could not base its decisions on the advice of Experts only, but must take public opinion into account.[24]

By the end of the month, therefore, Simon had produced a plan, the object behind which was 'to support the moral forces, namely, world opinion, and that part of public opinion in Germany which was opposed to rearmament.'[25] Shortly afterwards, on 10 November, Simon presented to the House of Commons a statement accepting Germany's moral right to equal treatment so long as Germany signed a 'Declaration of No Resort to Force' and Baldwin gave a famous speech in favour of abolition of aerial bombardment, declaring 'the bomber will always get through.'[26] By 24 November, Simon had persuaded leaders from France, Italy, the USA and Germany to meet him in Geneva the following month.

The Declaration of 11 December 1932

Now that attention had returned to Geneva, the transnational element of the disarmament campaign had a renewed role to play. The representatives of the five powers were presented with a detailed statement on security, equality and disarmament drawn up by the International Consultative Group, which the Group hoped would form the basis of agreement.[27] The statement included numerous specific proposals for qualitative disarmament as the means to accord recognition of equality, and bore many similarities to the detailed proposal suggested by the American representative Norman Davis in the ensuing discussions.[28]

---

[24] Cabinet meeting 53 of 19 Oct. 1932, CAB 23/72, National Archives, London.

[25] Cabinet meeting 56 of 31 Oct. 1932, CAB 23/72, National Archives, London.

[26] The text of Simon's speech is contained in columns 534–48 of House of Commons, *Parliamentary Debates*, fifth series, vol. 270 The text of Baldwin's speech is contained in columns 630–8 of the same volume.

[27] 'Disarmament, Equality and Security: Declaration by the International Consultative Group in Geneva, December 1st 1932,' box 5, ICG papers.

[28] *FRUS*, 1932, vol. 1, p. 492.

In the event, any detailed proposals suggested were sidelined and at the meeting of 6 December, Herriot's vague formula to the effect that 'one of the aims of the Conference of Disarmament is to accord to Germany and the other disarmed powers equal rights in a system which would provide security for all nations' was the only proposal taken by the Germans to be a productive starting point.[29] After five days of wrangling between Chancellor Schleicher and Prime Minister Herriot, the representatives of Britain, Italy, France and Germany managed with American assistance to agree on a declaration that stated: 'One of the principles that should guide the Conference on Disarmament should be the grant to Germany, and to other powers disarmed by treaty, equality of rights in a system which would provide security for all nations,' and that this principle should be embodied in the final convention. It continued: 'On the basis of this declaration, Germany had signified its willingness to resume its place at the Disarmament Conference.' Buelow felt able to declare to the German people that the principle of equal rights was established 'whether the conference succeeded or failed.'[30]

While it was meaningless in that it left all points of substance still to be debated, the declaration assured both the Germans on equality and the French regarding security, and an additional clause stating that all European states should reaffirm their commitment never to use force to settle disputes catered for British concerns. With Germany's participation ensured again, a full meeting was convened three days later. Rather than seizing this last opportunity to negotiate a final settlement, however, the Conference was instead adjourned until 31 January 1933, the day after Hitler had gained the German Chancellorship. As Walters argues: 'the first year of its work had ended where it should have begun. The fleeting opportunities which might have led to its success had been missed, and they were not destined to return.'[31]

The Reopening of the Disarmament Conference

Nevertheless, at the time the members of the International Consultative Group had not given up hope. On 15 December 1932, they drew up a

---

[29] Kimmich, *Germany and the League of Nations*, p. 170.
[30] Quoted in Kimmich, *Germany and the League of Nations*, p. 172.
[31] F. P. Walters, *A History of the League of Nations* (London, 1952), p. 515.

memorandum on what they hoped would constitute 'The Next Stage in Disarmament.' They argued that a disarmament convention was possible on the basis of the positions already outlined by the various governments. As regards security, all states appeared to agree on the consultative arrangements provided for in the French 'Constructive Plan,' while a set of measures for the realisation of qualitative disarmament had already been indicated in the Beneš resolution.[32]

ICG activists also agreed that something had to be done to mark the reopening of the Conference and the anniversary of the presentation of the petitions the year before. However, their confidence was weakening. It was thought that 'it would be worse than useless to have any action that would not be powerful,' so instead of a major demonstration to mark the anniversary of the Extraordinary Session, they merely agreed to host a luncheon with Conference President Arthur Henderson on 6 February 1933, as this was 'more apt to succeed.'[33] Despite this, Henderson still expressed the belief at this dinner that 'there existed today a volume of public opinion throughout the world which would support the Governments in any measure of reduction, however drastic, upon which they might agree.'[34] This was reflected when, the following month, the two main international ex-servicemen's organisations (known by their acronyms as CIAMAC and FIDAC) succeeded in staging a massive disarmament demonstration in Geneva attended by 4,500 delegates.[35]

Meanwhile, the Conference had restarted by considering the French 'Constructive Plan.' The German position had by now become particularly obstructive, with Nadolny suggesting that the proposal for the retention of 'offensive weapons' in League hands violated the principle of qualitative disarmament and thus denied German rights to equality. As for the question of security, it was impossible to get the Americans to make any firm commitment to consult because Hoover's Presidency was

---

[32] 'The Next Stage in Disarmament: A Statement from the International Consultative Group in Geneva, 15 December 1932,' box 5, ICG papers.

[33] Minutes of ICG meeting of 13 Jan. 1933, box 2, ICG papers.

[34] Henderson's speech at the ICG dinner of 6 Feb. 1933, box 5, ICG papers.

[35] The proceedings of this conference are provided in Conférence Internationale des Associations de Mutilés et Anciens Combattants and Fédération Interallié des Anciens Combattants, *Rassemblement International des Anciens Combattants et Victimes de la Guerre à Genève les 19 et 20 mars 1933* (Paris, 1933). The absence of German representatives at this gathering, however, was ominous (See Antoine Prost, *Les anciens combattants et la société française, 1914–1945*, vol. 1 (Paris, 1977), p. 153).

shortly to come to an end. In consequence, from 9 February onwards, the Conference instead debated a vague 'programme of work' summarising all the points on which progress had been made so far, and the discussions again became bogged down in the face of German intransigence on technical details.

The MacDonald Plan

With Henderson threatening to overcome the impasse with a new disarmament plan of his own, the last of the three Western powers felt it was time to present a plan to resolve the Conference: Great Britain. On 16 March 1933, British Prime Minister Ramsay MacDonald presented the last major disarmament plan.[36] The proposal came in the form of a complete Draft Convention.[37] Part I provided for 'security' by multilateralising Stimson's doctrine that the United States was obliged to consult with other signatories to the Kellogg-Briand Pact in the event of a breach. This conformed with the Paul-Boncour Plan, and additional concessions were given to the French in the form of supervisory arrangements through the establishment of a permanent disarmament commission and the maintenance of German arms at existing levels for two years. As for the disarmament measures outlined in Part II, all countries but Russia were to be allowed 200,000-strong land armies, and mobile guns were to be limited by calibre (4 inches) and tanks by weight (16 tons). The measures of the Treaty of London were to be used for naval armaments, while aerial bombardment was to be abolished except for 'policing' purposes. To satisfy German interests, the Draft Convention was to replace the Versailles disarmament obligations, and Germany could substitute a short-service army for the Reichswehr and gain actual equality of land effectives and armaments within five years.

MacDonald's proposal was the outcome of the work of two enthusiastic young men working in the Foreign Office, Anthony Eden and Alexander Cadogan. Despite not having close links with the disarmament activists, they felt that the public pressure that had been generated

---

[36] The text of MacDonald's speech is contained in *Documents on British Foreign Policy*, series 2, vol. iv, appendix iv.

[37] The complete text of the British Draft Convention can be found in John W. Wheeler-Bennett, *The Disarmament Deadlock* (London, 1934), pp. 267–92.

could not be ignored.[38] In late 1932, Eden had sent numerous letters to Baldwin urging that Britain should make a bold gesture such as total abolition of military aviation and tanks in order to place 'ourselves above any criticism which must otherwise be directed against Her Majesty's Government by our detractors at home and abroad.'[39]

With disarmament activists in Britain claiming in early 1933 that 'the time was ripe for a Draft Convention which could put the proposals in a coherent shape, and it does seem as if in the present chaos Great Britain was the only power which commanded something like general confidence and goodwill,'[40] Eden and Cadogan drew up a detailed Draft Convention and in February 1933, Eden thought that 'we should make an attempt to get it through the Conference. The reaction upon public opinion at home of such an attempt must be favourable, and for my part I am really very sad at the prospect for Europe if this Conference fails.'[41] He persuaded Cabinet to accept it by arguing that this would be much easier to accept than the draft plan that Henderson was about to present to the Conference, which was thought to involve greater security assurances for France.[42]

The International Consultative Group thought the MacDonald Plan was 'a genuinely courageous step' which had 'saved the Conference at least for the present.'[43] However, opinion in Britain was mixed: when Cecil told League of Nations Union Chairman Gilbert Murray that he thought the MacDonald Plan was 'a great deal better than nothing,'[44] Murray told him that he thought 'the Foreign Office scheme rotten as usual. Not a single sacrifice by England: all the reductions to be made by others.'[45] Anomalies such as the continuation of aerial bombardment 'for police purposes' seemed particularly geared towards British self-interest.

Furthermore, straight after the presentation of the Draft Convention to the Disarmament Conference, the British Prime Minister hastily left

---

[38] See David Carlton, *Anthony Eden: A Biography* (London, 1981), p. 37.

[39] Eden to Baldwin, 20 Oct. 1932, file 118, Stanley Baldwin papers, Cambridge University Library, Cambridge.

[40] Murray to Simon, 17 Feb. 1933, file 216, Murray papers.

[41] Eden to Baldwin, 24 Feb. 1933, file 129, Baldwin papers.

[42] Eden to Simon, 24 Feb. 1933, FO 800/291, Sir John Simon papers, National Archives, London.

[43] Meeting of 18 Mar. 1933, box 2, ICG papers.

[44] Cecil to Murray, 20 Mar. 1933, file 217, Murray papers.

[45] Murray to Cecil, 17 Mar. 1933, Add. MSS. 51132, Cecil papers.

for Rome, where Mussolini wanted to negotiate a Four Power Pact to supplant the League of Nations. This was a public sign of MacDonald's private feeling that the Draft Convention was not serious: it was 'designed not to achieve disarmament, but to prop up a conference which everyone knew was disintegrating.'[46] Officials in the Foreign Office had also noticed that the MacDonald Plan was 'simply a demonstration for internal consumption here…We have all been too late.'[47]

FURTHER AMERICAN CONCESSIONS

Despite MacDonald's cynicism, his plan had significant repercussions on American policy. By the time of its presentation, the Hoover Presidency had come to an end and Democrat Franklin Roosevelt had been sworn into office on 4 March 1933. He appeared to be as keen on disarmament as his predecessor, telling delegates that 'we should push the disarmament conference to the fullest extent.'[48] His Secretary of State was Cordell Hull, an advocate of an active role for the United States in world affairs who also thought that disarmament was 'an essential element to peace.'[49] Furthermore, to the delight of peace groups, Roosevelt had appointed a prominent internationalist, Norman Davis, to the Chairmanship of the American delegation to the Disarmament Conference.

The MacDonald Plan insisted on a greater US commitment to European security than had so far been proposed: it asked for the United States not to insist upon neutral rights when collective sanctions were being placed on aggressor nations in Europe. This was a policy both administrations had committed themselves to in their support of Congressional resolutions on the use of embargoes, which had been drawn up in response to the Chaco War.[50] Furthermore, junior members of the US delegation such as Hugh Wilson thought that agreement to

---

[46] Quoted in Carolyn Kitching, *Britain and the Geneva Disarmament Conference: A Study in International History* (Basingstoke, 2003), p. 135.

[47] Note of 13 Mar. 1933, FO 371/17353, Foreign Office General Correspondence.

[48] Roosevelt to Davis, 26 Nov. 1932, container 51, Norman Davis papers, Library of Congress, Washington, DC.

[49] Cordell Hull, *The Memoirs of Cordell Hull*, vol. 1 (London, 1948), p. 222.

[50] See Robert A. Divine, 'Franklin D. Roosevelt and Collective Security, 1933,' *Mississippi Valley Historical Review*, 48/1 (1961), pp. 45–7.

this policy could be used to revitalise the Disarmament Conference.[51] On 16 April 1933, therefore, Norman Davis proposed this policy to Washington on behalf of the entire delegation as their suggested response to Part I of the MacDonald Plan.[52] A month later, after being warned by Davis that 'it would be useless to continue as in the past,' Roosevelt formally announced the policy in a speech delivered on 16 May, followed by Davis' presentation of the policy in Geneva six days later.[53] For the time being, this represented a fundamental step forward in American interventionism.[54]

It should be noted that, while disarmament activists had played a crucial role in the origins of the Hoover Plan and of Stimson's declaration of an American commitment to consult, their role in the commitment not to impede sanctions was insubstantial. 'Right wing' organisations such as the League of Nations Association had corresponded with Hull on the subject in the months preceding the announcement and Hull declared himself in 'complete agreement' with them,[55] but the rest of the peace movement in America refused to speak of sanctions.[56]

Nevertheless, the American announcements had significant repercussions at the Conference. The day after Roosevelt's announcement, Hitler declared that 'Germany is at any time willing to undertake further obligations of international security if all the other nations are ready on their side to do the same' and German reservations about the MacDonald Plan were withdrawn.[57] On the other hand, Paul-Boncour

---

[51] Wilson to Moffat, 29 Mar. 1933, container 43, Davis papers. See also Hugh R. Wilson, *Diplomat Between Wars* (New York, 1941), pp. 285–6.

[52] Marriner to Hull, 16 Apr. 1933, *FRUS*, 1933, vol. 1, pp. 89–92.

[53] Davis to Roosevelt, 23 Apr. 1933, President's Secretary's File 130, Franklin D. Roosevelt papers, Franklin D. Roosevelt Presidential Library, Hyde Park, NY. For the speech, see Department of State, *Peace and War: United States Foreign Policy, 1931–1941* (Washington, DC, 1943), pp. 188–9.

[54] The Congressional resolution was later destroyed by Roosevelt's acceptance of an amendment by Hiram Johnson on 27 May 1933 which made the proposed embargo apply impartially to all belligerents. See Divine, 'Franklin D. Roosevelt and Collective Security,' p. 56.

[55] Hull to Strong, 20 Mar. 1933, document 500. A 15 A 4/1776, container 2393, Department of State Decimal File, 1930–9, National Archives 2, College Park, MD. See also Strong to Hull, 13 Mar. 1933, document 1765, container 2393, Department of State Decimal File, 1930–9, National Archives 2.

[56] The Interorganization Council split into 'right' and 'left' wings on this and other issues as early as May 1932. See the minutes of the meetings of 23 and 27 May 1932, Interorganization Council on Disarmament (ICD) papers, Swarthmore College Peace Collection, Swarthmore, PA.

[57] Arnold Toynbee, *Survey of International Affairs, 1933* (London, 1934), p. 270.

made it known that, although he welcomed the American commitment, the French government still insisted upon the reservation of 'offensive weapons' for use in a League police force. Because of this and other points of disagreement, the Conference was adjourned for the summer on 8 June, and on 27 June it was decided that the Conference would not reopen until mid-October.

RENUNCIATION OF FRENCH DEMANDS FOR SECURITY

In the meantime, efforts were made to resolve what appeared to be the last major sticking-point at the Disarmament Conference: the need for the French to disarm without first being assured of at least a continental European mutual assistance pact guaranteed by a League army. In the summer of 1933, this problem came to an end. Despite his delegation's stance at the Conference, at home the new Prime Minister Edouard Daladier had already been making more conciliatory statements. For instance, on 1 March 1933 he told the American Press Association in Paris that 'effective' supervision would be the most important step towards French agreement to disarm. This policy had been evident as early as 22 December 1932, when his predecessor had made a similar statement to the Chamber of Deputies. In June 1933, 'effective' supervision officially became the *sole* prior security commitment that the French government demanded in exchange for agreement to disarm, and by 'effective' was meant a four-year trial period.[58]

French disarmament activists had a role to play in this softening of the French position. For example, activist politicians Pierre Comert and Pierre Cot felt assured that the position taken in the speech of 22 December 1932 was the result of their pressure.[59] When Cot was made Daladier's Air Minister, he was better able to demand that the French government's response to the MacDonald Plan should be to change tactic from demanding security guarantees to merely strict supervision of all countries' armaments.[60] As Jules Prudhommeaux of the Federation of French League of Nations Associations pointed

---

[58] See *DDF*, vol. 3, pp. 897–9.

[59] See Memorandum by R. F. Wigram of conversations with Comert and Cot, 23 Dec. 1932, FO 371/16470, Foreign Office General Correspondence.

[60] Vaïsse, *Sécurité d'abord*, p. 435.

out, the way the disarmament activists exerted pressure here was very different from in the Anglo-Saxon countries: 'we have not held public demonstrations, but in face of difficult circumstances we have *acted*. And the way we have acted is through those who are rightly our delegates in Geneva: H. de Jouvenel, Paul-Boncour, Pierre Cot, Paganon, René Cassin. These are our best activists.'[61]

However, other motivations for the policy change also need to be taken into account. In particular, Daladier accepted supervision as the only possible way France could salvage something from the Conference: the assured inspection and maintenance of German armaments at existing levels. By insisting on a four year trial period, he could ensure the continuation of the status quo for long enough that the Anglo-Saxons might realise Hitler's intentions and take a more sympathetic line as regards French security demands.[62]

The new French policy was discussed with the British, Americans and Italians while the Conference was in recess and on 22 September 1933 these powers agreed that it should form the basis of agreement at the Conference when it reopened in October. The agreed policy was essentially the MacDonald Plan, but with the addition of the French proposal of a four-year trial period of supervision before implementation could take place.

ACTIVISM'S LAST STAND

While the negotiations ploughed on, the movement for disarmament ran into difficulties. By June 1933, activist Laura Puffer Morgan noted: 'There is no confidence whatever that anything *will* come of the Disarmament Conference. When I wrote in one of my last articles that the people would be disappointed to learn that the Conference had been adjourned, members of our own staff laughed.'[63] In her native America, the Interorganization Council in New York had ceased to exist because of the impossibility of 'keeping the various peace

---

[61] Prudhommeaux to Small, 28 Jun. 1932, box P.97, International Federation of League of Nations Societies (IFLNS) papers. League of Nations Archives, Geneva.

[62] See J. Néré, *The Foreign Policy of France from 1914 to 1945* (London, 1975), p. 127.

[63] Morgan to Livingstone, 11 Aug. 1933, box 6, ICG papers. The splits had emerged in the adoption of separate right and left wing platforms at the Jun. 1932 Chicago demonstrations.

organisations at peace with themselves.'[64] At the transnational level, meanwhile, some of the organisations began to run out of money, having expected the Disarmament Conference to last only a year. In the case of the Disarmament Committee of the Women's International Organisations, a desperate and ultimately unsuccessful attempt to secure the Nobel Peace Prize was the result.[65] The activists' trilingual journal, *Disarmament*, on the other hand, had lost interest in the subject of its title and was renamed *Recovery* to follow instead the proceedings of the London Economic Conference.

Nevertheless, the movement made one last great effort to push for disarmament in the summer of 1933. The primary driving force behind this was the International Consultative Group in Geneva, and its efforts to produce a transnational campaign to save the Conference reveal some of the difficulties faced in the pursuit of transnational activism.

On 9 June, the ICG sent a memorandum to the national societies, urging them to press their respective governments to make concessions on areas where they had been particularly obstinate. Once the date for the reconvening of the Disarmament Conference had been set for mid-October, the Consultative Group set aside 15 October for a mass demonstration. An organising committee was set up to arrange the demonstration, directed by Dame Adelaide Livingstone of the British League of Nations Union. In the meantime, meetings around the world were organised to send messages of support to the Geneva demonstration. It was hoped that every meeting would adopt a common six-point resolution advocating no rearmament, substantial reduction, qualitative disarmament, budgetary limitation, strict supervision and a permanent supervisory organisation.[66]

Preparations did not go as well as was hoped. Arthur Henderson, having initially invited the Group to present its demonstration at another special session of the Disarmament Conference like that of 6 February

---

[64] See Walter van Kirk to the Members of the Interorganization Council, 2 Jun. 1933, ICD papers. The quotation is from Walter van Kirk to Laura Puffer Morgan, 31 Mar. 1933, box 3, Subject File—Disarmament—Disarmament Congresses: Conference for the Reduction and Limitation of Armaments, Geneva, February 1932, Swarthmore College Peace Collection, Swarthmore, PA.

[65] See the 'Summary or Supplementary Report of Activities from June 1933 to March 1934' of the Disarmament Committee of Women's International Organisations, folios 1248–56, reel 99, Women's International League for Peace and Freedom papers on UMI microfilm.

[66] Minutes of the meeting of 14 Jul. 1933, box 2, ICG papers.

1932, told the Group's leaders in September 1933 that he no longer thought it advisable and that they had to hold the demonstration by themselves.[67] As for the six-point resolution, several versions of it were promoted according to the national preferences of the countries in which it was distributed. In Germany references to 'no rearmament' were purged, while in the United States any reference to security commitments was expunged.[68] Furthermore, with pacifists facing persecution in Germany, only state-sponsored groups such as the 'German Society for League of Nations Questions' had any role to play in this country, and unsurprisingly they did nothing.[69]

Nevertheless, outside Germany this last-ditch campaign was impressive in scale. In the weeks leading up to the Geneva demonstration, approximately one thousand meetings were held in each of the USA, France and the UK. In total, over six thousand messages of support were sent by branches of organisations in thirty countries to Geneva.[70] Furthermore, MacDonald, Daladier, Stimson and Molotov were all persuaded to send formal messages of support to the 15 October meeting—an unprecedented gesture in the history of *international* non-governmental demonstrations.[71] When Henderson received a deputation from the Group the day after, Cecil felt able to declare that the demonstration 'showed that public opinion was as strong as ever on behalf of disarmament.'[72]

The End of the Disarmament Conference

However, the demonstration took place at least a day too late. The German government had already made up its mind about the usefulness of the Disarmament Conference. At a public meeting of the Bureau on 14 October 1933, Simon had formally put forward the common plan agreed upon in September by Britain, France and the United States, and all but one delegate spoke in favour of it as the basis of

---

[67] Minutes of the meeting of 23 Sep. 1933, box 2, ICG papers.

[68] See Dame Adelaide Livingstone's correspondence in box 6, ICG papers.

[69] See Kirchoff to Ruyssen, 21 Sep. 1933, box P.102, IFLNS papers.

[70] Malcolm Davis to Vladimir Romm, 8 Mar. 1934, box 4, ICG papers.

[71] 'Public Opinion Speaks Again' (Memorandum 150 of the Disarmament Committee of Women's International Organisations, 19 Oct. 1933), box 2, ICG papers. The messages are contained in box 6 of the ICG papers.

[72] For a complete account of the event, see *Conference for the Reduction and Limitation of Armaments Journal*, Special Supplement, No. 5, 26 Oct. 1933.

a settlement. However, the German delegate, Baron von Rheinbaben rejected the four-year trial period and demanded immediate equality of status. Shortly after the meeting broke up that day the German Foreign Minister delivered the Conference's death-blow: a telegram stating that Germany had been 'compelled to leave the Disarmament Conference.' Furthermore, Hitler had the excuse he had been waiting for to leave the League of Nations, and announced his intention to do so that evening.[73]

Without German participation, it was generally agreed that the Conference could not possibly achieve productive results. However, Norman Davis pointed out that the activists did score a meagre final success in ensuring that the General Commission continued to meet despite the German withdrawal.[74] Nevertheless, no progress could be made and on 11 June 1934 the Disarmament Conference was adjourned *sine die*. As for the International Consultative Group, on 23 November 1933 it evolved from an activist organisation into 'a bureau for the collection of material on various subjects related to disarmament.'[75]

---

[73] Wheeler-Bennett, *Disarmament Deadlock*, pp. 181–3.

[74] See Laura Puffer Morgan's 'Weekly Report,' second series, no. 2, 27 Oct. 1933, box LON 28, Brochure and Pamphlet Collection, League of Nations Archives, Geneva.

[75] Minutes of the meeting of 23 Nov. 1933, box 2, ICG papers.

PART FIVE

ASSESSMENT: THE POSSIBILITIES OF
TRANSNATIONAL ACTIVISM

CHAPTER TEN

IMPACT OF THE DISARMAMENT CAMPAIGN

The last five chapters of this book have outlined the evolution, activities and achievements of the global disarmament campaign from the Paris peace settlement in 1919 to the collapse of the World Disarmament Conference in 1933. In Part V, the evidence presented in those chapters is used in two ways. First, the evidence is used in this chapter to draw conclusions on the extent of the interwar disarmament campaign's influence. Secondly, in chapter eleven, the evidence is used to test the factors facilitating and inhibiting achievement of activist objectives outlined in Part I, in order to find out if there are any general propositions about the role of transnational activism in world politics that are justified empirically. The propositions that are not eliminated by this test are also checked against the evidence of other existing case studies of activist influence. In the final chapter, the sole proposition that survives both of chapter eleven's tests is highlighted, and its implications are outlined.

Summary of the Influence of the Interwar Disarmament Campaign

The common aim of the movement examined in this study, as embodied in the Budapest programme, was the creation of an 'international convention' that would provide for 'a substantial reduction in armaments.'[1] This required action on the part of national governments, and in particular those of Great Britain, France and the United States. In this chapter, the impact of activist pressure on the policies of these countries is briefly summarised. The detailed evidence for the assertions of activist impact made here has been provided in Parts III and IV.

---

[1] Articles 1 and 2 of the Budapest Resolution in International Federation of League of Nations Societies, *XV Plenary Congress of the International Federation of League of Nations Societies, Budapest, 1931* (Brussels, 1931), p. 156. The complete text is reproduced in the sixth appendix to this book.

One of the most visible consequences of the disarmament campaign was the effort made by governments to appoint activists to national delegations to international conferences and commissions on disarmament. The French government, for example, appointed the trade union leader and disarmament activist Léon Jouhaux to the Temporary Mixed Commission. The British and US governments, for their part, responded positively to the request of the Liaison Committee of Women's International Organisations that women activists be appointed to serve in national delegations to the World Disarmament Conference by making Margery Corbett Ashby and Mary Woolley delegates.[2] In addition, British governments frequently appointed leaders of the League of Nations Union to serve on British delegations to League meetings, and the Prime Minister in 1932 expressed disappointment when Viscount Cecil refused to serve as a British delegate to the World Disarmament Conference.[3]

The principal reason for the appointment of activists to national delegations was the need to give the impression of activist approval of government policy. There was also a tendency on the part of government leaders to attempt to give the impression of governmental support for activist objectives. This was done in a number of superficial ways. In France, for example, the Foreign Ministry sponsored a booklet on the eve of the World Disarmament Conference describing the aims and activities of all the main peace groups in France, and inserted War Minister André Tardieu's photograph as the frontispiece.[4] In all three of the countries examined in this book, government leaders also felt compelled to address activist rallies in support of disarmament, the most prominent example being the 15 July 1931 Albert Hall demonstration organised by the League of Nations Union which was addressed by the leaders of all three of the main political parties in Great Britain.[5]

As for the impact of the disarmament campaign upon the *policies* of the three governments examined in this study, developments during the course of the World Disarmament Conference highlight its nature. As outlined in the eighth and ninth chapters of this book, the

---

[2] See page 107.

[3] MacDonald to Cecil, 22 Jan. 1932, Add. MSS. 51081, Cecil of Chelwood papers, British Library, London.

[4] *Nous voulons la paix: concentration des efforts universels des forces pacifistes sous le haut patronage du Ministère des Affaires Étrangères. 1932* (Paris, 1932).

[5] See page 105.

principal governmental response to activist pressure during the World Disarmament Conference was the presentation of wide-ranging 'plans' for the reduction and limitation of armaments: the Tardieu Plan of February 1932, the Hoover Plan of June 1932, the Paul-Boncour Plan of November 1932, and the MacDonald Plan of March 1933. In Great Britain and the United States, where the national movements for disarmament were most substantial, the plans were largely a response to domestic activism. In France, where the national campaign was comparatively weak, the proposals were primarily a response to transnational activist pressure.

The production of these plans clearly demonstrates that national governments had to alter the *presentation* of their policy. As Alan Leeper of the British Foreign Office noted, the disarmament proposals were produced in order to avoid 'being held responsible by world opinion...for the breakdown of the conference.'[6] However, no government was prepared to alter the *content* of its policy to a degree sufficient to make possible the activists' objective of agreement upon a multilateral disarmament convention. The plans put forward by Hoover and MacDonald failed to provide for the security guarantees and supervisory apparatus that could have made possible French agreement to a disarmament convention. As British Foreign Office officials remarked of the MacDonald Plan, it was 'simply a demonstration for internal consumption' rather than a serious attempt to forge agreement at the Disarmament Conference.[7] The plan put forward by Paul-Boncour, on the other hand, went further than any other scheme at the World Disarmament Conference in making concessions to the requirements of the other powers, the greatest concession being the abandonment of France's demand for mutual assistance commitments from Great Britain and the United States. However, even the changes embodied in this proposal were not far-reaching enough: some elements of the Paul-Boncour Plan, such as the maintenance of heavy weapons on French soil and the creation of national militias, were still unacceptable to the Anglo-Saxon delegations.

---

6 'Disarmament Conference in Extremis,' 29 May 1933, FO 371/17361, Foreign Office General Correspondence, National Archives, London.

7 Note of 13 Mar. 1933, W2738/40/98, FO 371/17353, Foreign Office General Correspondence.

So, none of the three principal governments targeted by the interwar disarmament campaign was prepared to make changes to national policy that were substantial enough to make possible the realisation of the activists' primary objective of a multilateral convention for general and comprehensive reduction and limitation of armaments. In fact, as Louis Aubert pointed out, the grandiose plans put forward by governments at the World Disarmament Conference were only 'real as a tactic' and 'the reality of the Conference [was] not everyday reality, but a demagogic and theatrical reality, determined by manoeuvres made in view of captivating universal public opinion with simple ideas.'[8]

---

[8] 'Note de M. Aubert remise au Président du Conseil le 6 janvier 1932: Observations à soumettre au CSDN (8 janvier),' cote 498, Tardieu papers, French Foreign Ministry Archives, Paris.

CHAPTER ELEVEN

TESTING THE FACTORS AFFECTING IMPACT

Since the previous chapter has summarised the impact of the interwar disarmament campaign, it is now possible to examine the implications of this evidence for the principal factors cited as affecting achievement of activist objectives in the existing literature on transnational activism. These factors are listed in table one in chapter one and are split into those that facilitate achievement of activist objectives and those that inhibit achievement of activist objectives. This chapter examines the implications of the evidence of the interwar disarmament campaign for each set of factors in turn, and subsequently assesses the implications of the evidence provided in other studies of activist campaigns.

Testing the Factors Facilitating Achievement of Activist Objectives

In the case of the factors cited as facilitating achievement of activist objectives, if any of these can be demonstrated to have been present in the case of the interwar disarmament campaign then they must be rejected as sufficient conditions for the realisation of activist goals. This is because, as the previous chapter has shown, the interwar disarmament campaigners failed to achieve their primary objective of a multilateral convention for the reduction and limitation of armaments. The following paragraphs will look at each of the nine factors outlined in table one and show that all but one of them were present in the case of the interwar disarmament campaign.

The first two factors relate to the characteristics of the international environment. One is 'the existence of international codes and legislation' that provide legitimacy for activist objectives.[1] These were clearly present in the case of the interwar disarmament campaign. Activists were able to draw on two important international legal documents to

---

[1] Jennifer Chapman, 'What Makes International Campaigns Effective? Lessons from India and Ghana' in Michael Edwards and John Gaventa (eds.), *Global Citizen Action* (London, 2001), p. 263.

support their goals. One was the Versailles Treaty, which stated that the disarmament of Germany was undertaken 'in order to render possible the initiation of a general limitation of the armaments of all nations.' The other was the Covenant of the League of Nations, Article 8 of which stated: 'The members of the League recognise that the maintenance of peace requires the reduction of national armaments to the lowest point consistent with national safety, and the enforcement by common action of international obligations.' Both of these commitments featured prominently in the propaganda of the interwar disarmament campaign, and were referred to at the start of the common 'Budapest' programme of the movement, which recalled 'the definite, unconditional pledge given by Members of the League of Nations in Article 8 of the Covenant' and 'the formal promise given to the States disarmed under the Treaties.'[2]

The second facilitator of activist influence at the international level that is commonly referred to in the literature is 'the presence of international governmental organisations...that facilitate network development.'[3] This factor was also present in the case of the interwar disarmament campaign. Unlike the movement for disarmament at the Hague Conferences before the First World War, the interwar disarmament campaign benefited from the facilitating presence and encouragement of the League of Nations. From January 1922 onwards, the Disarmament Section of the League of Nations distributed its documentation to national and international campaigning organisations in the hope that they might help 'spread the idea of disarmament.'[4] The Secretariat also passed on INGO resolutions on the issue to member governments at meetings of the League Council and its Commissions on disarmament, as well as through publication in the pages of the Assembly Journal.[5] At the World Disarmament Conference, the League of Nations provided 'special facilities' to the disarmament campaigners,

---

[2] Articles 1 and 2 of the Budapest programme, International Federation of League of Nations Societies (IFLNS), *XV Plenary Congress of the International Federation of League of Nations Societies, Budapest, 1931* (Brussels, 1931), pp. 156–7. The complete text of the resolution is reproduced in the sixth appendix to this book.

[3] Joe Bandy and Jackie Smith (eds.), *Coalitions Across Borders: Transnational Protest and the Neoliberal Order* (Lanham, MD, 2005), p. 232.

[4] C.T.A. 52, Geneva, 15 Feb. 1922: 'TMC for the Reduction of Armaments: Propaganda for the Reduction of Armaments,' R. 217, League of Nations Archives, Geneva; and Note by Aghnides, 30 Jan. 1922, R. 1595, League of Nations Archives.

[5] See pages 70–1.

and broke from established diplomatic practice to allow the presentation of the movement's petitions and resolutions to the national delegations at a Special Session at the beginning of the Conference.[6]

At the national level, table one indicates that there are two further factors that are frequently cited in the literature on transnational activism as facilitating achievement of activist objectives. Again, both factors were present in the case of the interwar disarmament campaign. First, the existence of a relatively open institutionalised political system for activists to target.[7] In the case of the interwar arms limitation movement, the principal states targeted were Great Britain, France and the United States. Although the definition of 'openness' is highly contested, there is no question that, of all the great powers in international society at the time, Great Britain, France and the United States were the most open and therefore the states that were most likely to be susceptible to the influence of activist campaigns.

The second facilitator of influence at the national level is the existence of 'a key element of the domestic political elite, one capable of exerting its authority over armed elements,' that is sensitive to activist demands.[8] This was undoubtedly the case in all three of the countries examined in this book. In France, Joseph Paul-Boncour was a prominent policymaker who was both responsive to activist demands and capable of overruling the armed services, characteristics that were demonstrated when he prevailed over the military chiefs and secured agreement to participate in the Preparatory Commission in 1925 and put forward the 'Constructive Plan' at the World Disarmament Conference in November 1932.[9] In Great Britain, a similar example was Foreign Secretary Sir John Simon, who was able to ignore his Cabinet instructions and promote the offensive/defensive distinction in his opening speech at the World Disarmament Conference in February 1932.[10] Thirdly, President Hoover in the USA was able to overrule both the War Department and

---

[6] See pages 113–7.

[7] John D. McCarthy, 'The Globalization of Social Movement Theory,' in Jackie Smith, Charles Chatfield, and Ron Pagnucco (eds.), *Transnational Social Movements and World Politics: Solidarity beyond the State* (Syracuse, NY, 1997), p. 255.

[8] Susan Burgerman, *Moral Victories: How Activists Provoke Multilateral Action* (Ithaca, NY, 2001), p. 5.

[9] See pages 134–6.

[10] See page 120.

the State Department when he put forward his wide-ranging disarmament plan in June 1932.[11]

As for the characteristics of the disarmament campaign itself, table one indicates that there are four features that are said to facilitate achievement of activist goals. These are: (i) the leadership of 'active individuals;' (ii) the existence of 'well-organised national movements;' (iii) the presence of 'an active international campaign;' and (iv) activist 'expertise,' 'experience, professionalism and work record.'[12] The inter-war disarmament movement undoubtedly had all four characteristics. First, it benefited from the inspired leadership of prominent individuals, among whom Viscount Cecil of Chelwood was the outstanding figure. According to his friend, Philip Noel Baker: 'From the First League Assembly onwards, he...laboured tirelessly to keep disarmament at the top of the international agenda....he inspired the masses..., [and]...but for him, the [World Disarmament] Conference would never have met at all.'[13] It was Cecil who launched the British disarmament campaign in 1927, spearheaded the global movement in February 1931, was responsible for the establishment of three of the four transnational disarmament committees, and drew up the common platform of the disarmament movement embodied in the 'Budapest proposals.'

In addition to Cecil's leadership, the movement was supported by large and well-organised national campaigns in all three of the principal countries targeted. In Great Britain and the United States, the primary peace movement was particularly substantial, led by the League of Nations Union with its 3,000 branches in Great Britain and the National Council for Prevention of War with its thirty national member organisations in the USA. The primary peace movement in these countries was assisted by powerful church organisations such as the Church Peace Union, as well as the leading women's and temperance organisations, both of which had a proven ability to influence government policy. It was out of the national campaigns in the two Anglo-Saxon countries that the global disarmament movement evolved. The British disarmament campaign provided the movement with its

---

[11] See pages 125–7.

[12] Chapman, 'What Makes International Campaigns Effective?,' p. 263; Bandy and Smith, *Coalitions Across Borders*, p. 233; Azeez Mehdi Khan, *Shaping Policy: Do NGOs Matter? Lessons from India* (New Dehli, 1997), pp. 19–20.

[13] Philip Noel-Baker, *The First World Disarmament Conference, 1932–1934, And Why It Failed* (Oxford, 1979), p. 75.

programme, while the US campaign provided the global movement with a model for interorganisational co-operation. As for the French movement, even though it could be said of its primary peace societies that 'few of these count[ed] for anything,'[14] the disarmament campaign in France was supported by large and influential secondary bodies including ex-servicemen's associations such as the *Union Fédérale des Anciens Combattants*, the principal trade unions, and Catholic women's organisations. A good example of the efficient organisational structure of the national campaigns in all three countries was the ability of each national movement to organise a thousand disarmament demonstrations in support of the International Consultative Group's objectives during the three months between 14 July and 15 October 1933.[15]

The most striking feature of the interwar disarmament campaign, however, was the scale of its transnational component. As Bertram Pickard of the International Consultative Group remarked: 'Never before has there been an *international* co-ordinated effort on so wide and effective a scale.'[16] In terms of the proportion of the total population of the world that the organisations that participated in the campaign could plausibly claim to represent, it has arguably never been matched since. Estimates of the combined membership of the groups that promoted disarmament at the special session of the World Disarmament Conference on 6 February 1932 vary considerably, with some as high as a thousand million.[17] A more realistic estimate is 200 million, which still made up approximately a tenth of the population of the world at the time.[18] In addition, a hundred organisations representing half of these people of a hundred nationalities combined to form the International Consultative Group, many more than the numbers currently represented

---

[14] 'Note on the prospects of the disarmament movement in France,' 28 Feb. 1931, box 209, Gilbert Murray papers, Bodleian Library, Oxford.

[15] See pages 145–7.

[16] 'Memorandum concerning future development,' 18 Nov. 1933, box 2, International Consultative Group papers, League of Nations Archives, Geneva.

[17] Noel-Baker, *First World Disarmament Conference*, pp. 73–4.

[18] This is the estimate of the Vox Populi Committee in *Vox Populi* (Geneva, 1932), p. 15. The membership of the constituent bodies of the International Consultative Group was 100 million, plus 70 million families in the International Co-operative Alliance, plus 25 million people in the International Union of Catholic Women's Organisations, and 21,500,000 workers represented by the Labour and Socialist International and the International Federation of Trade Unions. The estimate of the Vox Populi Committee allows for an overlap of 16.5 million people in the memberships of these organisations, but the actual overlap may have been greater.

in the international council and mobilization committees of the World Social Forum.[19]

As well as its scale, the interwar disarmament campaign undoubtedly possessed considerable expertise and experience in its field. The advice and reports of organisations such as the League of Nations Union and James Shotwell's American Committee on Disarmament were frequently sought by the British and American governments respectively.[20] Furthermore, individual activists such as Cecil and Shotwell had considerably greater experience in the field than the majority of government officials.

Even more importantly, the campaign for disarmament between the two World Wars could claim to have mass public support, not only indirectly through membership of the organisations that participated in the campaign, but also directly through writing letters, attending mass meetings and signing petitions in support of the movement's objectives. In the United States, for example, fourteen million items of correspondence were sent by members of the American public in support of disarmament at the Washington Conference.[21] The clearest evidence of *global* popular support, on the other hand, was the women's disarmament petition launched in 1930, which with over twelve million signatures remains 'the biggest international petition there has ever been' in terms of the proportion of the world's population that signed it.[22]

The only factor facilitating achievement of activist objectives cited in table one that was not present in the case of the interwar disarmament campaign relates to the nature of the issue-area targeted. By targeting the armaments of the principal great powers in the international system, the interwar disarmament campaigners clearly did not target the 'low-politics' issue-areas that are often said to be more susceptible to activist pressure.

---

[19] On the International Consultative Group's membership, see the totals in the third annex of *Vox Populi*, pp. 77–84, and the transcript of a radio interview given by Malcolm Davis on 22 Feb. 1933 in box 1 of the International Consultative Group papers, League of Nations Archives, Geneva. For statistics on the World Social Forum's international mobilization committees, see http://www.forumsocialmundial.org.br, last accessed on 30 April 2007.

[20] See pages 64–5 and 73.

[21] See pages 61–2.

[22] Noel-Baker, *First World Disarmament Conference*, p. 68. The Jubilee 2000 petition acquired twice as many signatures as the women's disarmament petition, and the 'Live 8 List' acquired 2½ times as many names, but world population had tripled between 1932 and 2000.

As for the other eight factors cited as facilitative of achievement of activist objectives, it is clear that they were all present in the case of the interwar disarmament campaign. Therefore, this book has shown that not one of those eight factors may be considered to be a sufficient condition for the realisation of activist goals, either alone or in combination. It is possible for activism to be characterised by active leadership and large and well-organised national and international campaigns—and to benefit from the facilitative presence of favourable international law, international institutions, open political systems and allies within these systems—and still not achieve its goals.

THE FACTORS INHIBITING ACHIEVEMENT OF ACTIVIST OBJECTIVES

In order to explain why, despite the clear presence of so many of the factors cited as facilitative of achievement of activist objectives, the interwar disarmament campaigners failed to secure their goals, it is necessary to turn to the factors cited as inhibiting achievement of activist objectives listed in table one. The following paragraphs will examine each of these factors in turn, in order to see if any of them help to explain the failure of the interwar disarmament campaign.

Starting at the international level, one of the principal factors cited as important in preventing achievement of activist goals is the presence of 'international political conflict.'[23] There is some evidence for the role of this factor in inhibiting the interwar disarmament campaign. Studies of the World Disarmament Conference have often argued that 'disarmament failed because the Disarmament Conference was convened too late, under inauspicious circumstances.'[24] Japanese actions in Manchuria disrupted the deliberations of the Disarmament Conference from the outset, while Germany's domestic political situation deteriorated during the course of the Conference culminating in the country's withdrawal that brought about the Conference's collapse. However, neither of these developments was crucial in preventing the realisation of a disarmament convention. The Manchurian situation was not a fundamental threat to the Disarmament Conference for the same reason that it failed

---

[23] Bandy and Smith, *Coalitions Across Borders*, p. 236.

[24] Maurice Vaïsse, 'Security and Disarmament: Problems in the Development of the Disarmament Debates, 1919–1934,' in R. Ahmann, A. M. Birke and M. Howard (eds.), *The Quest for Stability: Problems of West European Security, 1918–1957* (London, 1993), p. 184.

fully to undermine the collective security provisions of the Covenant of the League: it was too far removed from the principal interests of the Atlantic powers. As for the domestic political situation in Germany, far from hindering progress at the Conference, during the period before 30 January 1933 it was one of the principal reasons cited by policymakers in France, the United States and especially Great Britain as to why agreement upon a disarmament convention was necessary: in order to help prevent Hitler's rise to power.[25]

The other factor at the international level that is often said to hinder achievement of activist objectives is the presence of global economic crisis. Again, there is some evidence that this inhibited the interwar disarmament campaign: the World Disarmament Conference was held at the height of the Great Depression; governments were distracted by the convening of the World Economic Conference in London during the summer of 1933; and it was later discovered that one of the most successful means of national economic recovery was the manufacture of armaments.[26] However, the role of economic difficulties is another misleading explanation for the failure of the disarmament campaign. At the time the World Disarmament Conference took place, it was widely believed that multilateral disarmament would assist economic recovery by reducing government expenditure. Therefore the British Treasury was a crucial ally of the disarmament movement in Great Britain, while in the United States Herbert Hoover devised his disarmament scheme of June 1932 partly in order to combat 'the continued economic degeneration of the world.'[27]

As for the characteristics of the national environment that are said to inhibit achievement of activist goals, one of the most commonly cited is the presence of 'closed' political systems.[28] This cannot explain the failure of the interwar disarmament campaign because, as was outlined in the previous section of this chapter, the governments that the interwar disarmament activists targeted were the most open of all the great powers of the interwar period.

---

[25] See, for instance, the summary of the British government's disarmament discussions of 8 Dec. 1931, FO 800/285, Sir John Simon papers, National Archives, London.

[26] Subhakanta Behera, *The Politics of Disarmament, 1919–39: A Study of the World Disarmament Conference* (Vidyapuri, 1990), p. 80.

[27] Memorandum of 24 May 1932, *Papers Relating to the Foreign Relations of the United States*, 1932, vol. 1, pp. 180–3.

[28] McCarthy, 'Globalization of Social Movement Theory,' p. 255.

A better explanation at the national level is the existence of substantial opposition, in both government structures and society as a whole. The interwar disarmament activists themselves were concerned by the existence of two important forms of opposition: the influence of the armed services in national and international governmental committees on disarmament, and the influence of the armaments industry upon governments and society.

The armed services were given a very prominent role in the special committees in which disarmament policy was formulated in Great Britain, France and the United States: the Committee of Imperial Defence, the *Conseil Supérieur de la Défense Nationale*, and the Interdepartmental Conference. At the international level, too, representatives of the armed services were given a prominent position, with the exclusive privilege of sitting on the Permanent Armaments Commission of the League of Nations and the 'Committees of Experts' that examined the methods of arms reduction during the World Disarmament Conference. It was a privilege that exasperated British activist Professor Gilbert Murray, who asked: 'Suppose a Spanish reformer in the seventeenth century wanted to abolish or reduce religious persecution, would he take all his experts from members of the Inquisition?'[29]

As for the role of the armaments industry, activists in all three countries complained of its influence: those in the United States voiced concerns about the influence of arms lobbyists such as William Shearer during international disarmament conferences, activists in France complained of the influence of organisations such as the *Comité des Forges* over the Paris press, while British activists worried about the influence of Vickers, ICI and the Beaverbrook press.[30]

However, the significance of the opponents of a disarmament convention should not be exaggerated. For example, activists such as Cecil and Shotwell also played a role in the committees that formulated disarmament policy. Furthermore, the previous section of this chapter highlighted the ability of civilian policymakers such as Sir John Simon and Joseph Paul-Boncour to ignore the preferences of their service

---

[29] Murray to the editor of *Time & Tide*, 13 Aug. 1932, box 214, Murray papers.

[30] Richard W. Fanning, *Peace and Disarmament: Naval Rivalry & Arms Control, 1922–33* (Lexington, KY, 1995), pp. 118–9; Campbell to Simon, 7 Sep. 1932, FO800/291, Simon papers, National Archives, London; Leeper to Fletcher, 28 Feb. 1933, box 75, Simon papers, Bodleian Library, Oxford. On the role of arms interests in general, see Katherine Gibberd, *The League in Our Time* (Oxford, 1933), pp. 84–5.

departments. As for the armaments industry and its allies, they received far less popular support than the disarmament movement, even in France.[31] In consequence, the activities of lobbyists such as Shearer and companies such as ICI and Vickers often boosted the disarmament campaign by becoming the subject of much of the most successful disarmament propaganda, such as the US anti-Shearer campaign during the London Naval Conference and the highly popular pamphlet by the British Union of Democratic Control entitled *The Secret International* that was widely distributed during the World Disarmament Conference.[32]

With respect to the characteristics of the activists themselves, it is often argued that if they are susceptible to accusations of having a 'hidden' or self-serving agenda, the prospects for achievement of their goals are diminished.[33] There is a limited amount of evidence that this hampered the activities of the interwar disarmament movement. For example, parts of the continental peace movement were vulnerable to accusations of being state-sponsored, with the funds for many of the continental League of Nations societies coming from their respective foreign ministries, including that in France.[34] However, the argument that the disarmament campaigners had ulterior motives is much harder to make than the argument that the opposition to disarmament was sponsored by the vested interests of the armaments industry.

So, the six factors examined so far (international political and economic conflict, closed political systems, governmental and non-governmental opposition, and susceptibility to accusations of ulterior motives) do not explain the failure of the interwar disarmament campaigners to secure their goals. Since it remains possible that these factors may help to explain failure in other cases, their ability to prevent achievement of activist objectives has been neither confirmed nor denied by the evidence provided in this book so far. As for the remaining three factors that are listed in table one as inhibiting achievement of activist objectives, they are all supported by the evidence of the interwar disarmament campaign.

---

[31] Campbell to Simon, 7 Sep. 1932, FO800/291, Simon papers, National Archives, London; Drummond to Cadogan, 24 Apr. 1930, Add. MSS. 51112, Cecil of Chelwood papers, British Library, London.

[32] Union of Democratic Control, *The Secret International: Armament Firms At Work* (London, 1932).

[33] Khan, *Shaping Policy*, p. 21.

[34] John L. Hogge II, *Arbitrage, Sécurité, Désarmement: French Security and the League of Nations, 1920–1925* (DPhil thesis, New York University, 1994), p. 70.

With respect to the characteristics of the activists themselves, the evidence of the interwar disarmament campaign supports the assertion that promotion of an inconsistent or incoherent programme can help explain campaign failure. On first impression, there appears to have been transnational unity amongst the disarmament campaigners with respect to their promotion of a disarmament convention and their support for the Budapest programme of the International Federation of League of Nations Societies. However, a closer examination of the movement's propaganda reveals fundamental problems. The propaganda of the interwar disarmament campaign was either kept ambiguously vague or was twisted to suit the preferences of national audiences. For example, the principal text of the women's disarmament petition, with its simple declaration that the signatories 'stand for world disarmament' was, as Stanley Baldwin pointed out, imprecise to the point of being 'quite innocuous.'[35] As for the 'Budapest' programme of the League of Nations societies, although it provided a specific set of policies for the realisation of disarmament, it contained many different elements, so national League of Nations societies and their partners chose to promote only the elements that had greatest appeal to national public opinion in their respective countries. Thus the French societies emphasised the third part of the Budapest policy, which outlined the need to 'strengthen the mutual guarantees of security.'[36] In Great Britain, on the other hand, as Gilbert Murray noted: 'L. N. U. speakers as a whole… rather funked the question of security because audiences don't like it.'[37] The US movement, for its part, omitted all reference to the demand for non-naval disarmament in its propaganda. By the time of the International Consultative Group's last-ditch campaign to save the World Disarmament Conference in the summer of 1933, the attempt at promotion of a transnational programme was abandoned altogether in favour of completely separate national resolutions.[38] So, despite the apparent unity of the interwar disarmament activists around the objective of a multilateral convention and despite the coherence of the

---

[35] Reported in Norton to Fry, 26 Nov. 1931, box 129, Stanley Baldwin papers, Cambridge University Library, Cambridge.

[36] IFLNS, *XV Plenary Congress*, p. 158.

[37] Murray to Cecil, 18 Feb. 1933, file 216, Murray papers, quoted in Martin Ceadel, *Semi-Detached Idealists: The British Peace Movement and International Relations, 1854–1945* (Oxford, 2000), p. 301.

[38] See Dame Adelaide Livingstone's correspondence in box 6 of the International Consultative Group papers.

Budapest programme, the interwar disarmament campaigners in fact ended up promoting inconsistent goals, with the Anglo-Saxon movement promoting direct disarmament and the continental European movement promoting indirect disarmament subject to security assurances.[39]

The argument that the targeting of 'high politics' issue-areas such as security inhibits achievement of activist objectives is also supported by the evidence of the interwar disarmament campaign. It should be noted that the evidence of the interwar disarmament campaign does not support the argument that 'high policy' cannot be altered at all in response to activism. For example, civilian policymakers were able to overrule their armed services and alter disarmament policy in response to transnational activism when Joseph Paul-Boncour introduced his 'Constructive Plan' in November 1932. However, as has been shown in chapter ten, not one of the alterations made to disarmament policy in the interwar years was substantial enough to bring about agreement upon a multilateral convention for the reduction and limitation of armaments.

Thirdly, the evidence of the interwar disarmament campaign supports the proposition that achievement of activist objectives will be inhibited if these objectives would bring about fundamental change in international relations. Robert Gilpin has suggested that there are three types of such change: (i) systems change ('a change in the nature of the actors or diverse entities that compose an international system'); (ii) systemic change ('changes in the international distribution of power, the hierarchy of prestige, and the rules and rights embodied in the system'); and (iii) interaction change ('modifications in...the interactions or processes among the actors in an international system').[40] The goal of the interwar disarmament activists of a multilateral arms reduction convention is a clear example of interaction change whereby states rely less upon armaments in their relations with each other. Furthermore, multilateral disarmament is one of the most radical forms of interaction change possible: as US Secretary of State Henry Stimson stated in 1932, a multilateral disarmament convention is 'a proposal from Alice in Wonderland.'[41]

---

[39] The way in which this inconsistency contributed towards the interwar disarmament campaign's failure is explained in greater depth in the next chapter.

[40] Robert Gilpin, *War and Change in World Politics* (Cambridge, 1981), pp. 39–44.

[41] Entry for 24 May 1932, Henry L. Stimson diary, Vere Harmsworth Library, Oxford.

The Evidence of Other Studies of Activist Campaigns

The previous section of this chapter has shown that the evidence of the interwar disarmament campaign supports the proposition that three factors can inhibit achievement of activist goals: (i) promotion of an inconsistent programme; (ii) targeting 'high' political issues; and (iii) having goals that would fundamentally change international relations. However, if there is evidence in other studies of activist campaigns of achievement of activist objectives despite the presence of these inhibitory factors, then these factors cannot be considered to be sufficient conditions for the failure of activist campaigns.

The argument that activists cannot achieve their objectives if their goals lie in the field of military security is not supported by the evidence provided in studies of other campaigns. For example, numerous authors have pointed out the success of the International Campaign to Ban Landmines, with the 1997 Ottawa Convention on the Prohibition of the Use, Stockpiling, Production and Transfer of Anti-Personnel Mines and on their Destruction having been ratified by 144 countries (although not the United States, Russia or China).[42]

The proposition that activists cannot achieve their objectives if their goals would fundamentally alter international relations is harder to disprove. However, a possible counterexample is provided by the role of activism in the establishment of the League of Nations and the United Nations, if it is accepted that the creation of these actors is evidence of systems change in world politics.[43] A stronger counterexample is

---

[42] Information correct on 22 Dec. 2004. The numerous studies of the International Campaign to Ban Landmines include: Don Hubert, *The Landmine Ban: A Case Study in Humanitarian Advocacy* (Providence, RI, 2000); Maxwell A. Cameron, Robert J. Lawson and Brian W. Tomlin (eds.), *To Walk Without Fear: The Global Movement to Ban Landmines* (Toronto, 1998); Kenneth Anderson, 'The Ottawa Convention Banning Landmines, the Role of International Non-Governmental Organizations and the Idea of International Civil Society,' *European Journal of International Law*, 11/1 (2000), pp. 91–120; Nicole Short, 'The Role of NGOs in the Ottawa Process to Ban Landmines,' *International Negotiation*, 4/3 (1999), pp. 483–502; Motoko Mekata, 'Building Partnerships toward a Common Goal: Experiences of the International Campaign to Ban Landmines' in Ann M. Florini (ed.), *The Third Force: The Rise of Transnational Civil Society* (Tokyo, 2000), pp. 143–76; and Richard Price, 'Reversing the Gun Sights: Transnational Civil Society Targets Landmines,' *International Organization*, 52/3 (2000), pp. 613–44.

[43] On the role of activism in the origins of the League of Nations, see Peter Munch (ed.), *Les origines et l'oeuvre de la Société des Nations* (Copenhagen, 1923–4); Laurence Martin, *Peace Without Victory: Woodrow Wilson and the British Liberals* (New Haven, 1958); and Ruhl Jacob Bartlett, *The League to Enforce Peace* (Chapel Hill, NC, 1944). On the role of activism in the origins of the United Nations, see Dorothy Robins, *Experiment in*

arguably provided by Matthew Evangelista, whose work is said to justify the conclusion that non-governmental organisations such as the Pugwash Movement and International Physicians for the Prevention of Nuclear War 'contributed to...the end of the Cold War'—a classic case of systemic change in international relations.[44]

So, there are studies that appear to disprove the proposition that activists cannot achieve their objectives if their goals lie in the field of military security or if their objectives would fundamentally alter international politics. These studies also highlight the fact that activist goals can be realised despite the presence of many of the other inhibitory factors listed in table one. For example, the creation of the United Nations during the height of the Second World War is evidence that the existence of international political conflict is not a sufficient condition for the prevention of the achievement of activist goals. Evangelista's study of the impact of activism upon Soviet foreign policy towards the end of the Cold War, for its part, reveals that campaigners can have a significant impact even upon 'closed' regimes in which there is substantial opposition to activist objectives.

There is only one proposition that is both supported by the evidence of the interwar disarmament campaign and for which there are no counterexamples in other studies of activist influence: the claim that promotion of a programme with clear inconsistencies inhibits realisation of activist objectives. This claim is examined in greater depth in the final chapter, after a summary of the other conclusions of this book.

Democracy: The Story of U.S. Citizen Organizations in Forging the Charter of the United Nations (New York, 1971) and Clark Eichelberger, *Organizing for Peace: A Personal History of the Founding of the United Nations* (New York, 1977).

[44] Quotation from Thomas Risse-Kappen (ed.), *Bringing Transnational Relations Back In: Non-State Actors, Domestic Structures and International Institutions* (Cambridge, 1995), p. 280; the argument is most fully outlined in Matthew Evangelista, *Unarmed Forces: The Transnational Movement to End the Cold War* (Ithaca, NY, 1999).

CHAPTER TWELVE

SUMMARY OF CONCLUSIONS

Chapter eleven has demonstrated on the basis of the evidence of the interwar disarmament campaign that neither alone nor in combination are the following eight factors sufficient conditions for the realisation of activist objectives: (i) existence of international codes and legislation that provide legitimacy for activist goals; (ii) presence of international governmental organisations that facilitate network development; (iii) existence of open political systems in the countries targeted by activists; (iv) presence of key elements of the domestic political elites in the countries targeted that are capable of exerting their authority over armed elements and which are sensitive to activist demands; (v) leadership of the disarmament movement by talented and highly motivated individuals; (vi) existence of well-organised national movements; (vii) presence of an active international campaign; and (viii) existence of activist expertise and experience.

An examination of the literature on other activist campaigns reveals a brighter picture with respect to the role of many different factors that are supposed to inhibit achievement of activist objectives. This literature indicates that activists may still achieve their goals even when one or more of the following inhibitive factors is present: (i) existence of international political conflict; (ii) presence of closed political systems and substantial opposition in the states targeted by activists; and (iii) the targeting of 'high-political' issues or issues that would fundamentally change international politics.

The only proposition that is both supported by the evidence of the interwar disarmament campaign and not disproved by other case studies of activist influence is the argument that promotion of an incoherent programme inhibits achievement of activist objectives. Since this represents the only empirically supported generalisation with respect to the factors affecting realisation of transnational activist goals (outlined in table one in chapter one), this problem and its implications will now be examined in greater detail.

Essentially, the interwar disarmament campaigners faced a fundamentally important dilemma to which all activists have to respond if achievement of their goals requires a change in public attitudes towards a particular issue: without international public support activists cannot persuade governments to adopt their goals; but if these goals require a change in public attitudes the support will not be forthcoming.

When faced with this problem, activists have a choice between two options: (i) conducting a programme of education until public support for their goals reaches critical mass; or (ii) fudging their propaganda in order to give the impression of mass public support for their objectives which in fact does not exist. The interwar disarmament campaigners made the fundamental mistake of choosing the second option.

The dilemma with which the interwar disarmament activists were confronted came in the following form. Their goal was the creation of a convention for the reduction and limitation of armaments. However, there were two different views with respect to what should form the content of such a convention. One was the view held by the British and American governments: that the convention should simply contain figures for the reduction and limitation of each country's armaments. The other was the view held by the French government: that the convention should also contain measures that would assure states of their security once their armaments had been reduced and limited. The views of these governments reflected the preferences of public opinion in each of these countries.

Activists therefore had a choice between educating public opinion in France in support of direct disarmament without any security assurances, or educating public opinion in Great Britain and the United States in support of indirect disarmament accompanied by security provisions. Instead, activists chose to fudge the issue. The Budapest proposal that was the initial programme adopted by the majority of activists promoted both methods of disarmament: it proposed a 25% cut in global arms expenditure without new security commitments, as well as security measures to make possible greater disarmament. Because it promoted both methods of disarmament, campaigners selected for their propaganda whichever component had the greatest appeal in their national contexts. Therefore activists in Great Britain and the United States promoted the 25% cut proposal without mentioning the security-related clauses that were prioritised in France. As was noted in chapter eleven, by the time of the International Consultative Group's last-ditch campaign in the summer of 1933, even the semblance of a unified programme was abandoned, with campaigners in each country promoting completely separate programmes.[1]

The consequence of the activists' fudging of the issue was that public opinion in all of these countries was given the false expectation that a disarmament convention was possible without substantial alterations to national policy. This caused considerable frustration among government members who were placed in the difficult situation of having to appear in favour of a disarmament convention without being able to provide the concessions that would make such a convention possible. This frustration is shown in British Foreign Secretary Sir John Simon's comment at the peak of the campaign: 'I wish sometimes that there had been more public education as to the methods of disarmament and less public eloquence about the ideal of disarmament.'[2] It is also revealed in the much blunter comments of British Prime Minister Ramsay MacDonald in an unsent letter to Rev. Maldwyn Jones of the Congregational Union, who had posted him a standard resolution on the disarmament issue in October 1932:

> The government unfortunately cannot plume itself on passing or supporting a resolution. It has to get the hidden background of all resolutions settled as well. It is the old difficulty between the man who says, 'This is what I want; this is my ideal,' and the man who, accepting the ideal just as sincerely as the other, has got the task, not of declaring it, but of embodying it in the structure of a world such as that in which we live today. I wonder if you would take the trouble just to think out what are the problems of negotiation as well as the joys of declaration.[3]

So, much of the responsibility for the failure of the interwar disarmament campaign lies with the activists themselves. They failed in the task set for them in February 1931 by the future President of the World Disarmament Conference, Arthur Henderson: that of educating the public in order to 'show the Governments that however far they may be ready to go their people will be behind them.'[4] Instead, activists

---

[1] See pages 165–6.

[2] Simon to Murray, 24 May 1932, box 72, Sir John Simon papers, Bodleian Library, Oxford.

[3] MacDonald to Rev. Maldwyn Jones, 12 Oct. 1932 (unsent), PRO 30/69/678, Ramsay MacDonald papers, National Archives, London. A copy of the letter is also contained in box 73, Simon papers.

[4] Quoted in Martin Ceadel, *Semi-Detached Idealists: The British Peace Movement and International Relations, 1854–1945* (Oxford, 2000), p. 279; and in *Headway*, Mar. 1931, supplement, p. i.

chose to fudge the issue by promoting incompatible policies in different countries.[5]

The implication is clear: activism will be inhibited from achieving its goals if its propaganda is inconsistent. When faced with the problem of incompatible views held by public opinion in different countries, activists must make it their duty to educate public opinion in these countries rather than changing their propaganda to fit the demands of public opinion. It is a message that was understood at the time by the chief US delegate to the Preparatory Commission and the World Disarmament Conference, Hugh Gibson. In a speech to the Preparatory Commission in 1931, he said: 'it is not enough that public opinion be aroused. It is first of all necessary that it should be informed, for an aroused and uninformed public opinion may do infinitely more harm than good.'[6]

---

[5] The contrast with the more successful International Campaign to Ban Landmines (ICBL) in the 1990s is notable: as S. Neil MacFarlane has pointed out, in the case of the ICBL 'members subordinated their differences to the pursuit of the central objective' ('Preface by S. Neil MacFarlane,' in Don Hubert, *The Landmine Ban: A Case Study in Humanitarian Advocacy* (Providence, RI, 2000), p. xii).

[6] League of Nations, *Documents of the Preparatory Commission, Series X: Minutes of the Sixth Session (Second Part) of the Preparatory Commission for the Disarmament Conference* (Geneva, 1931), p. 409.

APPENDICES

APPENDIX I

THE PRINCIPAL ASSOCIATIONS

This appendix provides brief descriptions of the foundation, nature and contribution to the disarmament movement of the main international non-governmental organisations studied in this book. It has been necessary to limit this list to the organisations that participated in the principal global co-ordinating body of the campaign during the World Disarmament Conference—the International Consultative Group—together with the other organisations that were represented at the principal demonstration of pro-disarmament opinion of the inter-war years: the Special Session of the World Disarmament Conference of 6 February 1932.

I. International Co-ordinating Bodies

International Consultative Group (for Peace and Disarmament) [ICG]: established in Geneva on 23 July 1932 by representatives of most of the INGOs present at the Special Session of the World Disarmament Conference of 6 February 1932. The ICG functioned primarily to enable the leaders of its member organisations to pool their efforts during the remainder of the World Disarmament Conference. Its chief achievement was the Geneva disarmament demonstration of 15 October 1933. After the failure of the Disarmament Conference, the Group became a research organisation, issuing reports on international issues. Its activities ceased in June 1940. Participating organisations: Disarmament Committee of Christian International Organisations, Disarmament Committee of Students' International Organisations, Disarmament Committee of Women's International Organisations, International Conference of Disabled Soldiers and Ex-Servicemen (CIAMAC), International Federation of League of Nations Societies, Inter-Parliamentary Union, American Interorganization Council in Geneva, British Group, German Group.

Disarmament Committee of Christian International Organisations [DCCIO]: established in Geneva on 21 October 1931 to co-ordinate the disarmament efforts of the principal Geneva-based Christian international organisations. The committee provided a press service on the Disarmament Conference for Christian publications worldwide and arranged special services and lectures in Geneva during the Conference. Its activities ceased in June 1934. Participating organisations: Friends' International Service, International Fellowship of Reconciliation, Universal Christian Council for Life and Work, World Alliance for Promoting International Friendship through the Churches, World Student Christian Federation, World's Alliance of Young Men's Christian Associations, World's Alliance of Young Women's Christian Associations.

Disarmament Committee of Students' International Organisations [DCSIO]: established in Geneva on the initiative of the International Student Service in July 1931, this was a pseudo-organisation. It met intermittently before and during the World Disarmament Conference, and held a Conference on Moral Disarmament in March-April 1933. Participating organisations: International Confederation of Students, International Federation of Socialist Students, International Federation of University League of Nations Societies, International Federation of University Women, International Student Service, *Pax Romana*, World Student Christian Federation, World Union of Jewish Students.

Disarmament Committee of Women's International Organisations [DCWIO]: formally established in Geneva on 5 September 1931, this organisation's principal purpose was to arrange the presentation of the massive women's disarmament petition at the Special Session of the World Disarmament Conference held on 6 February 1932. It continued to apply pressure on delegates throughout the Conference, made declarations, and arranged conferences and weekly discussions. However, the Committee was cautious in its approach, arranging only a dinner to mark the anniversary of the presentation of the petitions. Although the organisation struggled after the collapse of the World Disarmament Conference, it survived until December 1940. Participating organisations: European Federation of Soroptimist Clubs, International Alliance of Women for Suffrage and Equal Citizenship, International Co-operative Women's Guild, International Council of Women, International Federation of Business and Professional Women, International Federation of University Women, International League of Mothers and of Women Teachers for the Promotion of Peace, League of Iberian and Latin-American Women, League of Jewish Women, Women's

International League for Peace and Freedom, World Organisation of Jewish Women, World Union of Women for International Concord, World Women's Christian Temperance Union, World's Alliance of Young Women's Christian Associations.

Joint Disarmament Commission [JDC] of the Labour and Socialist International [LSI] and the International Federation of Trade Unions [IFTU]: conceived in February 1931, the Joint Disarmament Commission held its inaugural meeting the following April. It organised a joint disarmament petition signed by local branches of the LSI and IFTU in 1931, held a mass demonstration in Zurich in May 1932, and formed common resolutions on the progress of the World Disarmament Conference for its duration. The JDC also participated in the special session of the World Disarmament Conference of 6 February 1932 but refused to co-operate with the rest of the disarmament movement on any other occasion. Participating organisations: Labour and Socialist International, International Federation of Trade Unions.

II. International Organisations Participating in the International Consultative Group

European Federation of Soroptimist Clubs: formed in London in February 1928 as part of the Soroptimist International Association. It consisted of a small number of service clubs for professional and managerial women, and played a peripheral role in the DCWIO. It is now known as Soroptimist International of Europe.

Friends' International Service: from 1926, Bertram and Irene Pickard ran a Quaker Centre in Geneva on behalf of the British Friends' Council of International Service and the American Friends' Service Committee. The Centre's purpose was to develop links between British and American Quakers and the League of Nations, and it is now succeeded by the Quaker United Nations Office in Geneva. The Centre's contribution to the disarmament movement was principally that of Bertram Pickard, who was President of the DCCIO.

International Alliance of Women for Suffrage and Equal Citizenship [IAW]: conceived in Washington in 1902 and fully established at a meeting in Berlin two years later, the Alliance was the principal INGO of the women's suffrage movement, with 38 member organisations by 1923. Several of its leaders founded WILPF in 1915, and in 1926 it created a special committee to stimulate peace activism among its members and to arrange conferences on arbitration, security and disarmament. It collaborated with the International Council of Women to create the Joint Standing and Liaison Committees of Women's International Organisations, which successfully promoted the appointment of women to official delegations to the World Disarmament Conference. The Alliance was one of the more prominent members of the DCWIO. In 1946 the organisation adopted its present name: International Alliance of Women—Equal Rights, Equal Responsibilities.

International Confederation of Students: founded in Strasbourg in 1919, this was the largest student INGO of the interwar years, with about a million members in forty-two national student unions by 1937. Its principal achievements lay in the facilitation of student travel and international student sport events. Although it was a member of the DCSIO, it was peripheral in the disarmament movement. The organisation was destroyed in 1940 when German troops occupied its Brussels headquarters.

International Conference of Disabled Soldiers and Ex-Servicemen [CIAMAC]: created in 1925 by René Cassin to promote Franco-German reconciliation, this was the second largest international ex-servicemen's organisation of the interwar years (the largest was the Interallied Federation of Ex-Servicemen [FIDAC], which also promoted disarmament during the World Disarmament Conference). Although not represented on 6 February 1932, CIAMAC gave a deputation to the President of the World Disarmament Conference the following day, became a member of the ICG, and held a massive disarmament demonstration with FIDAC in Geneva in March 1933. Like FIDAC, CIAMAC collapsed with the outbreak of the Second World War.

International Co-operative Women's Guild [ICWG]: an offshoot of the International Co-operative Alliance, the ICWG was founded in Bâle in 1921. Ten years later, it could claim to represent 'several' million women in the co-operative movements of 34 countries. It was one of the most active women's organisations in the disarmament movement, presenting demands for total disarmament at the opening session of the

Preparatory Commission in 1926 and a petition in support of the disarmament proposals of the Soviet government in 1927–8. The Guild's activities declined after the Second World War, and the organisation ceased to function in 1963. It was formally dissolved in 1966, when it was replaced by the Women's Advisory Council of the International Co-operative Alliance.

International Council of Women [ICW]: founded in Washington in 1888 and based in Paris, the ICW was the largest and most significant international women's organisation, with national councils in 41 countries in 1931. Although less radical than the International Alliance of Women (with which it frequently co-operated—see above), the ICW was one of the leading pro-disarmament organisations. It hosted its own peace conference at Wembley in 1924, organised peace days in the run-up to the World Disarmament Conference, and was vital in ensuring that the women's peace petitions acquired large numbers of signatures. The Council continues to promote peace, co-operation and women's rights today.

International Federation of Business and Professional Women: American lawyer Lena Madesin Philips established this business and professional women's service organisation in Geneva in August 1930 partly to promote women's economic independence. It had members in 15 countries by 1931, but although it helped gather signatures for the women's disarmament petitions it was of marginal importance in the disarmament movement. The organisation is now known as BPW International.

International Federation of League of Nations Societies [IFLNS]: founded in Paris in 1919, this was the leading international peace organisation of the interwar period, run by Secretary-General Théodore Ruyssen. It had a total membership of about 1.5 million people in forty countries by the time of the World Disarmament Conference. Although the British League of Nations Union could claim a paying membership of over 400,000 in 1931, many of the continental European societies were pseudo-associations that relied on government sponsorship to survive. The Federation's principal contribution to the disarmament movement was its 'Budapest programme,' which became the common agenda for much of the disarmament movement by the time that the World Disarmament Conference opened. The IFLNS was replaced by the World Federation of United Nations Associations in 1946.

International Federation of Socialist Students [IFSS]: reorganised in Amsterdam in 1926 with a membership of about eight thousand students, this was a peripheral member of both the socialist youth movement and the disarmament movement. Its activities appear to have ceased in 1940.

International Federation of University League of Nations Societies [IFULNS]: founded in Prague on 12 April 1924 and based in Paris, this organisation had about 20,000 members in 22 countries in 1933. Although it benefited from a close relationship with the International Institute of Intellectual Co-operation, the Federation's preference for formulating policy over active campaigning prevented it from playing a leading role in the disarmament movement.

International Federation of University Women [IFUW]: American and British women academics created this organisation in London in 1919 in the hope that it could help prevent another World War by facilitating international co-operation among women graduates. By 1933, its 36 national branches had a combined membership of 55,000 people. Although the Federation was important in promoting the intellectual co-operation activities of the League of Nations, its involvement in the disarmament movement extended little further than membership of the DCWIO. The organisation moved to Geneva in 1970, where it continues its work today.

International Fellowship of Reconciliation [IFoR]: a Christian pacifist and quietist organisation established in Holland in 1919 by representatives from a dozen countries, IFOR was a somewhat passive member of the DCCIO. Its work continues today.

International League of Mothers and of Women Teachers for the Promotion of Peace: founded in Douai, France, in May 1928 by Madame Eidenschenk-Patin, who became its secretary-general. The organisation's purpose was to ensure that mothers and women teachers educated a generation without prejudice against people from other nations. The League had 72,000 members in France in 1933, and it collected a large number of resolutions from French organisations for the ICG's disarmament demonstration of 15 October 1933. However, its influence outside of France was limited.

International Student Service [ISS]: initially known as European Student Relief, this organisation was created in Geneva in 1920 as a branch of the World Student Christian Federation. It became the International Student Service in 1925 and an autonomous organisation in 1931. Its principal purposes were material assistance for needy students and cultural exchange. Its secretary-general, Michel Poberezski, set up the DCSIO, but the overall contribution of the ISS to the disarmament movement was insubstantial. The organisation was renamed World Student Relief in 1943 and adopted its current name, World University Service, in 1950.

Inter-Parliamentary Union [IPU]: founded in Paris in 1889, the IPU was composed of approximately five thousand parliamentarians from thirty countries at the time of the World Disarmament Conference. It was created to work for peace and ultimately a world parliament. It consistently passed resolutions in support of disarmament at its annual conferences, and its secretary-general, Christian Lange, was influential in the establishment of the Temporary Mixed and Preparatory Commissions. It continues to promote peace and inter-parliamentary dialogue today.

League of Iberian and Latin-American Women: little is known about this organisation, but it is said to have been founded in 1922 and to have been feminist, pan-Hispanic and anti-US.[1] Its President in 1932 was Spanish author Carmen de Burgos, and the organisation was a peripheral member of the DCWIO.

League of Jewish Women: this Geneva-based organisation was founded in 1920 to combat anti-Semitism, and its membership was mainly Swiss and East European. It participated in the activities of the International Peace Bureau and it was a peripheral member of the DCWIO.

Pax Romana: established in Fribourg in 1921, this organisation's full name was '*Pax Romana*: International Secretariat for National Catholic University Federations.' It was a passive participant in the DCSIO,

---

[1] Christine Ehrick, '*Madrinas* and Missionaries: Uruguay and the Pan-American Women's Movement,' *Gender & History*, 10/3 (1998), p. 419.

and is now succeeded by the International Movement of Catholic Students and the International Catholic Movement for Intellectual and Cultural Affairs.

Universal Christian Council for Life and Work: created in Stockholm in 1925, this organisation was intended to promote the unity of Christendom and represented the Anglican, Protestant and Orthodox Churches. Its Geneva headquarters provided a base for the DCCIO. In 1948, it merged with the World Conference on Faith and Order to form the World Council of Churches.

Women's International League for Peace and Freedom [WILPF]: founded at the Hague in 1915, this was the leading women's peace organisation of the interwar years, with branches in 26 countries by 1931. Its relatively small membership was offset by the determined activism of its leaders, who initiated the International Disarmament Declaration in 1929. The different texts of this declaration highlight the organisation's division between pacifists and pacificists. It now has member organisations in thirty-seven countries.

World Alliance for Promoting International Friendship through the Churches: this organisation was founded at Constance in 1914 with the assistance of the American Church Peace Union on which it remained financially dependent. It had member organisations in thirty-seven countries, and was influential among Anglo-Saxon church leaders. However, the failure of the Roman Catholic Church to co-operate in its activities ensured that its influence in continental Europe was less substantial. The Alliance promoted the disarmament work of the League of Nations long before the establishment of the DCCIO. It was dissolved in 1948 when the World Council of Churches and the International Missionary Council set up the Commission of the Churches on International Affairs.

World Organisation of Jewish Women: created at the World Congress of Jewish Women in Vienna in 1923, this organisation was led by Rebekah Kohut of the American National Council of Jewish Women. Over a million Jewish women worldwide were affiliated to this organisation, but it was a peripheral member of the DCWIO.

World Student Christian Federation [WSCF]: founded in Vadstena (Sweden) in August 1895, the WSCF remains one of the principal elements of the ecumenical movement. It was a member of both the DCCIO and the DCSIO, and its Vaumarcus Conference of August 1931 stimulated the creation of the US Intercollegiate Council for Disarmament. Its member organisations in France, Czechoslovakia and Germany also conducted noteworthy disarmament campaigns.

World Union of Jewish Students: founded in Anvers on 6 May 1924 by Zvi Lauterpacht at a meeting of Jewish students from seventeen countries. This organisation's original purpose was to combat unfair restrictions on admission of Jews to universities. It was a member of the DCSIO, but not a prominent one. The Union's activities continue today.

World Union of Women for International Concord: created in Geneva on 9 February 1915, this women's peace organisation emphasised 'individual effort and responsibility.' It had over 25,000 subscribing members in 29 countries by 1931, together with a further 75,000 affiliated members. Although it was important in assisting the ICG's summer 1933 campaign in France, its overall contribution to the interwar disarmament movement was limited. The organisation was dissolved in 1958.

World Women's Christian Temperance Union: founded in Detroit in 1883, this organisation's primary objective remains the promotion of abstinence from alcoholic beverages. After the Eighteenth Amendment had been passed in the USA in 1919, disarmament became a new objective for the organisation to promote, hence its participation in the DCWIO. The Union had 700,000 members in 40 countries in 1931, but its membership was concentrated in the Anglo-Saxon and Scandinavian countries.

World's Alliance of Young Men's Christian Associations [World's YMCAs]: founded in Paris in 1855, this is arguably the world's oldest international non-governmental organisation. It published a bulletin on disarmament during the World Disarmament Conference, and a member of its secretariat, Joachim Mueller, was Secretary of the DCCIO.

World's Alliance of Young Women's Christian Associations [World's YWCAs]: created in London in 1894, this organisation had a membership of over a million women in seven thousand branches in over fifty countries in 1931. Disarmament was a prominent feature of its educational programmes, and one of its secretaries, Mary Dingman, was a leading disarmament activist and President of the DCWIO.

III. Other International Organisations
Represented at the Special Session of 6 February 1932

Confederation of Authors ('PEN Club'): now known as International PEN, this worldwide association of writers was founded in Great Britain in 1921. By 1932 it was composed of forty-five centres in thirty-six countries, and claimed to represent 'nearly all the leading poets and authors in the world.' Its involvement in the disarmament movement extended little further than a supportive resolution passed at its ninth annual congress.

International Co-operative Alliance [ICA]: founded in 1895, this was the largest INGO of the interwar period. At the time of the World Disarmament Conference (to which it sent a supportive resolution), it had a membership of seventy million families in forty-four countries and claimed to represent 250 million consumers. It still claims to be the world's largest INGO, representing more than 800 million people in eighty-five countries.

International Federation of Trade Unions [IFTU]: founded in 1919 as the successor to the International Secretariat of Trade Union Centres that had been established in 1901. Although its membership was predominantly European, the IFTU was the largest and most representative workers' organisation of the interwar years, with over fourteen million members in twenty-eight countries in 1932. Its agitation led to the appointment of three of its leaders to the Temporary Mixed Commission in 1921, and the IFTU held several demonstrations for peace and disarmament during the subsequent decade. In 1930, it joined with the Labour and Socialist International to promote the London Naval Conference, and the following year they collaborated in a Joint Commission to promote the success of the World Disarmament Conference (see JDC entry above). The IFTU was dissolved in 1945 when the World Federation of Trade Unions was created.

International League for the Rights of Man: founded in Paris in 1922 and reorganised 1928, this organisation was dominated by the French human rights body, the *Ligue des Droits de l'Homme*. It collected 200,000 signatures to a disarmament petition in the year preceding the World Disarmament Conference.

International Peace Bureau [IPB]: founded in Rome on 11 November 1891 to organise the Universal Peace Congresses, this Geneva-based organisation's influence declined sharply after the First World War. It set up a *Comité International de Co-ordination des Forces Pacifiques* on 7 June 1927, which its leaders hoped would co-ordinate the global disarmament campaign. Instead, it was bypassed by the IFLNS, WILPF and the International Consultative Group. After decades of decline, the IPB's membership rose after merging with the International Confederation for Disarmament and Peace in 1984.

International Union of Catholic Women's Organisations: founded in Brussels in 1910, this was one of the most substantial women's organisations of the interwar years. In 1932, it had twenty-five million members in fifty-four Catholic women's leagues in twenty-three countries. It was particularly influential in continental Europe, and its President, Madame Steenberghe-Engeringh, was the only Catholic representative at the Special Session of the World Disarmament Conference of 6 February 1932. It is now known as the World Union of Catholic Women's Organisations.

Labour and Socialist International [LSI]: the successor to the Second International, the LSI was founded in Hamburg in 1923. In 1932, it was composed of forty-seven national parties with a total of 7,500,000 members. In April 1926, the LSI's Executive Committee set up a commission to study the disarmament problem, and in February 1929 its braches sent 14,000 letters urging decisive action by the Preparatory Commission. From 1930 onwards, the LSI co-operated with the IFTU in order to promote disarmament jointly (see above). In 1948, the Labour and Socialist International became the International Socialist Conference, and its present name—Socialist International—was adopted in 1951.

Oecumentical Methodist Conference Eastern Council: the first Oecumenical Methodist Conference took place in London in 1881, and subsequent conferences were held every decade until 1931. The Eastern Council claimed to represent 50 million Methodists at the time of the World Disarmament Conference, to which it sent a resolution in favour of disarmament. Its role in the disarmament movement extended little further.

Rotary International: founded in Chicago in 1905 as the International Association of Rotary Clubs, this business and professional men's humanitarian service organisation adopted its present name in 1922. By that year it had member clubs in six continents. Its principal contribution to the disarmament movement was putting forward the first proposals and conducting the initial arrangements for the Trocadéro unofficial disarmament conference that was held in Paris in November 1931.

APPENDIX II

THE PRINCIPAL ACTIVISTS

This appendix provides brief details of the achievements of and positions held by 140 of the most significant activists in the interwar disarmament campaign.

Addams, Jane (1860–1935), American peace campaigner, reformer and lecturer. As co-founder and international president from 1915 of the Women's International League for Peace and Freedom, Addams was an inspirational figurehead for the women's pacifist movement. Poor health having forced her resignation from the presidency of WILPF in 1929, she was unable to play an active leadership role in the campaign during the World Disarmament Conference.

Adler, Friedrich (1879–1960), Austrian socialist leader and internationalist. Famous for having shot dead hardline Austrian Prime Minister Karl Stuergkh in 1916, Adler was general secretary of the Labour and Socialist International between 1923 and 1940. He was also co-secretary of the Joint Disarmament Commission of the Labour and Socialist International and the International Federation of Trade Unions with Walter Schevenels.

Aghnides, Thanassis (1889–1984), Greek diplomat. A long-term member of the Secretariat of the League of Nations, Aghnides became Director of the Disarmament Section in 1930 and was Secretary of the World Disarmament Conference.

Albarda, Johan Willem (1877–1957), Dutch socialist politician. Leader of the Dutch Social Democratic Party from 1925, Albarda was also President of the Disarmament Commission of the Labour and Socialist International from its foundation in 1926 and co-chairman of the Joint Disarmament Commission of the Labour and Socialist International and the International Federation of Trade Unions from 1931. He was the principal organiser of the international socialist movement's disarmament campaigning activities, and in May 1931 he drew up the common programme of action of the LSI and IFTU for the promotion of the World Disarmament Conference.

Albeniz, Alfonso, Spanish internationalist. The secretary-general of the Spanish League of Nations Society, Albeniz was a member of the League of Nations Secretariat and Spain's representative in the Disarmament Committee of the International Federation of League of Nations Societies.

Angell, Sir Norman [formerly Ralph Norman Angell Lane] (1872–1967), British peace activist and author. Owing to the popularity of his principal work, *The Great Illusion* (1910), Angell was one of the best-known peace propagandists of the early twentieth century. Although not prominent in the organisation of the interwar disarmament campaign, he was a popular speaker at British disarmament demonstrations and wrote influential pamphlets in support of disarmament, including *The Foreigner's Turn to Disarm?* (1931).

Apponyi, Count Albert (1846–1933), Hungarian internationalist. The head of the Hungarian delegation to the League of Nations (1924–33), Apponyi also led the Hungarian League of Nations movement and arranged the 1931 Budapest Conference of the International Federation of League of Nations Societies.

Arnold-Forster, William Edward (1886–1951), British peace publicist. Trained as a painter, Arnold-Forster became a propagandist on League of Nations issues for British organisations including the National Peace Council and the League of Nations Union (LNU). He was known principally for his promotion of the League's disarmament efforts, and was employed by Cecil to run the LNU's disarmament campaign in 1927. His career peaked during the World Disarmament Conference, during which he gave public lectures organised by the Disarmament Committee of Christian International Organisations, organised a memorial on disarmament signed by all the main peace activists in Geneva in July 1932, and provided reports on the proceedings of the Conference and the progress of activist goals for international and British peace organisations and publications.

Asch van Wijck, Cornelia Maria van (1890–1971), Dutch Christian women's movement leader. A leading Dutch feminist, Jonkvrouw van Asch van

Wijck served as President of the World's Alliance of Young Women's Christian Associations between 1930 and 1938.

Bailey, Vernon Gerald (1903–1972), British peace movement leader. Subsequently known for his work with Quaker groups to ease Cold War tensions, Bailey was secretary (later director) of the National Peace Council between 1930 and 1949.

Balch, Emily Greene (1867–1961), American economist and peace activist. After her anti-war activities caused the cessation of her employment at Wellesley College in 1918, Balch became WILPF's first international secretary between 1919 and 1922. She continued to work for WILPF, and resumed her position as international secretary in 1934–5.

Basch, Victor (1863–1944), French peace and human rights activist. A passionate Dreyfusard, Basch was Vice-President from 1909 and President from 1926 until 1940 of the *Ligue des Droits de l'Homme*. He ensured that this organisation promoted the League of Nations and its disarmament efforts, in addition to the *Ligue*'s primary goals of human rights and self-determination. He refused to leave France after Nazi occupation, and was murdered by the Gestapo in 1944.

Beneš, Edvard (1884–1948), Czechoslovak politician. Czech foreign minister between 1918 and 1935, Benes was the pre-eminent East European internationalist of the interwar years. As President of the Third Committee of the League Assemblies, Benes was central to the negotiation of the Draft Treaty of Mutual Assistance, the Geneva Protocol, and the establishment of the Preparatory Commission. As rapporteur-general of the World Disarmament Conference, he negotiated the compromise resolution of July 1932.

Bernstorff, Johann Heinrich von (1862–1939), German diplomat. As President of the *Deutsche Liga fuer Voelkerbund* and Germany's representative on the Preparatory Commission between 1926 and 1931, Bernstorff was one of the most vocal advocates of disarmament of the victors of the First World War.

Bliss, Tasker Howard (1853–1930), American General. Chief of Staff during the American intervention in World War One and a delegate at the Paris Peace Conference, Bliss became a prominent proponent of arms limitation in the aftermath of the Great War. He promoted disarmament during the Washington Conference in 1921, and participated in James Shotwell's American Committee on Disarmament that drew up the 'Draft Treaty of Disarmament and Security' which became one of the bases of the Geneva Protocol.

Blum, Léon (1872–1950), French Socialist leader. Elected to the Chamber of Deputies in 1919, Blum presided over the Socialist faction and in 1936 became Prime Minister in a Popular Front government. Throughout the period leading up to the World Disarmament Conference, Blum promoted disarmament and reconciliation with Germany. His daily editorials for *Le Populaire* were highly influential, and his promotion of disarmament in this journal on 6 October 1932 was one of the principal motivations for Joseph Paul-Boncour's 'Constructive Plan.'

Bodman, Baron Albert von (b. 1887), German peace activist. A leading figure in the *Deutche Liga fuer Voelkerbund*, von Bodman was one of the principal organisers of the Trocadéro Conference and a secretary of the International Federation of League of Nations Societies.

Boegner, Marc (1881–1970), French priest. A leader of the French ecumenical movement, Boegner was President of the *Fédération Protestant de France* between 1929 and 1961, and spoke on behalf of this organisation at the Trocadéro Conference.

Boissier, Léopold (1893–1968), Swiss professor, diplomat and internationalist. Known also for his later work as President of the International Committee of the Red Cross between 1955 and 1964, Boissier was a prominent internationalist in the interwar years. He was secretary from 1921 and secretary-general from 1933 until 1953 of the Inter-Parliamentary Union.

Borah, William Edgar (1865–1940), American Senator. A Republican Senator representing Idaho for 33 years from 1906, Borah made his name leading the successful campaign to prevent the United States from joining the League of Nations. However, his sponsorship in 1921 of a resolution promoting the convening of an international naval arms limitation conference led to the Washington Conference later that year.

Borel, Emile (1871–1956), French mathematician and politician. Best known for his mathematical research, Borel was also a radical-socialist deputy between 1924 and 1936 and a prominent advocate of the League of Nations and European unity. He founded the *Comité Français de Coopération Européenne* in 1927.

Bourgeois, Léon Victor Auguste (1851–1925), French statesman and internationalist. Elected to the Chamber of Deputies in 1888, Bourgeois was chief French delegate to the Hague Peace Conferences of 1899 and 1907. In 1910, he published *Pour la Société des Nations*, and he later became known in France as 'the father of the League of Nations' for his role in establishing the institution. He also founded the *Association Française pour la Société des Nations* in 1918, an organisation which he subsequently used to promote the ideals of disarmament and collective security.

Bovet, Ernest (1870–1941), Swiss academic and internationalist. A professor of literature at the University of Zurich, Bovet led the Swiss League of Nations movement and was Vice-President of the Disarmament Committee of the International Federation of League of Nations Societies.

Brossolette, Pierre (1903–1944), French journalist. A major contributor to left-wing French journals such as *Le Populaire*, Brossolette participated in the *Comité d'Action pour la Société des Nations*, served on the editorial board of *Disarmament*, and helped to organise the Trocadéro Conference. He committed suicide in 1944 after being tortured by the Gestapo.

Brouckère, Louis Gustave Jean Marie Théodore de (1870–1951), Belgian academic, diplomat, socialist and internationalist. A member of the Belgian senate between 1925 and 1933, de Brouckère led the Belgian disarmament movement and represented his country on the Preparatory Commission.

Butler, Nicholas Murray (1862–1947), American educator and internationalist. President of Columbia University between 1901 and 1945, Butler established the American branch of the Association for International Conciliation in 1905 and co-ordinated the efforts that led to the creation of the Carnegie Endowment for International Peace in 1910, of which he was president from 1925 to 1945.

Cantacuzino, Princess Alexandrina [known as Princess Cantacuzène] (1876–1944), Romanian feminist leader. One of the foremost East European political figures of the interwar years, Princess Cantacuzène led numerous Romanian women's organisations, including the National Orthodox Society of Romanian Women, the Romanian Women's Association, the 'Solidarity Society' and the Romanian National Council of Women. She was also President of the 'Little Entente of Women' from 1923 and a Vice-President of the International Council of Women from 1925.

Cassin, René-Samuel (1887–1976), French law professor, ex-servicemen's leader, and advocate of peace and human rights. Although now better known for his work in helping to draft the Universal Declaration of Human Rights in 1947, Cassin was a prominent figure in Third Republic France on account of his establishment in 1917 and subsequent leadership (1918–40) of that country's largest ex-servicemen's organisation, the *Union Fédérale des Anciens Combattants*. In order to promote Franco-German understanding, he also set up the International Conference of Disabled Soldiers and Ex-Servicemen (CIAMAC) in 1925. Under Cassin's guidance, the ex-servicemen's movement in continental Europe played a much more substantial role in mobilising public opinion in support of disarmament and security through the League of Nations than the primary peace movement. This is reflected in his appointment as a French delegate to the League of Nations between 1924 and 1938 and to the World Disarmament Conference between 1932 and 1934.

Catt, Carrie Chapman (1859–1947), American women's suffrage leader and peace activist. While she is best known for her successful leadership of the National American Woman Suffrage Association between 1900 and 1920, Catt also played a crucial role in persuading American women's organisations to turn their attention to the promotion of peace, the League of Nations and disarmament after the Nineteenth Amendment had been passed. Between 1925 and 1932 she chaired the National Committee on the Cause and Cure of War, an organisation which she founded and which pioneered the interorganisational co-operation that was one of the principal features of the interwar global disarmament campaign.

Cecil, (Edgar Algernon) Robert Gascoyne [known as Lord Robert Cecil and from 1923 as Viscount Cecil of Chelwood] (1864–1958), British statesman and internationalist. Having helped draft the Covenant of the League of Nations, Cecil became the world's foremost campaigner for peace and disarmament through the institution. Chairman 1919–23 and thereafter President of the League of Nations Union, Cecil developed the organisation into Britain's largest ever peace society. As a member of the Temporary Mixed Commission, he helped produce the Draft Treaty of Mutual Assistance; and as Chancellor of the Duchy of Lancaster responsible for British League policy between 1923 and 1927, he helped create the Preparatory Commission on which he represented Britain. His resignation from the British government over its policy at the Geneva Naval Conference in 1927 was the catalyst for his leadership of the non-governmental disarmament movement. In 1931, he became the principal driving force behind the international disarmament campaign: he designed its common programme (the Budapest resolution), organised a massive unofficial disarmament conference in the Paris Trocadéro, and helped establish the international committees that co-ordinated the campaign during the World Disarmament Conference. Although he returned to public office as an official British delegate to the League Assemblies and the Preparatory Commission from 1929 onwards, Cecil chose to promote disarmament at the World Disarmament Conference as an independent activist: he was President of the Disarmament Committee of the International Federation of League of Nations Societies and the keynote speaker at the special session of the World Disarmament Conference of 6 February 1932.

Challaye, Félicien (1875–1967), French teacher and pacifist polemicist. His experience in the trenches in the First World War made Challaye one of the leading exponents of integral pacifism in France throughout the interwar years. His principal contribution to the disarmament movement was literary, in the form of such works as *Pour la paix désarmée même en face d'Hitler* (1933).

Citrine, Walter McLennan (1887–1983), British trade union leader. Originally an electrician, Citrine rose through the ranks of the British trade union movement to become President of the International Federation of Trade Unions between 1928 and 1945. He co-chaired the massive disarmament demonstration held in Zurich on 22–23 May 1932 organised by the International Federation of Trade Unions and the Labour and Socialist International.

Clark, Hilda (1881–1955), British doctor and internationalist. The granddaughter of Quaker leader John Bright, Dr. Clark led the pacificist

wing of the British Women's International League and was a prominent figure in the Disarmament Committee of Women's International
Organisations.

Colban, Erik Andreas (1876–1956), Norwegian diplomat. After a career
in the Norwegian ministry of consular affairs, Colban entered the
Secretariat of the League of Nations in 1919. He directed the Disarmament Section between 1928 and 1930, and represented Norway
at the World Disarmament Conference.

Comert, Pierre (1880–1964), French journalist and internationalist spin-
doctor. After a career as a journalist and press officer for the French
government, Comert became director of the Information Section of
the League of Nations at its foundation, a position he relished with
idealism until forced to resign in 1933 when Joseph Avenol became
Secretary General of the League.

Corbett Ashby, Dame Margery Irene (1882–1981), British feminist and
internationalist. Known principally for her leadership of the women's
suffrage movement, and in particular the International Alliance of
Women for Suffrage and Equal Citizenship of which she was President
from 1923 to 1946, Corbett Ashby played a vital role in converting the
women's movement to internationalism in the 1920s. She chaired the
Disarmament Committee of Women's International Organisations during its 'temporary' phase between June and September 1931 and was
appointed a British substitute delegate for the duration of the World
Disarmament Conference, a position she resigned in 1935 for reasons
she outlined in the pamphlet *The Failure in Leadership at the Disarmament
Conference* (1935).

Cot, Pierre (1895–1977), French politician and internationalist. Elected
as a Radical-Socialist deputy in 1928, Cot dedicated himself to international issues from the outset. As Daladier's Air Minister, he was one
of the principal instigators of the French concessions at the World
Disarmament Conference in 1933.

Courtney, Dame Kathleen D'Olier (1878–1974), British feminist and peace
campaigner. A prominent member of the British women's suffrage
movement, Courtney helped found the Women's International League
for Peace and Freedom in 1915, and chaired the British section for a

decade until 1933. She ran the Central Disarmament Bureau that co-ordinated British pro-disarmament organisations during the build-up to the World Disarmament Conference, and was a Vice-President of the Disarmament Committee of Women's International Organisations from 1931.

Davies, David, first Baron Davies of Llandinam (1880–1944), British Liberal politician, philanthropist and internationalist. The chairman of the Welsh National Council of the League of Nations Union, Davies was primarily concerned with promoting the creation of an international armed force to strengthen the League of Nations. He attempted to persuade the League of Nations Union to adopt this goal, but when this effort failed he created his own New Commonwealth movement in 1932 to promote his collective security agenda.

Davis, Malcolm Waters (1889–1970), American journalist and internationalist. After a career as a journalist for the *New York Evening Post*, in 1922 Davis became managing editor of *Our World Magazine* which he hoped would stimulate internationalism in the USA by providing world news. In 1931, the Carnegie Endowment for International Peace sent him to Geneva, where he became director of the Geneva Research Center and Vice-Chairman of the American Interorganization Council in Geneva. In July 1932 he convened the first meeting of the International Consultative Group for Peace and Disarmament. He was the Group's first Chairman, holding this position until 1935 when he moved to Paris to become associate director of the Carnegie Endowment's European Center.

Davis, Norman Hezekiah (1878–1944), American banker, diplomat and internationalist. Owing to his banking experience, Davis was appointed financial adviser to the US delegation at the Paris Peace Conference. He subsequently represented the United States at the first World Economic Conference in 1927 and at the World Disarmament Conference in 1932–4, becoming Chairman of the US delegation when Roosevelt took over the Presidency. A committed internationalist, he helped organise the Council of Foreign Relations in 1921, and kept in close contact with the non-governmental campaigners during the World Disarmament Conference. In April 1933, he took the lead in ensuring US commitment not to insist upon neutral rights when collective sanctions were to be placed on aggressor nations in Europe.

Detzer, Dorothy (1893–1981), American peace campaigner. The leading activist of the US women's peace movement, Detzer was National Secretary of the US branch of the Women's International League for Peace and Freedom between 1924 and 1946. Her lobbying abilities were particularly impactful during the London Naval Conference and in helping to secure the appointment of a woman to the US delegation to the World Disarmament Conference.

Dickinson, Willoughby Hyett (1859–1943), British peace activist. A devout Christian, Dickinson assisted J. Allen Baker in forming in 1914 the organisation that became known as the World Alliance for Promoting International Friendship through the Churches, of which he was President between 1931 and 1943.

Dingman, Mary Agnes (1875–1961), American internationalist. After spending the 1920s working and lecturing internationally for the World's Alliance of YMCAs, Dingman became President of the Disarmament Committee of Women's International Organisations in 1931, a position she held until 1939.

Doyle, Michael Francis (1875–1960), American lawyer and internationalist. A lawyer known for having defended Irish revolutionary Roger Casement, Doyle was Chairman of the American Committee at the League of Nations in Geneva between 1923 and 1946. He founded the American Interorganization Council in Geneva in February 1932.

Drevet, Camille (1880–1969), French feminist and pacifist. Moved to pacifism and social work after the death of her husband in the First World War, Drevet was international secretary of the Women's International League for Peace and Freedom between December 1930 and May 1934.

Dreyfus-Barney, Laura Clifford (1879–1974), American Bahai teacher, philanthropist, and internationalist. Having served in the American Red Cross during the First World War, Mrs. Dreyfus-Barney remained in Europe in the 1920s and pioneered the collaboration of the women's movement with the League of Nations. She founded a 'Liaison Committee of Major International Associations' in 1925 and was a Vice-President of the Disarmament Committee of Women's International Organisations from 1931.

Duchêne, Gabrielle Laforcade (1870–1954), French feminist and pacifist. The founder of the French branch of the Women's International League for Peace and Freedom, Duchêne was its President between 1919 and 1954. A leading figure in the women's disarmament campaign in France, she secured 71,000 signatures to WILPF's petition and the participation of about forty groups in the *Comité d'Action pour le Désarmement*.

Duggan, Stephen Pierce Hayden (1870–1950). American educator and internationalist. Director of the Institute of International Education between 1919 and 1946, Duggan was also active in the Interorganization Council on Disarmament.

Dupuy, Jean [also known as Jean Dupuis] (b. 1903), French internationalist. As secretary-general of the *Comité d'Action pour la Société des Nations*, Dupuy was one of the principal organisers of the disarmament campaign in France. He also served as secretary-general and from 1932 President of the International Federation of University League of Nations Societies, and as President of the Disarmament Committee of Students' International Organisations.

Dupuy, Paul (1856–1948), French human rights activist. A passionate Dreyfusard, Dupuy was a member of the *Ligue des Droits de l'Homme* from its foundation. He spoke on behalf on the International League for the Rights of Man at the special session of the World Disarmament Conference of 6 February 1932.

Eidenschenk-Patin, Albertine-Louise (1864–1942), French educator and peace activist. Having lost her son in the First World War, Madame Eidenschenk-Patin, headmistress of the *Ecole Normale d'Institutrices de Douai* between 1905 and 1926, set up the International League of Mothers and Women Teachers for the Promotion of Peace in 1928 and served at its secretary-general.

Enfield, Alice Honora (1883–1935), British co-operative movement leader. Originally a schoolteacher, Honora Enfield (as she was known) dedicated her life to the co-operative movement from 1909 onwards. She was the secretary of the International Co-operative Women's Guild from its foundation in 1921, and reported for the organisation from Geneva during the World Disarmament Conference.

Eppstein, John Charles Newport (b. 1895), British internationalist. A devout Roman Catholic, Eppstein was a travelling secretary and lecturer for the League of Nations Union from 1921 onwards. He assisted Cecil during his 1931 tour of Europe that stimulated the principal elements of the global disarmament campaign.

Fosdick, Raymond Blaine (1883–1972), American internationalist. Under-Secretary-General of the League of Nations until the USA failed to ratify the organisation's Covenant, Fosdick became one of the principal proponents of US membership of the League in the interwar years. He helped form the League of Nations Non-Partisan Association in 1922–3, and served as its President between 1933 and 1935. He exploited his acquaintance with John Davison Rockefeller, Jr. to fund elements of the disarmament campaign, including the Trocadéro Conference.

Freundlich, Emmy (1878–1948), Austrian co-operative movement leader. A socialist Member of Parliament, Mrs. Freundlich was President of the International Co-operative Women's Guild between 1921 and 1948.

Garnett, (James Clerk) Maxwell (1880–1958), British peace movement administrator. Principal of Manchester College of Technology between 1912 and 1920, Garnett was secretary of the League of Nations Union between 1920 and 1938.

Giannini, Amedeo (1886–1960), Italian diplomat. President of the Italian League of Nations Association from 1924 onwards, Giannini was also Italy's delegate to the League of Nations in 1931–2.

Golay, Henri (1867–1950), Swiss peace movement leader. After serving as Head of the French section at the Swiss Foreign Ministry, he acted as secretary-general of the International Peace Bureau from 1911 until his death. During this time, he arranged a dozen international peace conferences, but his organisational skills were largely neglected by the disarmament movement.

Gorecki, Roman (1889–1946), Polish general and minister. As President of the Interallied Federation of Ex-Servicemen (FIDAC) in 1933, General Gorecki led the joint CIAMAC-FIDAC disarmament demonstration held in March that year.

Grant, Donald, British ecumenist. General secretary of the International Fellowship of Reconciliation between 1929 and 1933, Grant represented and reported for the organisation in Geneva during the World Disarmament Conference.

Green, James Frederick (b. 1910), American students' leader. In late 1931, Green helped organise the Intercollegiate Disarmament Council of the United States of America, which conducted a poll of 25,000 undergraduates on the disarmament issue. He presented the results at the special session of the World Disarmament Conference on 6 February 1932: 62% of those voting supported US unilateral disarmament.

Guillon, Charles-François (1883–1965), French priest and internationalist. Mayor of Chambon-sur-Lie, pasteur Guillon was a secretary of the World's Alliance of YMCAs and a participant in the Disarmament Committee of Christian International Organisations.

Gulick, Sidney Lewis (1860–1945), American ecumenist. Known for his promotion of friendly relations between the USA and Japan in the 1920s, Gulick was secretary of the Commission on International Justice and Goodwill of the Federal Council of the Churches of Christ in America and a participant in the Interorganization Council.

Guthrie d'Arcis, Clara (1879–1937), American peace activist. Born and raised in the USA, Clara Guthrie moved to Geneva in 1911 to run an American export house with her husband, Ludovic d'Arcis. In response to the First World War, she set up the World Union of Women for International Concord in 1915. She presided over the organisation from its foundation until her death in 1937. She also served as Treasurer of the Disarmament Committee of Women's International Organisations.

Henderson, Arthur (1863–1935), British socialist politician and internationalist. First elected to the House of Commons in 1903, Henderson was secretary of the Labour Party between 1911 and 1934 and Foreign Secretary between 1929 and 1931. He represented the Second International in its deputation to the council of four victor powers at the Paris Peace Conference and campaigned for the League from the time of its foundation. His appointment of Cecil to the Preparatory Commission ensured the convening of the World Disarmament

Conference, over which Henderson presided from its opening in 1932 until his death in 1935.

Heneker, Dorothy Alice, Canadian businesswoman, philanthropist and historian. After being appointed President of the Canadian Federation of Business and Professional Women's Clubs in 1930, Ms. Heneker became Assistant Secretary of the Disarmament Committee of Women's International Organisations the following year.

Hennessy, (Patrick) Jean (b. 1874), French internationalist. Born into the famous brandy family, Hennessy dedicated his life to political affairs: he was a member of the Chamber of Deputies and President of the *Fédération Française pour la Société des Nations.*

Henriod, Henry-Louis, Swiss ecumenist. One of the principal organisers of the ecumenical movement in the interwar years, Henriod was secretary-general of the World Student Christian Federation between 1920 and 1932 and secretary-general of both the World Alliance for Promoting International Friendship through the Churches and the Universal Christian Council for Life and Work between 1933 and 1938.

Hymans, Paul (1865–1941), Belgian internationalist. Minister of Foreign Affairs 1918–20, 1924–5 and 1927–35, Hymans represented Belgium at the Paris Peace Conference and the League of Nations. He was one of the leading advocates of disarmament and accompanying security measures, particularly the Geneva Protocol.

Jaeckh, Ernst (1875–1959), German internationalist. Originally a proponent of a German *Mitteleuropa*, Jaeckh became a leading proponent of disarmament and international co-operation after the death of his only son in the First World War. He founded the *Deutsche Liga fuer Voelkerbund* in 1918.

Jong van Beek en Donk, Benjamin de (1881–1948), Dutch pacifist journalist. Secretary of the *Nederlandsche Anti-Oorlog Raad* during the First World War, de Jong van Beek en Donk moved to Geneva in 1925 to report for the Dutch League of Nations and Peace Society's journal, *De Volkenbond.* He was President of the editorial board of the journal, *Disarmament,* between 1931 and 1933.

Jouhaux, Léon (1879–1954), French trade union leader and internationalist. One of the pre-eminent figures of interwar French politics, Jouhaux was secretary-general of the *Confédération Générale du Travail* between 1909 and 1947 and Vice-President of the International Federation of Trade Unions between 1919 and 1945. He devoted much of his time to the promotion of disarmament: he published a notable book on the subject, *Le Désarmement*, in 1927 and co-chaired the Joint Disarmament Commission of the International Federation of Trade Unions and the Labour and Socialist International from 1931. His efforts were recognised by the French government, and he was appointed a member of the Temporary Mixed Commission and subsequently a delegate to the League of Nations Assembly between 1925 and 1928.

Jouvenel, (Bertrand) Henry Léon Robert de, des Ursins (1876–1935), French statesman. One of France's foremost internationalists, Henry de Jouvenel was a senator and member of the Senate Foreign Affairs Committee between 1921 and 1935. A delegate to the League of Nations from 1920, his resignation from this position in 1927 stimulated the arbitration and disarmament campaigns in France. He founded and led the *Comité d'Action pour la Société des Nations* and collaborated with Cecil to convene the Trocadéro Conference in 1931.

Joxe, Louis (1901–1991), French diplomat and internationalist. Originally an historian, Joxe entered diplomacy in 1932. During the Daladier government, he assisted Air Minister Pierre Cot and served on the French delegation to the World Disarmament Conference.

Kayser, Jacques (1900–1963), French journalist and human rights activist. Editor-in-chief of *La République* and contributor to numerous progressive publications, Kayser served as secretary of the International League for the Rights of Man and represented this organisation at the World Disarmament Conference.

Keller, Adolf (1872–1963), Swiss ecumenist. General-secretary of the Universal Christian Council for Life and Work from 1925, Professor Keller chaired the first meeting of the organisations that became the Disarmament Committee of Christian International Organisations in 1931 and served as a member of its Executive Committee.

Kirchoff, Herman (b. 1892), German peace activist. A leading figure in the *Deutsche Liga fuer Voelkerbund*, Kirchoff was one of the most outspoken proponents of multilateral disarmament through the League of Nations. His pamphlet, *Wirkliche Abruestung* (1931), was published in many languages and was widely circulated.

Kirk, Walter William van (1891–1956), American ecumenist and peace movement organiser. Secretary of the Commission on International Justice and Goodwill of the Federal Council of Churches, van Kirk was one of the principal organisers of the churches' disarmament campaign in the USA. He was a member of the Executive Committee of the Interorganization Council on Disarmament from its foundation and served as its Chairman from October 1932 until its collapse in June 1933.

Kotschnig, Walter Maria (1901–1985), Austrian internationalist. Secretary-general of the International Student Service from 1927, Dr. Kotschnig was one of the organisers of the Disarmament Committee of Students' International Organisations.

La Fontaine, Henri (1854–1943), Belgian socialist politician and peace movement leader. A senator from 1895 to 1898, 1900 to 1932 and 1935 to 1936, La Fontaine was also a prominent figure in the international peace movement. He served as President of the International Peace Bureau between 1907 and 1943, but his considerable age prevented him from playing a leading role in the interwar disarmament campaign.

Lange, Christian Lous (1869–1938), Norwegian diplomat and internationalist. Secretary-general of the Inter-Parliamentary Union between 1909 and 1933, Lange used his participation in the Norwegian delegation to the League of Nations Assemblies from 1920 until his death to promote disarmament. He was central to the establishment of the Temporary Mixed and Preparatory Commissions in 1920 and 1925. He also served as President of the Disarmament Information Committee, which published the bulletin, *Disarmament*, in 1931–3.

Lange, Robert, French peace movement leader. One of the principal organisers of the League of Nations movement in France, Lange was secretary-general of the *Comité d'Action pour la Société des Nations*.

Lapierre, Georges (1886–1945), French teacher and trade unionist. The founder of the *Fédération Internationale des Associations d'Instituteurs*, Lapierre guided the campaign against war and fascism of the *Confédération Générale du Travail*.

Le Foyer, Lucien (1872–1952), French peace activist. Founder of the *Union Populaire pour la Paix Universelle*, Le Foyer was active in numerous French peace organisations in the interwar years as well as the International Peace Bureau. He was Vice-President of the *Association de la Paix par le Droit* and co-editor of its journal, *La Paix par le Droit*.

Libby, Frederick Joseph (1874–1970), American peace movement leader. Co-founder and executive secretary of the National Council for Prevention of War from 1921 until his death. Libby was one of the principal co-ordinators of the disarmament movement in the USA. He led the campaign during the Washington Naval Conference and served on the Executive Committee of the Interorganization Council.

Livingstone, Dame Adelaide Lord (1881–1970), British (by marriage; born American) peace campaigner. Honoured for her services to British prisoners of the First World War, Dame Livingstone joined the staff of the League of Nations Union in 1923. She was head of its special activities between 1928 and 1933 and subsequently organised the Peace Ballot in 1934–5. During the summer of 1933, she organised the transnational disarmament campaign of the International Consultative Group that culminated in the Geneva demonstration of 15 October 1933.

McDonald, James Grover (1886–1964), American internationalist. Chairman of the Board and President of the Foreign Policy Association between 1919 and 1933, McDonald was one of the principal advocates of US membership of the League of Nations. He led the multi-organisational campaign for ratification of the London Naval Treaty and in 1931 established the Interorganization Council on Disarmament (ICD). That year he led two ICD deputations to President Hoover, which appear to have influenced Hoover's disarmament plan of June 1932.

Madariaga Y Rojo, Salvador de (1886–1978), Spanish diplomat. Head of the League's Disarmament Section between 1922 and 1927 and chief Spanish delegate to the World Disarmament Conference between

1932 and 1934, Madariaga was one of the pre-eminent figures in the disarmament movement. He used his time as King Alphonso Chair of Spanish Studies at Oxford University between 1928 and 1931 to publish *Disarmament: Obstacles, Results, Prospects* (1929).

Malaterre-Sellier, Germaine (1889–1967), French nurse and internationalist. A Vice-President of the International Alliance of Women, she helped direct the organisation towards the promotion of peace and disarmament. She also served as a Vice-President of the *Ligue Internationale du Désarmement Moral par les Femmes*, the *Union Féminine pour la Société des Nations* and the International Federation of League of Nations Societies.

Manus, Rosette Susanna [known as Rosa Manus] (1881–1943), Dutch feminist and peace movement leader. Vice-President of the International Alliance of Women between 1923 and 1938, Rosa Manus served as secretary of its Committee for Peace and the League of Nations from 1926. She was also secretary of the Disarmament Committee of Women's International Organisations from 1931.

Margueritte, Victor (1866–1942), French pacifist author. One of the most prolific pacifist writers of interwar France, Margueritte advocated disarmament in the pages of *Evolution* and launched an 'Appeal to Good Sense' signed by many well-known 'intellectuals' to promote universal disarmament in 1928.

Marshall, Catherine E. (1880–1961), suffragist and peace movement organiser. A founder member of the Women's International League for Peace and Freedom, Marshall assumed many offices in the British and international sections of the organisation between 1919 and 1941.

Martin, William Louis (1888–1934), Swiss journalist. Foreign affairs editor of the *Journal de Genève* between 1924 and 1933, William Martin's reports on League of Nations affairs earned him a global reputation as an internationalist. He was one of the most popular speakers at non-governmental disarmament demonstrations in Geneva throughout the World Disarmament Conference, and he presided over the International Consultative Group's demonstration of 15 October 1933.

Massigli, René Daniel Lucien (1888–1988), French diplomat. An attaché to the French delegation at the Paris Peace Conference, Massigli was also a delegate at the London Naval and World Disarmament Conferences, and he served on the Preparatory Commission. He directed the *Service Français de la Société des Nations* from 1928 and together with Paul-Boncour used his participation in the *Conseil Supérieur de la Défense Nationale* to prevent the militarist faction from blocking proposals for disarmament and collective security through the League of Nations.

Méric, Victor (1876–1933), French pacifist journalist. A prolific writer for numerous socialist publications, Méric launched the *Ligue Internationale des Combattants pour la Paix* in 1930 as well as the journal, *La Patrie Humaine*, the following year.

Merriman, Christina (d. 1930), American peace movement leader. Secretary of the Foreign Policy Association between 1919 and 1928, Merriman was a co-founder and the first executive secretary of the National Council for Prevention of War in 1921.

Morgan, Laura Puffer (1874–1962), American peace activist. As well as presiding over the Committee on Permanent Peace of the American National Council of Women, Morgan was a disarmament expert and associate secretary of the National Council for Prevention of War (NCPW) throughout the 1920s and 1930s. She organised international fora for the NCPW during the Washington Naval Conference, and sent the organisation frequent reports on the development of the Washington, London and World Disarmament Conferences. She also headed the American Interorganization Council in Geneva from 1932 until 1940.

Morgan, Ruth (1880–1934), American feminist and peace activist. The chairman of the Committee for Peace and the League of Nations of the International Alliance of Women from 1926 until her death in 1934, Morgan led the Alliance's disarmament campaign. She chaired the Alliance's Belgrade conference for the promotion of disarmament in May 1931.

Motta, Giuseppe (1871–1940), Swiss diplomat. Principal Swiss delegate at every League Assembly, Motta was one of the most vocal advocates of the League and a popular orator at disarmament demonstrations.

Mueller, Joachim, German Christian internationalist. A member of the Secretariat of the World's Alliance of YMCAs, Mueller helped found the Disarmament Committee of Christian International Organisations in 1931. He served as the Committee's secretary and spoke at length on its behalf at the special session of the World Disarmament Conference of 6 February 1932.

Murray, (George) Gilbert Aimé (1866–1957), British classical scholar and internationalist. Regius Professor of Greek at Oxford University between 1908 and 1936, Murray was also British representative on the International Committee for Intellectual Co-operation from 1922 until 1939. As Chairman of the Executive Committee of the League of Nations Union between 1923 and 1938, his cautious approach to the organisation's activities complemented Cecil's zeal.

Nash, Philip Curtis (1890–1947), American internationalist. A prominent advocate of League membership in the USA, Nash was executive director of the League of Nations Association between 1929 and 1933. He was also a proponent of international disarmament and served as Chairman of the Interorganization Council from January until October 1932.

Noel Baker, Philip John (1889–1982), British athlete, politician and peace campaigner. The principal organiser of the Friends' Ambulance Unit in 1914, Baker subsequently became one of the world's foremost disarmament advocates. He assisted Cecil during the Paris Peace Conference, League Secretary-General Sir Eric Drummond between 1919 and 1922, Cecil again in 1923–4, and Henderson and Parmoor during the 1924 League Assembly. While Sir Ernest Cassell Professor of International Relations at the London School of Economics in 1924–9 he published *The Geneva Protocol* (1925), *Disarmament* (1926), and *Disarmament and the Coolidge Conference* (1927). As a Labour MP between 1929 and 1931 he served as Henderson's parliamentary private secretary, and during the World Disarmament Conference he was Henderson's chief assistant.

Paul-Boncour, Joseph (1873–1972), French socialist politician and internationalist. Although a socialist deputy between 1909 and 1931, Paul-Boncour served several bourgeois governments as a delegate to the League of Nations in 1924–8 and 1932–4. He chaired the League Committee that in 1925 established the Preparatory Commission (on which he subsequently served 1926–8), and as a delegate to the World Disarmament Conference (1932–4) he proposed the 'Constructive

Plan' of November 1932. He was France's War Minister in June-December 1932, Prime Minister for forty days between December 1932 and January 1933, and Foreign Minister from December 1932 until January 1934.

Perlen, Frida, German peace activist. A founder of the German branch of the Women's International League for Peace and Freedom (WILPF), Frau Perlen was the initiator of WILPF's disarmament petition in 1929.

Pichot, Henri (1884–1945), French ex-servicemen's leader and peace activist. Vice-President from 1919 of the *Union Fédérale des Anciens Combattants*, Pichot ensured that the organisation promoted peace and disarmament through participation in the French League of Nations movement. As President of CIAMAC, he represented the ex-servicemen's disarmament movement in a deputation to the President of the World Disarmament Conference on 7 February 1932 and at the International Consultative Group's disarmament demonstration on 15 October 1933.

Pickard, Bertram (1892–1973), British Quaker. Secretary of the London Friends Peace Committee from 1921, Pickard moved with his wife Irene to Geneva in 1926 to serve as Secretary of the Friends' Geneva Centre until 1940. During the World Disarmament Conference he was President of the Disarmament Committee of Christian International Organisations, and from 1935 until 1940 he was Chairman of the International Consultative Group.

Poberezski, Michel, students' leader. Assistant general secretary of the International Student Service, M. Poberezski organised the Disarmament Committee of Students' International Organisations in 1931 and served as the Committee's secretary throughout the World Disarmament Conference.

Politis, Nicolas Socrate (1872–1942), Greek diplomat. Greece's representative at the Paris Peace Conference and her delegate to the League of Nations between 1920 and 1937, Politis built a reputation as an expert on arbitration and disarmament. He helped draft the Geneva Protocol, was President of the Preparatory Commission in 1929, provided a definition of aggression for the World Disarmament Conference in May 1933, and published *The Problem of Disarmament* in 1934.

Potter, Pitman Benjamin (b. 1892), American academic and international-ist. A specialist in international organisation, Potter was Professor of Political Science at the University of Wisconsin between 1920 and 1932 and Professor of International Organisation at the Graduate Institute of International Studies in Geneva from 1930 until 1941. He was an active member of the American Interorganization Council on Disarmament in Geneva.

Prudhommeaux, Jules Jean (1869–1948), French peace activist. A founder member of the *Association de la Paix par le Droit*, Prudhommeaux was secretary-general of this organisation as well as of the *Fédération Française pour la Société des Nations* from 1920 onwards. He was a prolific lecturer and writer as well as organiser, providing much of the material for the journal *La Paix par le Droit*, which he co-edited with Lucien Le Foyer. He was central to the organisation of the *Cartels de la Paix* that promoted the World Disarmament Conference throughout France from 1931 onwards. As of 1911, he was also director of the European Center of the Carnegie Endowment for International Peace.

Quidde, Ludwig (1858–1941), German pacifist. The leading figure among the small number of genuine peace activists in interwar Germany, Quidde participated in the Inter-Parliamentary Union and the International Peace Bureau from the onset of the twentieth century. He led the German Peace Society between 1914 and 1929, and the German Peace Cartel between 1920 and 1929. He remained prominent in the International Peace Bureau after that date, and fled to Geneva in the spring of 1933. Disarmament was one of his principal objectives; he published *Erste Schritt zur Weltabruestung* in 1927.

Radziwill, Princess Gabrielle Jeanne Anne Marie (1878–1968), Lithuanian international civil servant. A member of the Information Section of the League of Nations Secretariat, Princess Radziwill was the liaison officer with the international peace and women's organisations.

Rankin, Jeannette (1880–1973), American suffragist and peace activist. After working as a field secretary for the Women's International League in 1920–5 and as a lobbyist for the Women's Peace Union in 1929, Rankin was the National Council for Prevention of War's Washington lobbyist and field organiser between 1929 and 1939.

Rheinbaben, Werner Freiherr von (1878–1975), German diplomat. As a German delegate to the League of Nations between 1926 and 1933, Baron von Rheinbaben was one of the most vocal proponents of disarmament of the victors of the First World War. He was a leading figure in the *Deutsche Liga fuer Voelkerbund* and a German representative on the Disarmament Committee of the International Federation of League of Nations Societies.

Rich, Raymond Thomas (1899–1959), American internationalist. Executive director of the World Peace Foundation between 1927 and 1936, Rich was one of the original participants in the Interorganization Council on Disarmament.

Rolin, Henri (1891–1973), Belgian internationalist. Belgian representative at every League Assembly between 1922 and 1932, Rolin was Vice-President of the Belgian League of Nations Union and was active in the disarmament work of the International Federation of League of Nations Societies. His proposals formed much of the basis of the Federation's Budapest Resolution.

Royden, (Agnes) Maude (1876–1956), British suffragist and pacifist. A devout Anglican, Royden helped found the Church League for Woman Suffrage in 1909 and the Fellowship of Reconciliation in 1914. She worked closely with Kathleen Courtney in the post-World War One British peace movement.

Ruyssen, Théodore Eugène César (1868–1967), French Kantian philosopher and internationalist. President of the *Association de la Paix par le Droit* between 1899 and 1948, Ruyssen was secretary-general of the International Federation of League of Nations Societies from 1921 until 1939.

Schevenels, Walther (1894–1966), Belgian trade union leader. General-secretary of the International Federation of Trade Unions between 1930 and 1945, Schevenels was the initiator and co-secretary of the Joint Disarmament Commission of the International Federation of Trade Unions and the Labour and Socialist International.

Schnee, Albert Heinrich (1871–1949), German diplomat. Governor of German East Africa from 1912 until 1918, Schnee was President of the *Deutsche Liga fuer Voelkerbund.* He represented Germany in the Disarmament Committee of the International Federation of League of Nations Societies.

Schwarz, Wolfgang, German internationalist. A leading member of the *Deutsche Liga fuer Voelkerbund,* Schwarz represented Germany in the International Consultative Group and the Disarmament Committee of the International Federation of League of Nations Societies.

Scialoja, Vittorio (1856–1933), Italian diplomat. A founder of the League of Nations and Italian delegate to the Assembly (1920–24) and the Council (1926–33), Scialoja sought to promote the success of the institution despite having to serve a fascist government. He addressed and helped organise the Trocadéro Conference in 1931.

Shotwell, James Thomson (1874–1965), Canadian-American internationalist. A professor of history at Columbia University from 1908 onwards, Shotwell was also one of the leading internationalists of the interwar years. He was director of Economics and History at the Carnegie Endowment for International Peace between 1924 and 1948 and was a leading advocate of US membership of the League of Nations. In 1924, he formed the 'American Committee on Disarmament and Security,' which produced the 'Draft Treaty of Disarmament and Security' that provided one of the principal bases for the Geneva Protocol. The establishment of the Preparatory Commission in 1925 was also partly in response to a memorandum by Shotwell. In 1927–8 Shotwell was central to the negotiations for the Kellogg-Briand Pact, and during the World Disarmament Conference his draft protocol on moral disarmament was adopted as the basis for discussion by the Committee on Moral Disarmament in 1933.

Small, Captain Lothian, British internationalist. Secretary of the International Federation of League of Nations Societies throughout the period of this book, Small was a Vice-President of the Federation's Disarmament Committee.

Smith, Fred Burton (1865–1936), American ecumenist and peace activist. Chairman of the Executive Committee of the American branch of the World Alliance for Promoting International Friendship through the

Churches, Smith led the 'right wing' (pacificists) of the Interorganization Council on Disarmament in 1933.

Smith, Tucker P., American pacifist. Secretary of the Committee on Militarism in Education between 1928 and 1933, Smith was a member of the Executive Committee of the Interorganization Council on Disarmament and led its 'left wing' (pacifist) faction in 1933.

Steenberghe-Engeringh, Petronille Aimée Florentine (b. 1875), Dutch Catholic women's movement leader. President of the World Union of Catholic Women's Organisations between 1922 and 1952, Madame Steenberghe-Engeringh was the only Catholic speaker at the Special Session of the World Disarmament Conference of 6 February 1932.

Swanwick, Helena Maria Lucy (1864–1939), British pacifist and feminist author. A member of the Executive Committee of the Union of Democratic Control from 1914, Swanwick was also President of the British branch of the Women's International League for Peace and Freedom between 1915 and 1922. She was a member of the Labour Party's advisory committee on international questions and served as a substitute delegate to the League Assemblies during the Labour governments of 1924 and 1929–31. She committed suicide after the outbreak of World War II in 1939.

Sweetser, Arthur (1888–1968), American journalist and international civil servant. Having produced some of the best journalism of the First World War, Sweetser was appointed to the League Secretariat in 1919 and subsequently served as a member of the Information Section. He was the most influential of the American members of the League Secretariat, acting as a liaison between it and US public figures. He helped secure US participation in the League's efforts towards disarmament in 1926.

Titulescu, Nicolae (1882–1941), Romanian diplomat. Romania's delegate to the Paris Peace Conference in 1919 and to the League of Nations between 1920 and 1936, Titulescu was one of the leading figures in the institution. He was best known for promoting gradual supplementation of the League's security provisions, including the Geneva Protocol (1924) and the Definition of Aggression (1933).

Vandervelde, Émile Guillaume (1866–1938), Belgian socialist statesman. As well as leading the Belgian socialist party from 1894 until his death, Vandervelde was President of the Labour and Socialist International from 1929 onwards. He was a delegate to the Paris Peace Conference, and as Foreign Minister between 1925 and 1927 helped negotiate the Locarno Treaties. He co-chaired the joint disarmament demonstration of the Labour and Socialist International and the International Federation of Trade Unions in 1932.

Vernet, Madeleine Cavelier (1878–1949), French pacifist. In order to promote total disarmament, Vernet established *Volonté de Paix* in 1927. She spent the subsequent years lecturing in support of disarmament, published *De l'objection de conscience au désarmement* in 1928, and organised two *Conférences libres du désarmement* in 1932.

Visser 't Hooft, Willem Adolf (1900–1985), Dutch ecumenist. As the first general secretary of the World Council of Churches between 1938 and 1966, Visser 't Hooft was one of the guiding figures of the twentieth century Protestant ecumenical movement. He was a secretary (general secretary from 1932) of the World Student Christian Federation between 1929 and 1938, and a prominent member of the Disarmament Committee of Christian International Organisations.

Watteville, J. Ch. de, ex-servicemen's leader. The secretary of the International Conference of Disabled Soldiers and Ex-Servicemen (CIAMAC), de Watteville was the principal organiser of the ex-servicemen's movement's disarmament campaign.

Weiss, Louise (1893–1983), French journalist and internationalist. The founder of the internationalist journal *L'Europe Nouvelle* in 1918 and of the *Nouvelle Ecole de la Paix* in 1930, Weiss organised the Trocadéro Conference in 1931.

Wilson, (Edward) Raymond (1896–1987), American pacifist. Field secretary of the peace section of the American Friends' Service Committee between 1931 and 1935, Wilson was in Geneva at the time of the World Disarmament Conference and participated in the American Interorganization Council in Geneva.

Wold, Emma (1871–1950), American feminist and peace activist. A researcher for the Women's Party in the 1920s, Wold founded the Women's Committee for National Disarmament in 1921 and toured the USA promoting disarmament in the build-up to the party conventions in Chicago in 1932.

Woolley, Mary Emma (1863–1947), American educator and internationalist. The President of Mount Holyoke College between 1900 and 1937, Woolley directed the World Alliance for Promoting International Friendship through the Churches and was President of the American Association of University Women between 1927 and 1933. Her involvement in the peace movement contributed towards her appointment as a delegate to the World Disarmament Conference.

APPENDIX III

ORGANISATIONS THAT PARTICIPATED IN THE TROCADÉRO CONFERENCE

This appendix lists the organisations that sent delegates to the unofficial World Disarmament Conference held in the Paris Trocadéro on 25–27 November 1931. Where known, the English names of international organisations have been provided. This list replicates the layout and spelling adopted in *L'Europe Nouvelle*, 5 December 1931, pp. 1617–21.

International Organisations (137 delegates)
All Peoples' Association International
Bulletin Catholique International
Bureau International Humanitaire Zoophile
Comité International d'Histoire
Comité International de Scoutisme
Comité International pour le Statut des Prisonniers Politiques
Correspondance Scolaire Internationale
Fédération Internationale des Escoutes Scolaires
Fédération Internationale des Femmes Avocats et Magistrats
Friends' International Service
Institut International de Christianisme Social
Institute of International Relations
Instituto Internationale de Risparmie
Inter-Alliance of Women's Suffrage
International Accountants Corporation
International Alliance of Women
International Arbitration League
International Association for the Promotion of Liberal Christianity
    and Religious Freedom
International Bureau of Education
International Confederation of Intellectual Workers
International Conference of Disabled Soldiers and Ex-Servicemen
    (CIAMAC)
International Co-operative Women's Guild
International Council of Women

International Federation of Journalists
International Federation of Leagues for the Rights of Man
International Federation of University Women
International Fellowship of Reconciliation
International League of Freemasons
International League of Mothers and of Women Teachers for the
  Promotion of Peace
International Order of Good Templars
International Peace Bureau
International Peace Press Bureau
International Pharmaceutical Federation
International Student Service
International Youth Circle
Ligue de Bonté Internationale
Rotary International
Union Universelle pour supprimer ce crime: la guerre
Universal Christian Council for Life and Work
War Resisters' International
Women's International League for Peace and Freedom
World Alliance for Promoting International Friendship through the
  Churches
World Student Christian Federation
World Union of Women for International Concord
World's Alliance of Young Men's Christian Associations
World's Alliance of Young Women's Christian Associations
World's Peace Union and Theosophical Order of Service

International and National Student Organisations (48 delegates)
Association Catholique de la Jeunesse Française
Association des Etudiants Bulgares
Association des Etudiants Polonnais de Paris
Association des Etudiants Tchécoslovaques
Association des Etudiants Yougoslaves à Paris
Austrian University League of Nations Society
Bulgarian University League of Nations Society
Correspondance Scolaire Internationale
Czechoslovakian University League of Nations Society
Eclaireurs Israélites de France
Etudiants de la Jeune République

Fédération des Eclaireurs de France
Fédération Universelle des Associations Chrétiennes d'Etudiants
Fondation des Etats-Unis à la Cité Universitaire
French University League of Nations Society
German University League of Nations Society
Greek University League of Nations Society
International Federation of University League of Nations Societies
International Federation of University Women
International Student Service
Jeunesse Démocrate Populaire
Ligue d'Action Universitaire Républicaine et Socialiste
National Confederation of Students
Pax Romana
Polish University League of Nations Society
Romanian University League of Nations Society
Swiss University League of Nations Society
World Union of Jewish Students

Argentina (3 delegates)
Association des Résidents de la Fondation Argentine

Australia (1 delegate)
Australian League of Nations Association

Austria (12 delegates)
Akademische Ver. fuer Volkenbundearbeit in Oesterreich
Arbeitsgemeinschaft Oesterreichische Juedensvereine
Bund Oesterreichische Frauenvereine
Oesterreichische Voelkerbundliga
Paneuropaeische Union
Tag des Guten Willens
Wikag Wishsnaplica Kulturelle Gesellschaft Wien

Belgium (9 delegates)
Groupe Cosmometapolis
Union Belge pour la Société des Nations
Verband V.O.S.
Vlaamsche Arbeid

Bulgaria (2 delegates)
Société Pacifique des Femmes en Bulgarie
Union des Femmes pour la Paix Bulgare

Canada (2 delegates)
Canadian Federation of Business and Professional Women's Clubs
Lyceum Club and Women's Art Association of Canada

Czechoslovakia (7 delegates)
Association Tchécoslovaque pour la Société des Nations
Peace Union of Moravia
Rada Obrodnych Organisaci
Société de la Paix (Prague)
Ukrainian Academic Committee (Czechoslovakia)
Zenska Narodnirada

Denmark (7 delegates)
Commission d'Action Danoise pour la Paix et la Société des Nations
Danish Radical Party and Danish Peace and League of Nations
    Union
Fédération des Instituteurs Danois
National Council of Women of Denmark
Union des Eglises du Monde—Danemark
Women's International League for Peace and Freedom—Denmark

Estonia (1 delegate)
National Council of Women in Estonia

Finland (1 delegate)
National Council of Women—Finland

France (605 delegates)
Alliance Française des Unions Chrétiennes de Jeunes Filles
Alliance des Unions Chrétiennes de Jeunes Gens de France
Alliance Sainte Jeanne d'Arc
Amitiés Internationales
Anciens Combattants Républicains Ardennes
Armée du Salut (France)
Association Amicale des Ingénieurs du Conservatoire National des
    Arts et Métiers

Association Amicale : Les Amis d'Emile Armand
Association des Etudiants Protestants de Paris
Association de Françaises Diplômées des Universités
Association des Mutilés et Anciens Combattants de Cosne-sur-Loire
(Nievre)
Association de Mutilés des Yeux
Association de la Paix par le Droit (Loire-Inférieure)
Association Polymathique
Association Française pour la Société des Nations
Association Française pour la Société des Nations (Alger)
Association Française pour la Société des Nations (Bordeaux)
Association des Volontaires du Service Social
Cartel Rouennais de la Paix
Cercle d'Etudiants de la Ligue des Droits de l'Homme
Combattants Républicains (Féd. Dépt. Somme)
Comité d'Action pour la Société des Nations
Comité Français de l'Entr'aide Universitaire
Comité Français de Secours aux Enfants
Confédération Française des Travailleurs Chrétiens
Confédération Générale des Anciens Combattants et de Toutes les
Victimes de la Guerre
Confédération Nationale des Anciens Combattants et Victimes de la
Guerre
Confédération des Travailleurs Intellectuels
Conseil National des Femmes Françaises (Montauban)
Démocratie Féminine
Ecole Normale de Foix (Ariège)
Ecole de la Paix (Marseille)
Eglise Réformée Evangélique Libre de la Vie Droite
Eglise Réformée de Saint-Affrique
Fédération Amicale des Mutilés 'Aide et Protection'
Fédération du Calvados de l'Association Française pour la Société des
Nations
Fédération Départementale des Associations de Victimes de la Guerre
Fédération Départementale des Associations de Victimes de la Guerre
(Loire)
Fédération Départementale des Mutilés et Ascendants du Lot
Fédération Européenne des Soroptimist Clubs
Fédération Française des Associations Chrétiennes d'Etudiants
Fédération Française des Associations pour la Société des Nations

Fédération des Jeunesses Laïques et Républicaines
Fédération Nationale des Agricultures
Fédération Nationale des Combattants Républicains
Fédération Nationale des Combattants Républicains (Nice)
Fédération Nationale des Trépanés et Blessés de la Tête (Lyon)
Fédération Universelle des Associations Chrétiennes d'Etudiants
Fondation Biermans-Lapotie
F. O. P. des Associations de Mutilés, Veuves, Orphelins de la Guerre
    et Anciens Combattants
Foyer de la Nouvelle Europe
Francs-Maçons—Loges Lalande—Les Trinitaires
Groupe Maçonnique Fraternité-Réconciliation
Groupe Oberlin (Marseille)
Groupe Rollin
Groupement du Lycée Rollin
Groupe Universitaire Franco-Allemand
Groupement Universitaire pour la Société des Nations
Groupement Universitaire pour la Société des Nations (Section
    d'Alger)
Groupement Universitaire pour la Société des Nations (Bonneville
    H-S)
Groupement Universitaire pour la Société des Nations (Section de
    Caen)
Groupement Universitaire pour la Société des Nations (Poitiers)
Institut de Coopération Internationale
Ligue des Anciens Combattants Pacifistes
Ligue des Catholiques pour la Justice et la Paix (Section de Paris)
Ligue des Catholiques pour la Justice et la Paix (Section de Bordeaux)
Ligue du Devoir Social
Ligue des Droits de l'Homme (Neuilly-sur-Seine)
Ligue d'Etudes Germaniques (Le Havre)
Ligue Française pour les Droits de la Femme
Ligue Française pour le Droit des Femmes (Amiens)
Ligue Internationale des Mères et Educatrices pour la Paix (Carcassonne)
Ligue de la Jeune République
Ligue du Libre-Echange
Notre Temps
Réconciliation

Rotary Club de Mulhouse
Section de l'Association Française pour la Société des Nations (Quency)
Section Française de la Ligue Internationale des Femmes pour la Paix
    et la Liberté
Section Française du Mouvement International de la Réconciliation
Section Grenoble du Groupement Universitaire pour la Société des
    Nations
Société d'Art Théâtral de Jeunesse
Société d'Enseignement Technique et Général (Section l' 'Essor Moderne')
Syndicat National des Institutrices et Instituteurs Publics
Trait d'Union
Union des A. B. de Guerre
Union Amicale des Mutilés de Ruelle (Charente)
Union des Anciens Prisonniers et Victimes de Guerre
Union Fédérale des Associations Françaises d'Anciens Combattants et
    Victimes de Guerre
Union Féminine pour la Société des Nations U. F. S. F.
Union Fraternelle des Femmes pour la France et les Colonies
Union Internationale de la Propriété Foncière Bâtie
Union des Mutilés et Anciens Combattants (Angoulême)
Union Nationale des Combattants
Union Nationale des Mutilés Réformés et Anciens Combattants
Union des Poilus d'Hénin-Liétard
Union Populaire pour la Paix
Uni Pax
Volonté de Paix

Georgia (1 delegate)
Georgian Association for the League of Nations

Germany (43 delegates)
Arbeitsgemeinschaft der Ver. Ehemaliger Deutscher Kriegsgefangegner
Aussenhandelsverband
Buero des Voelkerbundes Berlin
Bund Deutsche Frauenvereine
Bund der Kriegsdienstgegner
Bund Entschiedener Schulreformer und Arbeitsgemeinschaft der
    Vereinigungen Ehemaliger Deutscher Kriegsgefangegner
Deutscher Akademikerinnenbund

Deutscher Friedensbund
Deutsch-franz Gesellschaft Berlin
Deutsches Institut fuer Auslandskunde
Deutsche Liga fuer Voelkerbund
Deutscher Republikanischer Reichsbund
Deutsche Sekretariat fuer die Pariser Abruestungskundgebung
Deutsches Staatsburgerinnenverband
Deutsche Vereinigung fuer den Fuersorgedienst im Frankenhaus
Evangelische Jungmaennerbuende Deutschlands
Friedensbund Deutscher Katholiken
"Germania" Liga fuer Volkenbund
Gewerkschaft Deutscher Geistesarbeiter
Gruppe Rev. Pazifisten
Juedischer Frauenbund
Kartell der Republikanischen Verbaende Deutschland
Katholischer Deutscher Frauenbund
Katholische Gesellenvereine
Philosophische Hochschule Augsburg
Preusssischer Landesverband Juedischer Gemeindenbaende
Reichsarbeitsgemeinschaft der juedischen Landesverbaende
Reichsbanner Schwarz-Rot-Gold
Reichsbund der Deutschen Jungdemokraten Berlin
Reichsbund der Kriegsbeschaedigten, Kriegsteilnehmer und Krieger-
    hinterbliebenen
Reichsverband der Deutschen Industrie
Reichsverband der Deutschen Windhorstbunde
Reichsverband Deutscher Konsumvereine
Reichsverband der Katholischen Arbeitsvereine Deutschlands
Religioese Gesellschaft fuer Freunde
Republikanischer Richterbund Berlin
Soroptimistenvereinigung Berlin
Technische Hochschule Darmstadt
Universitaet Bonn
Vereinigung Katholischer Deutscher Lehrerinnen
Weltjugendliga
Zentralstelle der Katholischen Jungfrauenvereine
Zentralstelle der Vilksvereine fuer das Katholische Deutschland
Zentralstelle fuer Studentische Voelkerbundsarbeit in Deutschland
Zentralverband Deutscher Staatsbuerger Juedischen Glaubens

Great Britain and Ireland (79 delegates)
All Peoples' Association
Auxiliary Movement
Baptist Union of Great Britain and Ireland
British Council on Interchange
British Federation of University Women
Christian Science Committees on Publications
Christian Social Council
Council of Ministers on Social Questions
Educational Institute of Scotland
English Speaking Union
Fellowship of Reconciliation
Headmasters' Conference
Kendall Branch of the Wives Fellowship
Industrial Christian Fellowship
Jewish Peace Society
League of Nations Union (Chelsea Branch)
League of Nations Union (East of Scotland Distr. Council)
League of Nations Union (Highgate Branch)
League of Nations Union (Kent Federation Council)
League of Nations Union (Letchworth Branch)
League of Nations Union (N. and N.W. of Scotland Distr. Council)
League of Nations Union (Surrey Federation)
Letchworth Disarmament Council
Letchworth Women's Liberal Association
National Adult School Union
National Council of Prisoners of War
National Council of Women (Great Britain)
National Council of Women of Ireland
National Federation of Women's Institutes
National Peace Council
National Union of Distributive and Allied Workers
National Union of Seamen
National Union of Societies for Equal Citizenship
National Union of Teachers
North Herts. Liberal Association
North Wales Women's Peace Council
Overseas League
Parents' National Educational Union

Primitive Methodist Church
Rotary Club (Chelsea)
Rotary Club (Stockton and Thornaby)
Rotary International (Great Britain)
St. Joan's Social and Political Alliance
Salvation Army
Society of Friends Peace Centre
Student Christian Movement of Great Britain
Trades Union Congress General Council
Union of Jewish Women
University League of Nations Society (Dublin)
Wesleyan Methodist Church Social Welfare Dept.
Women's Club of Newcastle
World's Committee Y.N.C.
Y.M.C.A. British National Council
Y.M.C.A. of Great Britain

Greece (3 delegates)
Greek University League of Nations Society
National Council of Greek Women
Société Hellenique des Amis de la Paix

Holland (31 delegates)
Algemeene Nederlandsche Vrouwen Vredesbond
Bond ter Behartiging van de Belangen van het Kind
Bond van Ambtenaren in Dienst van bij de Nederlandsche Spoorwegen
Dutch Girl Guides
Federatie van Christelijke Vereenigingen van en voor Vrouwen en
   Meisjes
Groupe des Mennonistes contre le service militaire
Jongeren Vredesfederatie
Kerk en Vrede
Liberale Staatspartij 'De Vrijhedsbond'
National Council of Women (Netherlands)
Nederlandsche Christen-Studenten Vereeniging
Nederlandsche Esperantisten Vereeniging
Nederlandsche Journalisten Kring
Nederlandsche Ver. voor Vrouwenbelangen
Nooit meer Oorlog

Roomsch Katholieke Volkspartij in Holland
Roomsch Katholieke Vredesbond in Nederland
Theosophische Vereeniging
Vereeniging 'Het Nederlandsche Meisjesgilde'
Vereeniging voor Volkenbond en Vrede
Vredeskamer
Vrijzinnige Christelijke Jongerenbond

Hungary (2 delegates)
All Peoples' Association (Hungarian Branch)
Comité de Contrôle de la Société des Nations

India (2 delegates)
National Council of Women (India)

Italy (4 delegates)
Academia pro Interligua (Torino)
Association Slave pour la Société des Nations (Italie)
Socièta per la Pace et la Giustitia Internazionale
Socièta per la S. d. N.

Lithuania (3 delegates)
Chamber of Commerce and Industry
National Committee of World Alliance

Luxemburg (1 delegate)
Protestantische Kirche in Luxemburg

Norway (3 delegates)
Association Norvégienne des Instituteurs
Commission Nationale Norvégienne de Coopération Intellectuelle
National Council of Women
Norwegian Federation of University Women

Poland (9 delegates)
Association des Amis de la Paix
Association des Femmes pour le Service Social en Pologne
Conseil des Associations Pacifistes Polonaises
Fédération des Associations Polonaises des Mutilés et Anciens Combattants

Fédération Polonaise pour la Société des Nations
Union Pan-Européenne (Pologne)

Romania (2 delegates)
Association Roumaine pour la Société des Nations
Conseil National des Femmes Roumaines

Spain (2 delegates)
Spanish League of Nations Association

Sweden (8 delegates)
Forbundel for Krisbet Samhallsliv
Swedish Council: World Alliance for International Friendship through
    the Churches
Swedish Council: Life and Work
Swedish School Peace League
Swedish Section of World's Women's Christian Temperance Union
Swedish Section of Women's International League for Peace and
    Freedom
Teachers' Peace Association of Scandinavia
Verein Schwedisches Informationsburo fuer Friedensfragen
Vita Bandet

Switzerland (13 delegates)
Alliance Nationale de Sociétés Féminines
Association Suisse de Femmes Universitaires
Association Suisse pour la Société des Nations
Secrétariat de Suisses à l'Etranger de la Nouvelle Société Helvétique
Suffrage Suisse
Swiss Branch of Women's International League for Peace and Freedom
Union Mondiale de la Femme pour la Concorde Internationale

Ukraine (2 delegates)
Association Ukrainienne pour la Société des Nations

USA (53 delegates)
American Academy of Political and Social Science
American Friends Service Committee
American Students Atelier
American University Union

American University Women's Peace Centre
American Women's Club (London)
American Women's Club (Paris)
Fondation des Etats-Unis
Foreign Policy Association
League of Nations Association
Pennsylvania USA
Schoolworld Friendship League
Unit-Western Branch of National Association
University Women of the USA
Women's International League USA
Women's Peace Society USA

Yugoslavia (2 delegates)
Association Yougoslave pour la Société des Nations
Women's International League for Peace and Freedom (Yugoslavia)

ORGANISATIONS THAT PARTICIPATED IN THE INTERORGANIZATION COUNCIL ON DISARMAMENT

(List of members on 29 September 1931)

American Association of University Women
American Community
American Friends' Service Committee
Anglo-American Committee
Catholic Association for International Peace
Church Peace Union
Committee on Educational Publicity in the Interests of World Peace
Committee on Militarism in Education
Council of Christian Associations
Council of Women for Home Missions
Federal Council of Churches of Christ in America
Fellowship of Reconciliation
Foreign Policy Association, Inc.
Friends' Peace Committee of Philadelphia
Intercollegiate Disarmament Council
Jewish Religious Institute
League for Independent Political Action
League for Industrial Democracy
League of Nations Association
National Committee on the Cause and Cure of War*
National Council for Prevention of War**
National Council of Jewish Women
National Federation of Temple Sisterhoods
Pacifist Action Committee
People's Lobby
War Resisters' League
Women's International League for Peace and Freedom
Women's Peace Society
Women's Peace Union
World Alliance for International Friendship through the Churches

World Peace Commission, Methodist Episcopal Church
World Peace Committee, First Humanist Society of New York
World Peace Posters, Inc.
Young Men's Christian Associations (National Council)
Young Women's Christian Associations (National Board)
Young Women's Christian Associations (National Student Council)

* The National Committee on the Cause and Cure of War consisted
in turn of:

American Association of University Women
Council of Women for Home Missions
Federation of Woman's Boards of Foreign Missions of North America
General Federation of Women's Clubs
National Board of Young Women's Christian Associations
National Council of Jewish Women
National Federation of Business and Professional Women's Clubs
National League of Women Voters
National Woman's Christian Temperance Union
National Women's Conference of American Ethical Union
National Women's Trade Union League

** The National Council for Prevention of War consisted of:

American Association of University Women
American Federation of Teachers
American Friends Service Committee
American School Citizenship League
Church of the Brethren, Board of Religious Education
Committee on Militarism in Education
Fellowship of Reconciliation
General Alliance of Unitarian Women, Committee on Social Service
General Conference of the Religious Society of Friends
International New Thought Alliance
National Board YWCA
National Council of Jewish Juniors
National Council of Jewish Women
National Education Association
National Federation of Temple Sisterhoods
National Reform Association
National Women's Trade Union League

Peace Association of Friends in America
Society to Eliminate Economic Causes of War
Woman's Missionary Union of Friends in America
Women's International League for Peace and Freedom

APPENDIX V

THE WOMEN'S DISARMAMENT PETITION

The petition presented by the Disarmament Committee of Women's
International Organisations on 6 February 1932 was composed of four
different texts. This appendix provides the four texts and the geographical distribution of signatures to each text.[1]

The Four Texts

I. *British text of the Declaration of the Women's International League
for Peace and Freedom*

The undersigned men and women without distinction of party stand
for world disarmament. They are convinced: (i) that competition in
armaments is leading all countries to ruin without bringing them security; (ii) that this policy renders further wars inevitable; (iii) that wars
in future will be wars of indiscriminate destruction of human life; (iv)
that the governments' assurances of peaceful policy will be valueless
as long as those measures of disarmament are delayed that should be
the first result of the Pact for the Renunciation of War.

II. *Continental text of the Declaration of the Women's International
League for Peace and Freedom*

The undersigned men and women, irrespective of party, are convinced:
(i) that competition in armaments is leading all countries to ruin without
giving security; (ii) that this policy renders future wars inevitable and
that these will be wars of extermination; (iii) that governmental assurances of peaceful policy will be valueless as long as those measures of
disarmament are delayed that should be the first result of the Pact for
the Renunciation of War. They therefore ask for total and universal

---

[1] Source: Disarmament Committee of the Women's International Organisations,
*Official Record of the Declarations and Petitions presented by the Disarmament Committee of the
Women's International Organisations to the Disarmament Conference, Geneva, February 6th, 1932*
(Geneva, 1932).

disarmament and request their government formally to instruct its delegates to the International Disarmament Conference, meeting in February, 1932, to examine all proposals for disarmament that have been or may be made and to take the necessary steps to achieve real disarmament.

III. *Text of the Petition adopted at Belgrade, May 1931, by the Committee on Peace and the League of Nations of the International Alliance of Women for Suffrage and Equal Citizenship*

Since the Treaty of Versailles disarmed certain nations in order to further general disarmament, according to the solemn promise contained in Article 8 of the Covenant of the League of Nations; since the states signatories of the Kellogg Pact have renounced war as a means of settling their disputes; since the success of the Conference is all-important in order to reaffirm confidence, relieve the world's economic situation and stop the dangerous competition in armaments which will inevitably involve the world in another catastrophe; we the undersigned men and women urge the members of the Disarmament Conference not to disappoint the earnest hopes of the people and not to disband without achieving a first, important reduction of armaments.

IV. *Text of the Petition drawn up by the United States National Committee on the Cause and Cure of War and adopted in other countries*

We, the undersigned women hereby petition the International Disarmament Conference to gratify the expectations and hopes of the world by putting into immediate and unhesitating effect the pledges already made for the reduction of national armaments. The Allied and Associated Nations pledged world disarmament to their adversaries; the Covenant of the League of Nations promised it; great nations have solemnly agreed that international disputes shall be settled by peaceful methods without resort to war; and, lastly, through the Kellogg-Briand Pact, war has been renounced. Clearly, the next step is the bold reduction of every variety of armament. To do less would violate treaty obligations, awaken suspicion and incite fresh war talk. The assurances of peace will become invincible when the reduction of armament for which we plead has been secured. Wars will cease when governments so resolve.

[German signatories to the text of the Cause and Cure of War petition added that they: 'associate themselves with the Petition for Disarmament, only on the understanding that negotiations of the Disarmament Conference are based on unconditional equality between the nations already disarmed and the others;' and that they 'consider that the Draft Convention of the Preparatory Commission which in its present form would only produce an illusory and not a real disarmament cannot form the basis of any genuine reduction of armaments.']

Distribution of Signatures

(RECEIVED BY 6 FEBRUARY 1932)

Country	Text of Petition				Total Signatures
	I	II	III	IV	
Albania		10			10
Argentina	2 165				2 165
Australia	112 108				112 108
Austria		45 508			45 508
Belgium		17 153			17 153
Brazil		2 937	2 079		5 016
Bulgaria		43 927			43 927
Canada	490 888			172	491 060
Ceylon	86		7		93
Chile	227				227
Colombia		20			20
Cuba		31			31
Czechoslovakia		485 000			485 000
Denmark	380 049				380 049
Egypt		420	1 893		2 313
Estonia	150 997		1 859		152 856
Fiji	330				330
Finland		93 126			93 126
France		70 992	463 840		534 832
Germany		241 345	800 000		1 041 345
Great Britain	2 141 176	4 886			2 146 062
Greece		98			98
Haiti	129				129
Hawaii	130				130
Hungary		7 782	22 700		30 482
Iceland		111			111
India	4 668				4 668
Indonesia	3 000	127	4 617		7 744
Ireland		19 298			19 298
Italy	342		6 270		6 612

Table (*cont.*)

Country	Text of Petition				Total Signatures
	I	II	III	IV	
Jamaica	83		4 656		4 739
Japan	172 915				172 915
Latvia		100			100
Lithuania		241			241
Luxemburg	315		38 109		38 424
Madagascar	5				5
Mexico	20				20
Netherlands		115 538			115 538
New Zealand	41 725				41 725
Newfoundland	43				43
Nigeria	2 000				2 000
Norway		65 370			65 370
Palestine	8 545				8 545
Poland	8 333	19 631	13 784		41 748
Portugal		5 159			5 159
Romania	5 000	5 597	6 743		17 340
South Africa	81 254		4 031		85 285
Spain	297				297
Sweden		301 654	479		302 133
Switzerland	1 132	339 922			341 054
Syria	61				61
Tunisia		1 346			1 346
Turkey	100				100
Uruguay			40		40
USA		500 153		635 300	1 135 453
Others		449			449
TOTAL	3 609 165	2 387 931	1 371 107	635 472	8 003 675

[The final total number of individual signatures received was over 12 million]

In addition to the individual signatures tabulated above, the Disarmament Committee of Women's International Organisations received petitions signed by organisations on behalf of their members from the following countries:

Argentina: collective petition signed by 1 200 organisations;
Bulgaria: petition signed by 212 organisations representing 663 000 people;
France: 360 610 collective signatures from the *Union Féminine pour la Société des Nations*;
Lithuania: resolutions adopted by 14 women's organisations;
Netherlands: petition from the Netherlands Association of Christian Women representing 4144 women;
Uruguay: collective signatures from 32 national organisations.

THE 'BUDAPEST' RESOLUTION

'General Resolution: Programme for Disarmament' passed at the XV Plenary Congress of the International Federation of League of Nations Societies

XV Plenary Congress,

Recalling the resolutions adopted at its previous Congresses,

Considering that the Council of the League of Nations has definitely convened the first Disarmament Conference for 2 February 1932,

Endorses the recommendation of the French delegate, M. Aristide Briand, according to which: 'Between now and the opening of the Conference a great propaganda effort must be undertaken to enlighten the mind of the public on this important question.'

Urges Societies to launch at once and to maintain without intermission until the opening of the Conference a methodical campaign with the public and their governments; and

Adopts as basis of it the following principles:

I. *The necessity of the Conference culminating in a positive result, viz. an International Convention*

In this connection should be recalled:

i) the definite, unconditional pledge given by Members of the League of Nations in Article 8 of the Covenant to reduce armaments within certain limits and thereafter not to exceed these without the concurrence of the Council;

ii) the formal promise given to the States disarmed under the Treaties that the exceptional regime applied to them is only a stepping stone to a general system of universal limitation and reduction;

iii) the opinions expressed by statesmen, economists, jurists, publicists regarding the mad race in armaments;

iv) the pronouncements of contemporary historians upon the extent to which this race was responsible for the last war;

v) the disastrous effect that a failure of the Conference would have on the peace of the world.

II. *Necessity for a substantial reduction in armaments*

Article 8 of the Covenant provides that the limits fixed for armaments in each country shall be 'the lowest consistent with national safety and the enforcement by common action of international obligations.'

 i) This safety is increased by the mere existence of the League of Nations, which, in ten years, has gained experience, affirmed its authority and perfected its organisation.
ii) Since 1924 it has been recognised by the Assembly of the League of Nations that progress in arbitration has generally implied progress in security. Moreover since 1928, the majority of the States have adhered to the Optional Clause of the Statute of the Permanent Court of International Justice; an increasing number have adhered, or announce their intention of adhering, to the General Act of Arbitration; special agreements of conciliation and arbitration have been multiplied.
iii) At Locarno, where special guarantees were given to certain States, it was expressly declared that the entry into vigour of the treaties and conventions there concluded would strengthen the peace and security of Europe and would effectively hasten the Disarmament envisaged in Article 8 of the Covenant.
iv) The outlawry of war was realised by the Paris Pact (Briand-Kellogg).
 v) A convention for financial assistance has been signed.

The situation is such as to justify even now a considerable reduction of armaments and the Federation esteems that apart from the reduction of personnel and material which should be effected, provided suitable proportions are laid down for the different States under the conditions mentioned in Section IV hereunder, the Conference should achieve an all-round reduction of 25% on the total amount budgeted for armaments.

III. *Development of the factors for more complete disarmament*

In order to facilitate still further reductions in armaments means should be sought to strengthen the mutual guarantees of security and loyal observance of the treaties, as, for instance,

 i) the universalisation of the League of Nations;
ii) the adherence of all States to the General Act of Arbitration, the complement of the Paris (Briand-Kellogg) Pact;

iii) the inclusion in the Covenant of the League of Nations of the definite prohibition to resort to war, subject to the general sanctions of the Covenant;

iv) the reinforcement of the action of the Council in preventing war and in defining aggression;

v) failing this general measure, the extension of the system of special guarantees by special agreements for guarantee and security;

vi) the international organisation of aviation, under the auspices of the League of Nations, in order to ensure to the Council the best means of communication and supervision;

vii) the prohibition of all preparation for chemical and bacteriological warfare;

viii) an advance in moral disarmament through the abandonment of bellicose or aggressive propaganda and the consideration by the League of Nations of measures appropriate to that end.

IV. *Advance towards international equality*

The International Federation of League of Nations Societies is convinced that it is indispensable that the League of Nations should officially recognise the principle of equality in disarmament between the 'vanquished' and 'the victorious' powers and that the 1932 Conference must begin to effect such equality.

This equality must not be attained by increasing armaments already reduced under the treaties but by the proportionate reduction of those of other States.

In any case, the Federation considers that the principle of limitation and reduction of armaments should be the same for all States and consequently, that:

i) each State should be bound to limit the amount budgeted for its navy, army and air force;

ii) the prohibition of certain material, naval, land, or air, enjoined in the treaties should apply to all States signatory to the Convention;

iii) the observance of the obligations thus contracted by the States should be ensured by a Permanent Disarmament Commission established at the seat of the League of Nations and exercising its control equally over all nations.

BIBLIOGRAPHY

1. Unpublished Primary Sources

France

Archives du Ministère des Affaires Étrangères, Paris
League of Nations Files: Series SDN: IH: Arbitration, Security, Disarmament
                         Series SDN: II: Disarmament
Official Correspondence: Series Y: International
Private Papers: Edouard Herriot
               Henry de Jouvenel
               Joseph Paul-Boncour
               André Tardieu

Archives Nationales, Paris
Edouard Daladier papers
Joseph Paul-Boncour papers
André Tardieu papers

Bibliothèque de Documentation Internationale Contemporaine, Nanterre
Gabrielle Duchêne papers
Ligue des Droits de l'Homme archives
Jules Prudhommeaux papers

Bibliothèque Nationale de France, Paris
Henry de Jouvenel manuscripts
Louise Weiss papers

Centre d'Histoire de Sciences Po, Paris
Pierre Cot papers

Service Historique de l'Armée de Terre, Vincennes
Conseil Supérieur de la Défense Nationale minutes

Netherlands

International Institute of Social History, Amsterdam
International Co-operative Alliance collection
International Federation of Trade Unions archives
International Fellowship of Reconciliation collection
Labour and Socialist International archives
Liaison Committee of Women's International Organisations archives

Switzerland

League of Nations Archives, Geneva
League of Nations Files: Disarmament Section
                         General
                         Information Section
                         International Bureaux and Intellectual Co-operation

Permanent Advisory Commission minutes
Temporary Mixed Commission minutes

Peace Group Archives: International Consultative Group
International Federation of League of Nations Societies
International Peace Bureau

Private Papers: Thanassis Aghnides
Erik Colban
Arthur Henderson
Laura Puffer Morgan
Nicolas Politis

World Union of Women for International Concord collection

Women's International League for Peace and Freedom, Geneva
Women's International League for Peace and Freedom archives (UMI microfilm)

World Council of Churches, Geneva
International Student Service archives
Universal Christian Council on Life and Work archives
World Alliance for Promoting International Friendship through the Churches archives
World Student Christian Federation archives

World's Young Men's Christian Association, Geneva
World's YMCA archives—Mueller correspondence

World's Young Women's Christian Association, Geneva
World's YWCA archives—Dingman correspondence

United Kingdom

Birmingham University Library
Austen Chamberlain papers

Bodleian Library, Oxford
Willoughby Dickinson papers
Gilbert Murray papers
Sir John Simon papers

British Library, London
Viscount Cecil of Chelwood papers
Marquess of Reading papers

British Library of Political and Economic Science, London
League of Nations Union archives
National Peace Council archives
Women's International League for Peace and Freedom archives

Brynmor Jones Library, Hull
International Co-operative Women's Guild archives

Cambridge University Library
Stanley Baldwin papers
Cordell Hull papers (microfilm from Library of Congress)

Churchill Archives Centre, Cambridge
Philip Noel Baker papers

National Archives, London
Cabinet & CID committees on disarmament minutes (CAB 16 & CAB 27)
Cabinet memoranda (CAB 24)
Cabinet minutes (CAB 23)
Committee of Imperial Defence (CID) minutes & memoranda (CAB 2 & CAB 4)
Foreign Office Confidential Print (FO 425)
Foreign Office General Correspondence (FO 371)
Private Papers: Austen Chamberlain
             Baron Cushendun
             Arthur Henderson
             James Ramsay MacDonald
             Sir John Simon

Vere Harmsworth Library, Oxford
Henry L. Stimson diaries (microfilm from Sterling Library, New Haven, CT)

Women's Library, London
Margery Corbett Ashby papers
Kathleen Courtney papers
International Alliance of Women for Suffrage and Equal Citizenship archives
Maude Royden papers

United States of America

Columbia University, New York, NY
League of Nations Association archives
James T. Shotwell papers

Hoover Institution, Stanford, CA
Hugh Gibson papers
Herbert Hoover papers

Hoover Presidential Library, West Branch, IA
Herbert Hoover papers
Hugh R. Wilson papers

Library of Congress, Washington, DC
Norman H. Davis papers

National Archives 2, College Park, MD
Department of State Decimal File, 1930–1939 (RG 59)

Roosevelt Presidential Library, Hyde Park, NY
Franklin D. Roosevelt papers

Swarthmore College Peace Collection, Swarthmore, PA
American Interorganization Council in Geneva files
Interorganization Council on Disarmament files
National Council for Prevention of War archives
Subject File: Disarmament—Disarmament Congresses: Conference for the Reduction
  and Limitation of Armaments, Geneva, 1932
Women's International League for Peace and Freedom archives

2. Published Primary Sources

Published Government Documents

Akten zur Deutschen Auswaertigen Politik
British Documents on Foreign Affairs
Conference for the Reduction of Armaments Plenary Meetings Verbatim Records
Conference for the Reduction and Limitation of Armaments Journal
Documents Diplomatiques Français
Documents on British Foreign Policy
Documents on German Foreign Policy
Documents of the Preparatory Commission for the Disarmament Conference
Hansard
Journal Officiel de la République Française
League of Nations Official Journal
Papers Relating to the Foreign Relations of the United States
Records of the League of Nations Assemblies

Periodicals

Bulletin of International Associations
Cahiers des Droits de l'Homme
Le Christianisme Social
CIAMAC Bulletin
Daily Herald
Disarmament
Essential News
L'Etude Socialiste
L'Europe Nouvelle
FIDAC: Interallied Review of the Five Continents
Foreign Affairs
Foreign Policy Association Information Service
Foreign Policy Association News Bulletin
Friedens-Warte
The Friend
Friendship
Headway
International Affairs
International Conciliation
International Co-operative Women's Guild Disarmament Information Bulletin
International Federation of League of Nations Societies Bulletin
International Federation of League of Nations Societies Disarmament Bulletin
International Information
The International Trade Union Movement
Journal des Nations
Labour and Socialist International Bulletin
Labour Magazine
League of Nations Chronicle
Le Mouvement Pacifiste
Nation (London and New York)
National Council for Prevention of War News Bulletin
New York Herald (Paris)
New York Times
La Paix par le Droit
Pax International

The Peace Review
The Peace Year Book
The Political Quarterly
Le Populaire
Pour la Paix et la Société des Nations
Problems of Peace
Quarterly Bulletin of the Work of International Organisations
Recovery
La Renaissance
Round Table
The Student World
The Times
Towards Disarmament
Voelkerbund
WILPF International Circular Letter
The World Outlook
World's YMCAs Bulletin on Disarmament
The World's Youth

Articles, Books and Pamphlets

Addams, Jane, *The Selected Papers of Jane Addams* (Urbana, IL, 2003)
Aigner, Lucien, *Nous désarmons: visions de la Conférence pour la Réduction et Limitation des Armements, Genève, 1932* (Geneva, 1932)
Allen, Lord Clifford, *Peace in Our Time* (London, 1936)
Angell, Sir Norman, *After All* (New York, 1951)
——, *The Foreigner's Turn to Disarm?* (London, 1931)
——, *The Great Illusion, 1933* (London, 1933)
——, 'Man Can Abolish War,' *Spectator*, 150. 1933, pp. 207–8
Anon., *Abruesten! Eine Vortragsdisposition* (Berlin, 1931)
——, *Germany demands universal disarmement* [sic] *in the name of her menaced security, in the name of justice, in the interest of true peace* (Amsterdam, 1932)
——, *Nous voulons la paix: concentration des efforts universels des forces pacifistes sous le haut patronage du Ministère des Affaires Étrangères. 1932* (Paris, 1932)
——, *World Airways—Why Not?* (London, 1934)
Arnold-Forster, Will, *The Disarmament Conference* (London, 1931)
——, *The Disarmament Crisis: Level Up or Level Down?* (London, 1933)
——, *The First Stage in Disarmament: A Commentary on the Continuing Programme of the Conference* (Geneva, 1932)
——, *How Should We Answer Hitler?* (London, 1933)
——, 'A Policy for the Disarmament Conference,' *The Political Quarterly*, 2/3, 1933, pp. 378–93
——, *Why Have We Failed to Disarm?* (London, 1927)
Association Française pour la Société des Nations, *Manifestation en l'honneur de la Société des Nations, 30 Janvier 1920* (Paris, 1920)
——, *Troisième Conférence Interalliée des Associations pour la Société des Nations* (Paris, 1920)
Bailey, Gerald, & F. W. Norwood, *SOS: The Disarmament Conference* (London, 1932)
Bartlett, Vernon, *What Disarmament Means* (London, 1930)
Batho, Edith C., *A Lamp of Friendship: A Short History of the International Federation of University Women, 1918–1968* (London, 1968)
Beaton, Grace M., *Twenty Years Work in the WRI* (Enfield, 1945)
Beneš, Edvard, *Le Dilemme Européen: la Guerre où la Paix* (Prague, 1932)
Berenstein, Alexandre, *Les Organisations Ouvrières, Leurs Compétences et Leur Rôle dans la Société des Nations* (Paris, 1936)

Blesch, J., 'Die Voelkerbundligen zur Abruestung,' *Staat seid Ihr*, 1, June 1931, pp. 248–9

Blum, Léon, 'French Socialism and Disarmament,' *Labour Magazine*, 9, January 1931, pp. 416–8

——, *L'oeuvre de Léon Blum* (Paris, 1954–1972)

——, *Peace and Disarmament* (London, 1932)

——, *Les problèmes de la paix* (Paris, 1931)

Bourgeois, Léon, *Discours prononcé à l'Assemblée Générale Constitutive du 10 Novembre 1918 par M. Léon Bourgeois* (Paris, 1918)

——, *L'Etat Actuel de la Société des Nations* (Paris, 1922)

——, *L'Oeuvre de la Société des Nations, 1920–1923* (Paris, 1923)

——, *Le Pacte de 1919 et la Société des Nations* (Paris, 1919)

Brailsford, Henry N., *The War of Steel and Gold* (London, 1917)

Briand, A., *Paroles de Paix* (Paris, 1931)

Brock, C. J. L., *Peace and Disarmament* (London, August 1928)

Brockway, A. Fenner, *The Bloody Traffic* (London, 1933)

——, *Can Britain Disarm?* (London, 1930)

Brouckère, Louis de, 'Les travaux de la Société des Nations en matière de désarmement,' *Académie de droit international, recueil de cours, 1928*, v. 5, pp. 369–446

Brown, Arthur Joseph, *Disarmament or Disaster? A review of the first phase of the Disarmament Conference and an indictment of the British government's policy* (London, 1932)

Buell, Raymond Leslie, *Isolated America* (New York, 1940)

——, *The Washington Conference* (New York, 1922)

Bullard, Arthur, *The A B C's of Disarmament and the Pacific Problems* (New York, 1921)

Bureau International de la Paix, *Bulletin Officiel du Troisième Congrès International de la Paix tenu à Rome, Novembre 1891* (Rome, 1891)

——, *Résolutions adoptées de 1843 à 1931 par les Congrès Universels de la Paix concernant le désarmement* (Geneva, 1931)

——, *Texte des resolutions adoptées par le XVIIIe Congrès Universel de la Paix (Bruxelles, 5–10 juillet 1931)—Désarmement* (Berne, 1931)

Butler, Nicholas Murray, *The Path to Peace* (New York, 1930)

Buxton, Charles Roden, *Labour's Work for Peace at Geneva* (London, 1924)

Carnegie Endowment for International Peace, *Carnegie Endowment for International Peace: Summary of Organization and Work, 1911–1941* (Washington, DC, 1941)

Cassin, René, *Les anciens combattants français et la Société des Nations* (Paris, 1925)

——, *Nobel Lecture* (http://www.nobel.se/peace/laureates/1968/cassin-lecture.html)

Cecil, R. A. T. G., *Disarmament and the League of Nations* (New York, 1923)

Cecil of Chelwood, Viscount Robert, *All the Way* (London, 1949)

——, 'The Conference Must Succeed,' *Nation*, 25 March 1931, pp. 319–20

——, *The Disarmament Conference: Speech* (London, 1932)

——, *Draft Treaty of Mutual Assistance, with an explanatory note by the Rt. Hon. Viscount Cecil* (London, 1924)

——, 'Facing the World Disarmament Conference,' *Foreign Affairs*, October 1931, pp. 13–22

——, *A Great Experiment* (London, 1941)

——, *A Letter to an MP on Disarmament* (London, 1931)

——, *Lord Cecil describes the work of the Preparatory Commission for the Disarmament Conference* (London, 1931)

——, *Peace and Pacifism* (London, 1938)

——, 'Public Opinion and Disarmament,' *Nation*, 3 January 1931, pp. 451–2

——, and Norman H. Davis, *Disarmament* (Worcester, MA, 1932)

Challaye, Félicien, *Pour la paix désarmée même en face d'Hitler* (Paris, 1933)

Chilton, C. B., *Believe It And Act, Or—Perish* (Geneva, 1933)

Chopine, Paul, *Six Ans chez les Croix de Feu* (Paris, 1935)

Churchill, Winston S., *Arms and the Covenant* (London, 1938)
——, *The Second World War: Volume 1: The Gathering Storm* (London, 1948)
Comité National d'Etudes Sociales et Politiques, *L'Etat Actuel du Problème du Désarmement* (Paris, 1929)
Commission de la Conférence Libre du Désarmement (ed.), *Pour un désarmement réelle. Compte-rendu de la conférence libre du désarmement tenue à Paris, les 23 et 24 avril 1932 sous la présidence de Félicien Challaye* (Levallois-Perret, 1932)
Conférence Internationale des Associations de Mutilés et Anciens Combattants and Fédération Interallié des Anciens Combattants, *Rassemblement International des Anciens Combattants et Victimes de la Guerre à Genève les 19 et 20 mars 1933* (Paris, 1933)
Corbett Ashby, Margery, *The Failure in Leadership at the Disarmament Conference* (London, 1935)
Cot, Pierre, 'Disarmament and French Public Opinion,' *Political Quarterly*, 2, July–September 1931, pp. 367–77
——, *Le Procès de la République* (New York, 1944)
Cushendun, Baron, 'Disarmament,' *International Affairs*, 7, March 1928, pp. 77–90
Daladier, Edouard, *The Defence of France* (London, 1939)
Davies, David, *Suicide or Sanity? An Examination of the Proposals before the Geneva Disarmament Conference. The Case for an International Police Force* (London, 1932)
Davis, Malcolm, 'Unofficial International Agitation,' *Recovery*, 1/11–12, 10 November 1933, pp. 9–10
——, 'Voicing the People's Arms Policy,' *Recovery*, 1/9, 13 October 1933, p. 14
Davis, Norman, *The Disarmament Problem* (New York, 1935)
Dawson, William Harbutt, *The Future of Empire and the World Price of Peace* (London, 1930)
Debeney, Général, *Sur la sécurité militaire de la France* (Paris, 1930)
Denvignes, Général, *La farce du désarmement* (Paris, 1930)
Detzer, Dorothy, *Appointment on the Hill* (New York, 1948)
Deutsche Liga fuer Voelkerbund, *Abruestungsvorschlaege der Deutschen Liga fuer Voelkerbund* (Berlin, 1926)
Dickinson, W. H., *Disarmament and a League of Nations* (London, 1918)
Disarmament Committee of the Women's International Organisations, *Documents Illustrative of the Activities of the Committee, 1931–1937* (Geneva, 1937)
——, *Official Record of the Declarations and Petitions presented by the Disarmament Committee of the Women's International Organisations to the Disarmament Conference, Geneva, February 6th, 1932* (Geneva, 1932)
——, *Peace and Disarmament Committee of the Women's International Organizations* (Geneva, 193–)
——, *Statement by the Disarmament Committee of the Women's International Organisations in relation to the Conference for the Reduction and Limitation of Armaments* (Washington, DC, 1931)
Disarmament Information Committee, *Disarmament in 1932* (Geneva, 1932)
Drevet, Camille, *Désarmons d'abord les Profiteurs de Guerre* (Geneva, 1932)
Drew, G. A., *Salesmen of Death* (Toronto, 1933)
Dupuy, Jean, *Désarmement et sécurité après 18 mois de conférence: action nationale et internationale des associations pour la Société des Nations* (Paris, 1933)
Eddy, Sherwood, *A Century with Youth* (New York, 1944)
Eichelberger, Clark, *Organizing for Peace: A Personal History of the Founding of the United Nations* (New York, 1977)
Einstein, Albert, 'The 1932 Disarmament Conference,' *Nation* (New York), 133, 23 September 1933, p. 300
Einzig, Paul, *The Economics of Rearmament* (London, 1934)
Engelbrecht, H. C., and F. C. Hanighen, *The Merchants of Death* (New York, 1934)
Enock, Arthur G., *The Problem of Armaments* (London, 1923)
——, *This War Business* (London, 1932)

Entr'Aide Universitaire Internationale, *Conférence des représentants des organisations internationales d'étudiants sur une action universitaire internationale en faveur du désarmement* (Geneva, 1931)

Eppstein, John (ed.), *Ten Years Life of the League of Nations* (London, 1929)

Europe Nouvelle, *Comment et pourquoi désarmer: avec le texte intégral du mémorandum français sur le désarmement* (Paris, 1931)

Fanshawe, Maurice, *World Disarmament: A Handbook on the Reduction and Limitation of Armaments* (London, 1931)

Federal Council of Churches of Christ in America, *Achievements of the Conference* (New York, 1922)

Fédération des Institutions Internationales Privées et Semi-Officielles avec Siège à Genève, *Fédération des Institutions Internationales Privées et Semi-Officielles avec Siège à Genève: Ses Buts et Son Activité* (Geneva, 1937)

Fédération Universitaire Internationale pour la Société des Nations, *Fédération Universitaire Internationale pour la Société des Nations: Principes essentiels des Statuts, Organisation, Activité* (Paris, 1930)

Ferlin, Charles R., *World Voices against War: A symposium of newspaper and magazine articles, addresses and statements à propos of international limitation of arms and the general Disarmament Conference* (London, 1931)

Fischer, Louis, *The Soviets in World Affairs* (London, 1930)

Friends' Peace Committee, *The Campaign for World Disarmament* (London, 1932)

——, *Germany and Disarmament* (London, 1932)

Forcart-Respinger, E., *À Côté de la Conférence du Désarmement* (Geneva, 1932)

Foreign Policy Association, *Protocol for the Pacific Settlement of International Disputes; Commentary on the Protocol prepared in collaboration with Dr. James T. Shotwell* (New York, October 1924)

——, *Text of the Draft Treaty of Disarmament and Security Prepared by an American Committee and Submitted Officially by the Council of the League of Nations to the Governments represented by it with a Commentary Prepared in Consultation with Dr. James T. Shotwell* (New York, June 1924)

Fox, Henry Watson, *The Religious Basis of World Peace* (London, 1929)

Freundlich, Emmy, *Hausfrauen Bauen Eine Neue Welt! Die Geschichte der nationalen und internationalen genossenschaftlichen Frauenbewegung* (Prague, 1935)

Fund to Continue the International Work of the Churches, *The Churches in Action for World Peace* (New York, n. d.)

Galpin, Perrin C. (ed.), *Hugh Gibson, 1883–1954: Extracts from his letters and anecdotes from his friends* (New York, 1973)

Gardes, André, *Le désarmement devant la Société des Nations* (Paris, 1929)

Gibberd, Katherine, *The League in Our Time* (Oxford, 1933)

Gibson, Hugh, *The Road to Foreign Policy* (Garden City, NY, 1944)

——, and Herbert Hoover, *The Problems of Lasting Peace* (Garden City, NY, 1943)

Glinberg, Aron, *Le problème du désarmement devant la Société des Nations et en dehors d'elle* (Paris, 1930)

Gooch, G. P., *In Pursuit of Peace* (London, 1933)

Hankey, Lord, *Diplomacy by Conference: Studies in Public Affairs, 1920–1946* (London, 1946)

Harris, Lilian, *Disarmament and Security* (London, n.d.)

——, *Notes on the Draft Disarmament Convention* (London, 1931)

Headlam-Morley, James, *A Memoir of the Paris Peace Conference, 1919* (London, 1972)

Heald, Stephen, *Memorandum on the Progress of Disarmament, 1919–1932* (London, 1932)

Henderson, Arthur, *Consolidating World Peace* (Oxford, 1931)

——, *Labour and the Geneva Protocol* (London, 1924)

——, *Labour's Peace Policy: Arbitration, Security, Disarmament* (London, 1934)

——, *The New Peace Plan* (London, 1924)

Herriot, Edouard, *Jadis: volume 2: d'une guerre à l'autre, 1914–1936* (Paris, 1952)

Hoetzsch, Otto, *Abruestung und Sicherheit* (Leipzig, 1932)

Hooker, Nancy Harvison (ed.), *The Moffat Papers: Selections from the Diplomatic Journals of Jay Pierrepont Moffat, 1919–1943* (Cambridge, MA, 1956)

Hoover, Herbert, *The Memoirs of Herbert Hoover, Volume Two: The Cabinet and the Presidency, 1920–1933* (London, 1952)

Hosono, Gunji, *Histoire du désarmement* (Paris, 1933)

House, Edward M., and Charles Seymour (eds.), *What Really Happened at Paris: The Story of the Peace Conference, 1918–1919, by American Delegates* (London, 1921)

Hull, Cordell, *The Memoirs of Cordell Hull* (New York, 1948)

Ingram, A. Kenneth, *50 Years of the National Peace Council* (London, 1958)

Innes, G. A., *Disarmament: The Question of the Day* (London, 1931)

International Consultative Group for Peace and Disarmament, *The Draft Disarmament Convention: A Synthesis of Conference Decisions* (Geneva, 1932)

——, *The International Consultative Group (for Peace and Disarmament): Its Origins, Aims and Development* (Geneva, 1937)

International Council of Women, *The Prevention of the Causes of War: Addresses delivered at the Conference held at the British Empire Exhibition, Wembley, May 2nd to 8th, 1924* (London, 1924)

——, *Women in a Changing World: The Dynamic Story of the International Council of Women since 1888* (London, 1966)

International Federation of League of Nations Societies, *Disarmament: Notes for Speakers* (Brussels, 1932)

——, *Plenary Congress Proceedings and Resolutions* (Brussels and Geneva, 1925–34)

International Federation of Trade Unions, *Report of the International Peace Congress held at the Hague under the auspices of the International Federation of Trade Unions, December 10–15, 1922* (Amsterdam, 1923)

——, *Report on Activities* (1919–21, 1924–6, 1927–30, 1930–2, 1933–5)

International Federation of University Women, *Report of the Fifth Conference, Geneva, August 7 to August 14, 1929* (London, 1929)

International Fellowship of Reconciliation, *Immediate International Issues* (Vienna, 1931)

——, *The International Fellowship of Reconciliation: Looking Towards 1932* (Vienna, 1931)

International Institute of Intellectual Co-operation, *Les associations internationales d'étudiants* (Paris, 1931)

International Student Service, *The Right to Think: International Student Service—What it has done, is doing and must do* (Geneva, [1943])

Internationale Ouvrière Socialiste, *Le mouvement ouvrier international et le désarmement: décisions de la conférence commune de l'Internationale Ouvrière Socialiste et de la Fédération Syndicale Internationale pour le désarmement, Zurich, les 22 et 23 mai, 1932* (Zurich, 1932)

Inter-Parliamentary Union, *The Inter-Parliamentary Union, 1889–1939* (Geneva, 1939)

——, *The Inter-Parliamentary Union: Its Work and Organisation*, third edition (Geneva, 1930)

Jacobs, Ida T., and John J. DeBoer (eds.), *Educating for Peace: A Report of the Committee on International Relations of the National Council of Teachers of English* (New York, 1940)

Johnsen, Julia E., *Disarmament* (New York, 1930)

——, *Selected Articles on National Defence* (New York, 1928)

Jouhaux, Léon, *Le Désarmement* (Paris, 1927)

Jouvenel, Henry de, *La paix française: témoignage d'une génération* (Paris, 1932)

——, *La Position de la France dans la question du désarmement* (Bordeaux, 1931)

Kautsky, Benedikt, *Reparationen und Ruestungen* (Vienna, 1931)

Kirchoff, Dr. Herman, *Wirkliche Abruestung* (Berlin, 1931)

Kirk, Walter van, and Sidney L. Gulick, *Churches and the World Disarmament Conference. Factual Material and Questions for Discussion* (New York, 1931)

Kohut, Rebekah, *Jewish Women's Organizations in the United States* (New York, 1931)

———, *More Yesterdays: An Autobiography* (New York, 1950)

Labour and Socialist International, *The Disarmament Problem in the League of Nations: Memorandum on the Present Position adopted by the Executive of the Labour and Socialist International at its Meeting in Berlin, May 11–13, 1930* (Zurich, [1930])

———, *Reports and Proceedings of the Congresses of the Labour and Socialist International* (Zurich, 1925, 1928, 1932)

Labour Party, *Disarm?* (London, 1931)

———, *Disarm! Disarm! Disarm! World Labour's Demands to the Disarmament Conference* (London, 1931)

———, *'National' Government's Disarmament Record* (London, 1935)

Lamb, Beatrice Pitney, *Disarmament and the World Conference of 1932* (New York, 1931)

Lange, Christian L., *La Société des Nations et le problème des armements* (Copenhagen, 1924)

Lansing, Robert, *The Peace Negotiations: A Personal Narrative* (London, 1921)

Latané, John Holladay, *Development of the League of Nations Idea: Documents and Correspondence of Theodore Marburg* (New York, 1932)

Lavallaz, M. de, *Essai sur le désarmement et le Pacte de la Société des Nations* (Paris, 1926)

Lawrence, Martin, *The Soviet Union and Peace* (London, 1930)

League of Nations, *Handbook of International Organisations* (Geneva, 1929)

———, *Preliminary Report of the Work of the Conference for the Reduction and Limitation of Armaments* (Geneva, 1936)

League of Nations Association, *Disarmament* (New York, 1931)

League of Nations Library, *Annotated Bibliography on Disarmament and Military Questions* (Geneva, 1931)

League of Nations Union, *Armaments Can Be Reduced* (London, 1921)

———, *Armaments: Their Reduction and Limitation* (London, October 1926)

———, *Arms and the Churches* (London, 1931)

———, *Arms and the People* (London, 1931)

———, *The Churches' Call for International Disarmament* (London, January 1932)

———, *Disarmament* (London, February 1927)

———, *The Effect of National Armament upon the People's Life and Work* (London, 1927)

———, *Final Report of the Committee on Limitation of Armaments* (London, 1921)

———, *The League, Manchuria and Disarmament* (London, December 1931)

———, *The National Disarmament Demonstration of July 11, 1931, to promote the success of the World Disarmament Conference* (London, July 1931)

———, *Speakers' Notes on International Disarmament* (London, 1927)

Lefebure, Victor, *Common Sense about Disarmament* (London, 1932)

———, *Scientific Disarmament* (London, 1931)

Lehmann-Russbueldt, Otto, *Denkschrift zum Reparations- und Abruestungsproblem auf der Deutschen Liga fuer Menschenrecht* (Berlin, 1932)

Libby, Frederick, *To End War: The Story of the National Council for Prevention of War* (Nyack, NY, 1969)

Liddell Hart, B. H., *The Memoirs of Captain Liddell Hart*, volume one (London, 1965)

Ligt, Barthélemy de, *La paix créatrice: histoire des principes et des tactiques de l'action directe contre la guerre* (Paris, 1934)

Link, Arthur Stanley (ed.), *The Papers of Woodrow Wilson* (Princeton, NJ, 1966)

Lloyd George, David, *Memoirs of the Peace Conference* (New Haven, CT, 1939)

Lutz, George, *Où en est la Fédération universitaire internationale pour la S.d.N.?* (Paris, 1934)

Lyon, Jacques, *Les problèmes du désarmement* (Paris, 1931)

MacDonald, Ramsay, Stanley Baldwin and David Lloyd George, *We Want Disarmament All Round* (London, 1931)

Madariaga, Salvador de, *Disarmament: Obstacles, Results, Prospects* (London, 1929)

———, *Morning Without Noon: Memoirs* (Westmead, 1973)

Mantoux, Paul, *Le désarmement et l'opinion internationale* (Paris, 1932)
Margueritte, Victor, *La patrie humaine* (Paris, 1931)
Martin, William, *Disarmament and the Inter-Parliamentary Union* (Lausanne, 1931)
McDonald, James G., *My Mission in Israel* (New York, 1951)
Merriman, Christina, *The Significance of Locarno* (New York, 1925)
Miller, David Hunter, *My Diary at the Conference of Paris, with documents* (New York, 1924)
Moley, Raymond, *After Seven Years* (London, 1939)
Monteilhet, J., *La Paix par le Désarmement* (Paris, 1933)
Morgan, Laura Puffer, *The Background of the London Naval Conference, with Comparative Statistics on the Five Navies Illustrated by Tables and Charts* (Washington, DC, 1930)
——, 'Disarmament,' in Harriet Eager Davis (ed.), *Pioneers in World Order: An American Appraisal of the League of Nations* (New York, 1944)
——, *The Issues of the General Disarmament Conference. What should be the position of the United States?* (Washington, DC, 1931)
——, *A Possible Technique of Disarmament Control: Lessons from League of Nations Experience in Drug Control* (Geneva, 1940)
Morrison, Charles Clayton, *The Outlawry of War* (Chicago, IL, 1927)
Mott, John R., *The World Student Christian Federation: Origin, Achievement, Forecast* (London, 1920)
Murray, Gilbert, *An Unfinished Autobiography with Contributions by his Friends* (London, 1960)
——, *The League of Nations Movement: Some Recollections of the Early Days* (London, 1955)
Myers, Denys Peter, *World Disarmament: Its Problems and Prospects* (Boston, MA, 1932)
Naidoo, Kumi, *Reflections on the G8 Summit*, (http://www.whiteband.org/specialIssues/G8/gcapnews.2005-07-14.5388032995/en)
National Committee on the Cause and Cure of War, *Findings of the Conference on the Cause and Cure of War held in Washington, DC, January 18–24 1925* (Washington, DC, 1925)
——, *The National Committee on the Cause and Cure of War: Origins, Aims, Program* (New York, 1931)
——, *Proceedings of the Conference on the Cause and Cure of War* (Washington, DC, 1928, 1929, 1930)
National Council for the Limitation of Armaments, *National Council for the Limitation of Armaments* (Washington, DC, 6 December 1921)
National Council for Prevention of War (UK), *Disarmament and the World Conference of 1932* (London, 1931)
——, *Ourselves and Disarmament* (London, 1931)
National Council for Prevention of War (USA), *It Depends on Public Opinion whether the Disarmament Conference Succeeds or Fails* (Washington, DC, 1931)
——, *Peace Resolutions of Women's Organizations, Covering 1930–31–32 and the First Quarter of 1933* (Washington, DC, 1933)
——, *Resolutions in Support of International Reduction of Armaments* (Washington, DC, 1931)
——, *What are you doing for Disarmament?* (Washington, DC, 1931)
National Peace Council, *Disarmament: Britain Must Give a Lead* (London, 1922)
——, *1932—A Vital Year* (London, 1932)
——, *The Problem of Disarmament* (London, 1921)
New Commonwealth, *The Aims and Objects of the New Commonwealth* (London, 1932)
No More War Movement, *Conservatives and Disarmament* (London, 1929)
——, *No More War and Universal Disarmament Demonstrations* (London, July 1923)
——, *Your Country is in Danger* (London, 1932)
Nobs, Marguerite, *Étapes vers la Paix: Un Effort Féminin* (Geneva, 1960)

Noel Baker, Philip, *The Arms Race: A Programme for World Disarmament* (London, 1958)
——, *Challenge to Death* (London, 1934)
——, 'Disarmament,' *International Affairs*, January–February 1934, pp. 3–25
——, *Disarmament* (London, 1926)
——, *Disarmament and the Coolidge Conference* (London, 1927)
——, *The First World Disarmament Conference, 1932–1934, And Why It Failed* (Oxford, 1979)
——, *The Geneva Protocol for the Pacific Settlement of International Disputes* (London, 1925)
——, *The Private Manufacture of Armaments* (New York, 1937)
——, *War in the Air?* (London, 1933)
Nollet, General Charles, *Une Expérience de désarmement* (1932)
Northcroft, D. M., *Women at Work in the League of Nations* (Wadsworth, 1926)
Oertzen, K. L. von, *Abruestung oder Kriegsvorbereitung?* (Berlin, 1931)
Oertzen, P. W. von, *Das ist die Abruestung!* (Oldenburg, 1931)
Office Central de la Confédération Internationale des Etudiants, *Annuaire 1931* (Brussels, 1931)
Paul-Boncour, Joseph, *Entre-Deux Guerres* (Paris, 1945–7)
Petit Parisien, *Les instructions secrètes de la propagande allemande: texte complet des documents confidentiels* (Paris, 1933)
Philip, André, *Sécurité et Désarmement* (Paris, 1932)
Pichot, H., *Les combattants avaient raison* (Paris, 1940)
Pickard, Bertram, *The Greater League of Nations: A Brief Survey of the Nature and Development of Unofficial International Organisations* ([Zurich], 1936)
——, 'Pre-UN Contacts between INGOs and Intergovernmental Organizations,' *Transnational Associations*, 9, 1955, pp. 575–81
Politis, Nicolas, *The Problem of Disarmament* (Worcester, MA, 1934)
Ponsonby, Lord Arthur, *Disarmament: A Discussion* (London, 1932)
——, *Disarmament By Example* (London, 1927)
Puech, J.-L., *La tradition socialiste en France et la Société des Nations* (Paris, 1923)
Quidde, Ludwig, *Der erste Schritt zur Weltabruestung* (Berlin, 1927)
Ramel, Frédéric (ed.), *Philosophie des Relations Internationales* (Paris, 2002)
Rappard, William E., *International Relations as Viewed From Geneva* (New Haven, CT, 1925)
——, *Uniting Europe: The Trend of International Cooperation Since the War* (New Haven, CT, 1930)
Reely, M. K., *Selected Articles on Disarmament* (New York, 1921)
Reiss, Hans (ed.), *Kant: Political Writings* (Cambridge, 1991)
Réquin, Edouard, *D'une guerre à l'autre, 1919–1939: souvenirs* (Paris, 1949)
——, *La Société des Nations* (Paris, 1923)
——, 'Traité d'assistance mutuelle et réduction des armements,' *Revue militaire française*, 93, 19 November 1923, pp. 226–237
Rheinbaben, Werner Frhr. von, *Genfer Abruestungskonferenz—und was nun? Der deutsche Kampf um Abruestung und Gleichberechtigung* (Berlin, 1932)
Rolin, Henri, *Abruestung: Rede von Henri Rolin* (Glarus, 1931)
Romains, Jules, *Cela dépend de vous* (Paris, 1939)
Ruyssen, Théodore, *Is Unofficial International Collaboration passing through a Crisis?* (Geneva, 1939)
——, 'Le mémorandum français sur le désarmement,' *Cahiers des Droits de l'Homme*, 31/22, 30 August–10 September 1931, pp. 508–10
Saint-Aulaire, Auguste, *Genève contre la Paix* (Paris, 1936)
Salter, Arthur, *Memoirs of a Public Servant* (London, 1961)
——, *Slave of the Lamp: A Public Servant's Notebook* (London, 1967)
Sassenbach, Johann, *Twenty-Five Years of International Trade Unionism* (Amsterdam, 1926)

Schaer, Wilhelm, *Development of the disarmament deliberations from the beginning of the Conference to the end of 1932* (Berlin, 1933)

Schevenels, Walther, *Forty-Five Years: International Federation of Trade Unions: A Historical Précis* (Brussels, 1945)

Schmidt, Richard, *Disarmament and Equal Rights* (Berlin, 1934)

Schreiber, Dr. Georg, *Christentum und Abruestung* (Cologne, 1932)

Schuecking, Walther, *Das Abruestungsproblem. Vortrag* (Berlin, 1932)

Schwendemann, K., *Abruestung und Sicherheit: Handbuch der Sicherheitsfrage und der Abruestungskonferenz* (Leipzig, 1933)

Scott, James Brown, 'Disarmament through International Organization,' *Annals of the American Academy of Political and Social Science*, 126, 1926, pp. 146–50

Sée, Henri, *Histoire de la Ligue des Droits de l'Homme, 1898–1926* (Paris, 1927)

Shillock, John C., Jr., 'The Postwar Movements to Reduce Naval Armaments,' *International Conciliation*, 245, 1928, pp. 9–92

Shotwell, James T., *Arms and the World: Problems that a Conference must Face* (New York, 1926)

——, *At the Paris Peace Conference* (New York, 1937)

——, *The Autobiography of James T. Shotwell* (Indianapolis, 1961)

——, *Commentary on the Protocol* (New York, 1924)

——, *On the Rim of the Abyss* (New York, 1936)

——, *War as an Instrument of National Policy and its Renunciation in the Pact of Paris* (New York, 1929)

Simon, Viscount John Allsebrook, *Retrospect* (London, 1952)

Smith, Rennie, *General Disarmament or War?* (London, 1927)

Spaull, Hebe, *Women Peace-Makers* (London, 1924)

Stimson, Henry L., *The Pact of Paris: Three Years of Development [Department of State Publication No. 357]* (Washington, DC, 1932)

——, and McGeorge Bundy, *On Active Service in Peace and War* (New York, 1947)

Suttner, Bertha von, *Die Haager Friedenskonferenz: Tagebuchblaetter* (Dresden, 1900)

——, *Memoirs* (London, 1910)

Swanwick, H. M., *I Have Been Young* (London 1935)

Tatlow, Tissington, *The Story of the Student Christian Movement in Great Britain and Ireland* (London, 1933)

Temperley, Major-General Arthur Cecil, *The Whispering Gallery of Europe* (London, 1938)

Temple, William, *Sermon on the Occasion of the Disarmament Conference* (London, 1933)

Trade Union Congress General Council, *Disarm!* (London, 1934)

Union of Democratic Control, *Patriotism Ltd.: An Exposure of the War Machine* (London, 1933)

——, *The Secret International: Armament Firms At Work* (London, 1932)

Union of Soviet Socialist Republics, *The Soviet Union and Peace* (London, 1929)

Union of Soviet Socialist Republics Delegation to the Disarmament Conference, *L'URSS et le désarmement* (Paris, 1928)

United States Department of State, *Peace and War: United States Foreign Policy, 1931–1941* (Washington, DC, 1943)

Vandervelde, Emile, 'Belgian socialism and disarmament,' *Labour magazine*, 9, January 1931, pp. 419–21

——, *Souvenirs d'un militant socialiste* (Paris, 1939)

Vansittart, Baron Robert Gilbert, *The Mist Procession: The Autobiography of Lord Vansittart* (London, 1958)

Vernet, Madeleine, *De l'objection de conscience au Désarmement* (Paris, 1928)

Viala, Léon, *Les relations internationales entre les associations de mutilés de guerre et d'anciens combattants* (Paris, 1939)

Visser 't Hooft, W. A., *Students Find the Truth to Serve: The Story of the World's Student Christian Federation, 1930–1935* (Geneva, 1935)

Voigt, F. A., *Unto Caesar!* (London, 1938)

Vox Populi Committee, *Vox Populi* (Geneva, 1932)

Waldman, Seymour, *Death and Profits* (New York, 1932)

Wehberg, Hans, *The Limitation of Armaments: A Collection of the Projects Proposed for the Solution of the Problem, Preceded by an Historical Introduction* (Washington, DC, 1921)

Weiss, Louise, *Mémoires d'une Européenne, tome 2: 1919–1934* (Paris, 1970)

Weygand, *Mémoires: Mirages et Réalité* (Paris, 1957)

White, Andrew D., *Autobiography*, volume two (London, 1905)

Williams, Benjamin H., *The United States and Disarmament* (New York, 1931)

Wilson, Hugh R., *Diplomat Between Wars* (New York, 1941)

——, *Disarmament and the Cold War in the Thirties* (New York, 1963)

Women's International League (UK), *The Draft Treaty of Mutual Assistance* (London, 1924)

Women's International League for Peace and Freedom, *Report of the International Congress of Women, The Hague, April 28th to May 1st 1915* (Chicago, IL, 1915)

——, *Women's International League for Peace and Freedom, 1915–1938: A Venture in Internationalism* (Geneva, 1938)

Women's Peace Crusade, *Women and Disarmament: The Deputation of American, British, French and Japanese Women received by the Chairman of the London Naval Conference at St. James' Palace on February 6th 1930* (London, 1930)

Woolf, Leonard (ed.), *The Intelligent Man's Way to Prevent War* (London, 1933)

Woolley, Mary E., *Internationalism and Disarmament: An Address Given at the Kappa Delta Pi Dinner, February 27, 1934, enlarged and brought up to January 13, 1935* (New York, 1935)

World Peace Foundation, *The Staggering Burden of Armament* (Boston, MA, April 1921)

World Union of Women for International Concord, *The World Union of Women for International Concord* (Geneva, 1915)

World's Alliance of YWCAs, *Report by the General Secretary on the Work of the Executive Committee, June 1930—June 1934* (Geneva, 1934)

Zangwill, Edith, *The Story of the Disarmament Declaration* (London, 1932)

3. Secondary Sources

Articles

Altbach, Philip G., 'The International Student Movement,' *Journal of Contemporary History*, 5/1, 1970, pp. 156–74

Anderson, Kenneth, 'The Ottawa Convention Banning Landmines, the Role of International Non-Governmental Organizations and the Idea of International Civil Society,' *European Journal of International Law*, 11/1, 2000, pp. 91–120

Bariéty, Jacques, 'Les relations internationales en 1932–33: documents français: études étrangères,' *Revue Historique*, 238/2, 1967, pp. 347–64

Betsill, Michele M., and Elisabeth Corell, 'NGO Influence in International Environment Negotiations: A Framework for Analysis,' *Global Environmental Politics*, 1/4, 2001, pp. 65–85

Bettez, David J., 'Unfulfilled Initiative: Disarmament Negotiations and the Hague Peace Conferences of 1899 and 1907,' *RUSI Journal*, 133/3, 1988, pp. 57–62

Blair, Scott G., 'Les Origines en France de la SDN: La Commission Interministérielle d'Etudes pour la Société des Nations, 1917–1919,' *Relations Internationales*, 75, 1993, pp. 277–92

Bouchard, Carl, 'Le "Plan Américain" Shotwell-Bliss de 1924: une initiative méconnue pour le renforcement de la paix,' *Guerres Mondiales et Conflits Contemporains*, 202–203, 2002, pp. 203–225

Bull, Hedley, 'International Theory: The Case for a Classical Approach,' *World Politics*, 18, 1966, pp. 361–77

Burns, Richard Dean, 'On Power and Purpose,' *Review of Politics*, 26/4, 1964, pp. 558–62

Burroughs, John, and Jacqueline Cabasso, 'Confronting the Nuclear Armed States in International Negotiating Forums: Lessons for NGOs,' *International Negotiation*, 4/3, 1999, pp. 459–82

Carette, Gabriel, 'La Force internationale de police dans le cadre de la Société des Nations: Concepts et réalités au seuil des années vingt,' *Relations Internationales*, 75, 1993, pp. 293–300

Carlton, David, 'Disarmament with Guarantees: Lord Cecil, 1922–1927,' *Disarmament and Arms Control*, 3/2, 1965, pp. 143–64

Ceadel, Martin, 'Interpreting East Fulham,' in Chris Cook and James Ramsden (eds.), *By-Elections in British Politics*, second edition (London, 1997), pp. 94–111

Chapman, Jennifer, 'What Makes International Campaigns Effective? Lessons from India and Ghana,' in Michael Edwards and John Gaventa (eds.), *Global Citizen Action* (London, 2001), pp. 259–73

Charnovitz, Steve, 'Two Centuries of Participation: NGOs and International Governance,' *Michigan Journal of International Law*, 18/2, 1997, pp. 183–286

Chatfield, Charles, 'Intergovernmental and Nongovernmental Associations to 1945' in Jackie Smith, Charles Chatfield and Ron Pagnucco (eds.), *Transnational Social Movements and World Politics: Solidarity Beyond the State* (Syracuse, NY, 1997), pp. 19–41

Clark, Ann Marie, 'Non-Governmental Organizations and their Influence on International Society,' *Journal of International Affairs*, 48/2, 1995, pp. 507–25

——, Elisabeth J. Friedman, and Kathryn Hochstetler, 'The Sovereign Limits of Global Civil Society: A Comparison of NGO Participation in UN World Conferences on the Environment, Human Rights, and Women,' *World Politics*, 51/1, 1998, pp. 1–35

Cohen, Cynthia P., 'The Role of Nongovernmental Organizations in the Drafting of the Convention on the Rights of the Child,' *Human Rights Quarterly*, 12, 1990, pp. 137–47

Cortright, David, and Ron Pagnucco, 'Limits to Transnationalism: *The 1980s Freeze Campaign*' in Jackie Smith, Charles Chatfield and Ron Pagnucco (eds.), *Transnational Social Movements and World Politics: Solidarity Beyond the State* (Syracuse, NY, 1997), pp. 159–74

Davies, Thomas R., 'France and the World Disarmament Conference of 1932–34,' *Diplomacy & Statecraft*, 15/4, 2004, pp. 765–780

DeBenedetti, Charles, 'The Origins of Neutrality Revision: The American Plan of 1924,' *The Historian*, 35, 1972, pp. 75–89

Deist, Wilhelm, 'Bruening, Herriot und die Abruestungsgespraeche von Bessinge 1932,' *Vierteljahrshefte fuer Zeitgeschichte*, 5/3, 1957, pp. 265–72

——, 'Schleicher und die Deutsche Abruestungspolitik im Juni/Juli 1932,' *Vierteljahrshefte fuer Zeitgeschichte*, 7/2, 1959, pp. 163–76

Divine, Robert A., 'Franklin D. Roosevelt and Collective Security, 1933,' *Mississippi Valley Historical Review*, 48/1, 1961, pp. 42–59

Duelffer, Jost, 'Efforts to Reform the International System and Peace Movements before 1914,' *Peace & Change*, 14/1, 1989, pp. 25–45

Eckstein, Harry, 'Case Study and Theory in Political Science,' in Fred I. Greenstein and Nelson W. Polsby (eds.), *Handbook of Political Science*, volume 7, *Strategies of Inquiry* (Reading, MA, 1975), pp. 79–138

Ehrick, Christine, '*Madrinas* and Missionaries: Uruguay and the Pan-American Women's Movement,' *Gender & History*, 10/3, 1998, pp. 406–24

Falnes, Oscar J., 'Christian Lange and his Work for Peace,' *American Scandinavian Review*, 57, 1969, pp. 226–74

Fanning, Richard W., 'Peace Groups and the Campaign for Naval Disamament, 1927–1936,' *Peace & Change*, 15/1, 1990, pp 26–45

Finnemore, Martha, and Sikkink, Kathryn, 'International Norm Dynamics and Political Change,' *International Organization*, 52/4, 1998, pp. 887–917

Ford, Thomas K., 'The Genesis of the First Hague Peace Conference,' *Political Science Quarterly*, 51/3, 1936, pp. 354–82

Gibbs, Norman, 'The Naval Conferences of the Interwar Years,' *Naval War College Review*, 30, 1977, pp. 50–63

Grossi, Verdiana, 'Une Paix Difficile: Le Mouvement Pacifiste International pendant l'Entre-Deux Guerres,' *Relations Internationales*, 70, 1988, pp. 23–35

Haywood Hunt, H., 'Edouard Daladier and French Foreign Policy in 1933: From the Disarmament Conference to the Four Power Pact,' *Proceedings of the Annual Meeting of the Western Society for French History*, 7, 1979, pp. 162–72

Hermon, Elly, 'Le désarmement moral, facteur dans les relations internationales pendant l'entre-deux-guerres,' *Guerres Mondiales et Conflits Contemporains*, 39/156, 1989, pp. 23–36

Howlett, Charles F., 'Nicholas Murray Butler and the American Peace Movement,' *Teachers College Record*, 85/2, 1983, pp. 291–313

Huntington, Samuel P., 'Transnational Organizations in World Politics,' *World Politics*, 25, 1973, pp. 333–68

Hyman, Richard, 'The International Labour Movement on the Threshold of Two Centuries: Agitation, Organisation, Bureaucracy, Diplomacy,' (http://www.arbarkiv. nu/pdf_wrd/Hyman_int.pdf)

Jablon, Howard, 'The State Department and Collective Security, 1933–34,' *Historian*, 33/2, 1971, pp. 248–63

Jackson, Peter, 'France and the Problems of Security and Disarmament after the First World War,' *The Journal of Strategic Studies*, 29/2, 2006, pp. 247–280

Jenkins, Julia, 'A Forgotten Challenge to German Nationalism: The World Alliance for International Friendship through the Churches,' *Australian Journal of Politics and History*, 37/2, 1991, pp. 286–301

Kaetzel, Ute, 'A Radical Women's Rights and Peace Activist: Margarethe Lenore Selenka, Initiator of the First Worldwide Women's Peace Demonstration in 1899,' *Journal of Women's History*, 13/3, 2001, pp. 46–69

Kaldor, Mary, 'Global Civil Society,' in David Held and Anthony McGrew (eds.), *The Global Transformations Reader: An Introduction to the Globalization Debate*, second edition (Cambridge, 2003), pp. 559–63

Kennedy, Gregory C., 'Britain's Policy-Making Elite, the Naval Disarmament Puzzle, and Public Opinion, 1927–1932,' *Albion*, 26/4, 1994, pp. 623–43

Kircheneisen, Peter, 'Zwischen Landesverteidigung und Pazifismus: Die Sozialistische Arbeiter Internationale zur Frage Krieg und Frieden,' *Martin-Luther-Universitaet Halle-Wittenberg. Wissenschaftliche Zeitschrift. Gesellschafts- und Sprachwissenschaftliche Reihe*, 25/5, 1976, pp. 95–105

Krull, Catherine, and B. J. C. McKercher, 'The Press, Public Opinion, Arms Limitation, and Government Policy in Britain, 1932–34: Some Preliminary Observations,' *Diplomacy and Statecraft*, 13/3, 2002, pp. 103–36

Kuehl, Warren F., 'Internationalism and Peace,' in Otis L. Graham, Jr., and Meghan Robinson Wander (eds.), *Franklin D. Roosevelt: His Life and Times* (1985), pp. 205–8

Lipschutz, Ronnie, 'Reconstructing World Politics,' *Millennium*, 21, 1992, pp. 389–420

Lloyd, Lorna, 'Le règlement pacifique des conflits,' *Etudes Internationales*, 31/4, 2000, pp. 709–726

———, 'Le Sénateur Dandurand, pionnier du règlement pacifique des différends,' *Etudes Internationales*, 23/3, 1992, pp. 581–606

Lynch, Cecelia, 'A Matter of Controversy: The Peace Movement and British Arms Policy in the Interwar Period' in B. J. C. McKercher (ed.), *Arms Limitation and Disarmament: Restraints on War, 1899–1939* (Westport, CT, 1992), pp. 61–82

Malanowski, Wolfgang, 'Die Deutsche Politik der Militaerischen Gleichberechtigung: von Bruening bis Hitler,' *Wehrwissenschaftliche Rundschau*, 5/8, 1955, pp. 351–64

Martens, Kerstin, 'NGO Participation at International Conferences: Assessing Theoretical Accounts,' *Transnational Associations*, 3, 2000, pp. 115–27

Matthews, Jessica T., 'Power Shift: The Rise of Global Civil Society,' *Foreign Affairs*, 76/1, 1997, pp. 50–66

McCarthy, John D., 'The Globalization of Social Movement Theory,' in Jackie Smith, Charles Chatfield and Ron Pagnucco (eds.), *Transnational Social Movements and World Politics: Solidarity Beyond the State* (Syracuse, NY, 1997), pp. 243–59

McKercher, B. J. C., 'Of Horns and Teeth: The Preparatory Commission and the World Disarmament Conference, 1926–1934' in B. J. C. McKercher (ed.), *Arms Limitation and Disarmament: Restraints on War, 1899–1939* (Westport, CT, 1992), pp. 173–201

Mechoulan, Eric, 'L'incompréhension diplomatique franco-américaine, 1932–1933,' *Revue d'Histoire Moderne et Contemporaine*, 42/4, 1995, pp. 577–92

Mekata, Motoko, 'Building Partnerships toward a Common Goal: Experiences of the International Campaign to Ban Landmines' in Ann M. Florini (ed.), *The Third Force: The Rise of Transnational Civil Society* (Tokyo, 2000), pp. 143–76

Miller, Carol, '"Geneva—the Key to Equality:" Interwar Feminists and the League of Nations,' *Women's History Review*, 3/2, 1994, pp. 219–45

Miller, Robert Moats, 'The Attitudes of the Major Protestant Churches of America towards War and Peace, 1929–1939,' *The Historian*, 19, 1956, pp. 13–38

Morrill, Dan L., 'Nicholas II and the Call for the First Hague Conference,' *Journal of Modern History*, 46/2, 1974, pp. 296–313

Morris, A. J. A., 'The English Radicals' Campaign for Disarmament and the Hague Conference of 1907,' *Journal of Modern History*, 43/3, 1971, pp. 367–93

Naquet, Emmanuel, 'Éléments pour l'étude d'une génération pacifiste dans l'entre-deux-guerres: La LAURS et le rapprochement franco-allemand (1924–1933),' *Matériaux pour l'Histoire de Notre Temps*, 18, 1990, pp. 50–8

Perkins, Dexter, 'The Department of State and American Public Opinion' in Gordon A. Craig and Felix Gilbert (eds.), *The Diplomats, 1919–1939* (Princeton, NJ, 1953), pp. 282–308

Piper, Nicola, and Anders Uhlin, 'New Perspectives on Transnational Activism' in Nicola Piper and Anders Uhlin (eds.), *Transnational Activism in Asia: Problems of Power and Democracy* (London, 2004), pp. 1–25

Price, Richard, 'Reversing the Gun Sights: Transnational Civil Society Targets Landmines,' *International Organization*, 52/3, 2000, pp. 613–44

——, 'Transnational Civil Society and Advocacy in World Politics,' *World Politics*, 55, 2003, pp. 579–606

Pugh, Michael, 'Pacifism and Politics in Britain, 1931–1935,' *Historical Journal*, 23/3, 1980, pp. 641–656

Rainbolt, Rosemary, 'Women and War in the United States: The Case of Dorothy Detzer, National Secretary, WILPF,' *Peace & Change*, 4, 1977, pp. 18–22

Richardson, Dick, 'The Geneva Disarmament Conference, 1932–34' in Dick Richardson and Glyn Stone (eds.), *Decisions and Diplomacy: Essays in Twentieth Century International History: In Memory of George Grun and Esmonde Robertson* (London, 1995), pp. 60–82

——, and Carolyn Kitching, 'Britain and the World Disarmament Conference' in P. Catterall and C. J. Morris (eds.), *Britain and the Threat to Stability in Europe, 1918–1945* (Leicester, 1993), pp. 35–56

Risse, Thomas, 'Transnational Actors and World Politics' in Walter Carlsnaes, Thomas Risse, and Beth A. Simmons (eds.), *Handbook of International Relations* (London, 2002), pp. 255–74

Ruggie, John Gerard, 'Reconstructing the Global Public Domain: Issues, Actors and Practices,' *Harvard University John F. Kennedy School of Government Faculty Research Working Paper Series*, RWP04–031, July 2004, pp. 1–48

Rupp, Leila J., 'Constructing Internationalism: the Case of Transnational Women's Organisations, 1888–1945,' *American Historical Review*, 99/5, 1994, pp. 1571–1600

Schoenleitner, Guenther, 'World Social Forum: Is Another World Possible?' in John Clark (ed.), *Globalizing Civic Engagement: Civil Society and Transnational Action* (Sterling, VA, 2003), pp. 127–49

Scholte, Jan Aart, 'Civil Society and Democracy in Global Governance,' *Global Governance*, 8, 2002, pp. 281–304

——, 'Global Civil Society,' in Ngaire Woods (ed.), *The Political Economy of Globalization* (Oxford, 2000), pp. 173–201

Short, Nicole, 'The Role of NGOs in the Ottawa Process to Ban Landmines,' *International Negotiation*, 4/3, 1999, pp. 483–502

Snider, Christy Jo, 'The Influence of Transnational Peace Groups on US Foreign Policy Decision-Makers during the 1930s: Incorporating NGOs into the UN,' *Diplomatic History*, 27/3, 2003, pp. 377–404

Swerczek, Ronald E., 'Hugh Gibson and Disarmament: The Diplomacy of Gradualism,' in Kenneth Paul Jones (ed.), *U.S. Diplomats in Europe, 1919–1941* (Santa Barbara, CA, 1981), pp. 75–90

Tate, Merze, 'Disarmament,' in Alexander DeConde (ed.), *Encyclopedia of American Foreign Policy: Studies of the Principal Movements and Ideas* (New York, 1978), pp. 244–52

Thompson, J. A., 'Lord Cecil and the Pacifists in the League of Nations Union,' *Historical Journal*, 20/4, 1973, pp. 949–959

Thorne, Christopher, 'The Quest for Arms Embargoes: The Failure in 1933,' *Journal of Contemporary History*, 5, 1970, pp. 129–50

Vaïsse, Maurice, 'Continuité et discontinuité dans la politique française en matière de désarmement (février 1932–juin 1933): l'exemple du contrôle,' in Comité d'Histoire de la Deuxième Guerre Mondiale, *La France et l'Allemagne, 1932–1936: communications présentées au colloque franco-allemand tenu à Paris (Palais du Luxembourg, salle Medicis) du 10 au 12 mars 1977* (Paris, 1980), pp. 27–47

——, 'Le pacifisme français dans les années trente,' *Relations Internationales*, 53, 1988, pp. 37–52

——, 'Security and Disarmament: Problems in the Development of the Disarmament Debates, 1919–1934,' in R. Ahmann, A. M. Birke and M. Howard (eds.), *The Quest for Stability: Problems of West European Security, 1918–1957* (London, 1993), pp. 173–200

Venkataramani, M. S., 'Ramsay MacDonald and Britain's Domestic Politics and Foreign Relations, 1919–1931: A Study Based on MacDonald's Letters to an American Friend,' *Political Studies*, 8/3, 1960, pp. 231–49

Webster, Andrew, 'An Argument without End: Britain, France and the Disarmament Process, 1925–34,' in Martin S. Alexander and W. J. Philpott (eds.), *Anglo-French Defence Relations between the Wars, 1919–1939* (Basingstoke and London, 2001), pp. 49–71

——, 'The Disenchantment Conference: Frustration and Humour at the World Disarmament Conference, 1932,' *Diplomacy & Statecraft*, 11/3, 2000, pp. 72–80

——, 'The Transnational Dream: Politicians, Diplomats and Soldiers in the League of Nations' Pursuit of International Disarmament, 1920–1938,' *Contemporary European History*, 14/4, 2005, pp. 493–518

Winkler, Fred H., 'Disarmament and Security: The American Policy at Geneva, 1926–1935,' *North Dakota Quarterly*, Autumn 1971, pp. 21–33

——, 'The War Department and Disarmament,' *Historian*, 28/3, 1966, pp. 426–46

Winkler, Henry R., 'Arthur Henderson,' in Gordon A. Craig and Felix Gilbert (eds.), *The Diplomats, 1919–1939* (Princeton, NJ, 1953), pp. 311–43

Yearwood, Peter, '"On the Safe and Right Lines:" The Lloyd George Government and the Origins of the League of Nations, 1916–1918,' *Historical Journal*, 32/1, pp. 131–55

Books

Abs, Robert, *Emile Vandervelde* (Brussels, 1973)

Adamthwaite, Anthony, *Grandeur and Misery: France's Bid for Power in Europe, 1914–1940* (London, 1995)

Adler, Selig, *The Uncertain Giant, 1921–1941: American Foreign Policy between the Wars* (New York, 1965)

Agi, Marc, *René Cassin: Prix Nobel de la Paix: 1887–1976: Père de la Déclaration Universelle des Droits de l'Homme* (Paris, 1998)

Ahmann, R., A. M. Birke and M. Howard (eds.), *The Quest for Stability: Problems of West European Security, 1918–1957* (Oxford, 1993)

Aiftinca, Marin, *Nicolae Titulescu: précurseur de l'unité européenne* (Bucharest, 1993)

Allison, Graham, *Essence of Decision: Explaining the Cuban Missile Crisis* (New York, 1971)

Alonso, Harriet Hyman, *Peace as a Women's Issue: A History of the U.S. Movement for World Peace and Women's Rights* (Syracuse, NY, 1993)

——, *The Women's Peace Union and the Outlawry of War, 1921–1942* (Knoxville, TN, 1989)

Ambrosius, Lloyd E., *Woodrow Wilson and the American Diplomatic Tradition: The Treaty Fight in Perspective* (Cambridge, 1987)

Anheier, Helmut, and Mary Kaldor, *Global Civil Society, 2004–5* (London, 2005)

——, and Jeremy Kendall, *Third Sector Policy at the Crossroads: An International Nonprofit Analysis* (London, 2001)

Arnoldson, Klas Pontus, *Pax mundi, a concise account of the progress of the movement for peace by means of arbitration, neutralization, international law and disarmament* (London, 1892)

Arts, Bas, *The Political Influence of Global NGOs: Case Studies on the Climate and Biodiversity Conventions* (Utrecht, 1998)

——, Math Noortman, and Bob Reinalda (eds.), *Non-State Actors in International Relations* (Aldershot, 2001)

Ashley, LeRoy, *The Spearless Leader: Senator Borah and the Progressive Movement in the 1920s* (Urbana, IL, 1972)

Baer, George W., *International Organizations, 1918–1945: A Guide to Research and Research Materials* (Wilmington, DE, 1981)

Bailey, Thomas Andrew, *Woodrow Wilson and the Lost Peace* (Chicago, IL, 1963)

Baker, Gideon, and David Chandler (eds.), *Global Civil Society: Contested Futures* (Abingdon, 2005)

Baker, Ray Stannard, *Woodrow Wilson and World Settlement* (Garden City, NY, 1922)

Baker, Roscoe, *The American Legion and American Foreign Policy* (New York, 1954)

Bandy, Joe, and Jackie Smith (eds.), *Coalitions Across Borders: Transnational Protest and the Neoliberal Order* (Lanham, MD, 2005)

Bankwitz, Philip Charles Farwell, *Maxime Weygand and Civil-Military Relations in Modern France* (Cambridge, MA, 1967)

Bariéty, Jacques, *Les Relations Franco-Allemandes après la Première Guerre Mondiale* (Paris, 1977)

Barros, James, *Betrayal From Within: Joseph Avenol, Secretary-General of the League of Nations, 1933–1940* (New Haven, CT, 1969)

——, *Office Without Power: Secretary-General Sir Eric Drummond, 1919–1933* (Oxford, 1979)

Bartlett, Ruhl Jacob, *The League to Enforce Peace* (Chapel Hill, NC, 1944)

Batliwala, Srilatha, and L. David Brown, (eds.), *Transnational Civil Society: An Introduction* (Bloomfield, CT, 2006)

Beales, A. C. F., *The History of Peace: A Short Account of the Organised Movements for Peace* (London, 1931)

Behera, Subhakanta, *The Politics of Disarmament, 1919–1939: A Study of the World Disarmament Conference* (Vidyapuri, 1990)

Bennett, Edward W., *German Rearmament and the West, 1932–1933* (Princeton, NJ, 1979)

Bialer, Uri, *The Shadow of the Bomber: The Fear of Air Attack and British Politics, 1932–1939* (London, 1980)

Binion, Rudolph, *Defeated Leaders: The Political Fate of Caillaux, Jouvenel, and Tardieu* (Morningside Heights, NY, 1960)

Birchall, Johnston, *Co-op: The People's Business* (Manchester, 1994)

Birn, Donald S., *The League of Nations Union, 1918–1945* (Oxford, 1981)

Blumenthal, Henry, *Illusion and Reality in Franco-American Diplomacy, 1914–1945* (Baton Rouge, LA, 1986)

Boli, John, and George M. Thomas (eds.), *Constructing World Culture* (Stanford, CA, 1999)

Bongiorno, Joseph, *Fascist Italy and the Disarmament Question, 1928–1934* (New York, 1991)

Bonnet, Georges E., *Le Quai d'Orsay sous trois Républiques, 1870–1961* (Paris, 1961)

Bréal, Auguste, *Philippe Berthelot* (Paris, 1937)

Brock, Hugh, *The Century of Total War* (London, 1962)

Brock, Peter, *Pacifism in Europe to 1914* (Princeton, NJ, 1972)

——, and Thomas Socknat (eds.), *Challenge to Mars: Essays on Pacifism from 1918 to 1945* (Toronto, 1999)

Buckley, Thomas H., *The United States and the Washington Conference, 1921–1922* (Knoxville, TN, 1970)

Bull, Hedley, *The Control of the Arms Race: Disarmament and Arms Control in the Missile Age* (London, 1961)

Burgerman, Susan, *Moral Victories: How Activists Provoke Multilateral Action* (Ithaca, NY, 2001)

Bussey, Gertrude, and Margaret Tims, *Pioneers For Peace: The Women's International League for Peace and Freedom, 1915–1965* (London, 1980)

Cameron, Elizabeth R., *Prologue to Appeasement: A Study in French Foreign Policy* (Washington, DC, 1942)

Cameron, Maxwell A., Robert J. Lawson and Brian W. Tomlin (eds.), *To Walk Without Fear: The Global Movement to Ban Landmines* (Toronto, 1998)

Carlton, David, *Anthony Eden: A Biography* (London, 1981)

——, *MacDonald versus Henderson: The Foreign Policy of the Second Labour Government* (London, 1970)

Carr, Edward Hallet, *International Relations Between the Two World Wars, 1919–1939* (London, 1947)

——, *The Twenty Years' Crisis: An Introduction to the Study of International Relations* (London, 1939)

Castellan, G., *Le réarmement clandestin du Reich, 1930–1935, vu par le 2. Bureau de l'État-major français* (Paris, 1954)

Ceadel, Martin, *The Origins of War Prevention: The British Peace Movement and International Relations, 1730–1854* (Oxford, 1996)

——, *Pacifism in Britain, 1914–1945: The Defining of a Faith* (Oxford, 1980)

——, *Semi-Detached Idealists: The British Peace Movement and International Relations, 1854–1945* (Oxford, 2000)

Centre for the Study of Global Governance, London School of Economics and Political Science, *Global Civil Society Yearbooks* (Oxford and London, 2001–2007)

Chaput, Rolland A., *Disarmament in British Foreign Policy* (London, 1935)

Chatfield, Charles, *For Peace and Justice: Pacifism In America, 1914–1941* (Knoxville, TN, 1971)

—— (ed.), *Peace Movements in America* (New York, 1973)

Chavez-Pirson, Maria Elena, *The League of Nations and Private International Organisations* (Geneva, 1991)

Chickering, Roger, and Stig Forster (eds.), *The Shadows of Total War: Europe, East Asia and the United States, 1919–1939* (Cambridge, 2003)

Chuter, David, *Humanity's Soldier: France and International Security, 1919–2001* (Providence, RI, 1996)

Clark, John (ed.), *Globalizing Civic Engagement. Civil Society and Transnational Action* (Sterling, VA, 2003)

Clay, Kenneth, *Les Rapports Politiques Franco-Allemands à la Conférence du Désarmement* (Geneva, 1939)

Cohrs, Patrick O., *The Unfinished Peace after World War I: America, Britain and the Stabilisation of Europe, 1919–1932* (Cambridge, 2005)

Colas, Alejandro, *International Civil Society: Social Movements in World Politics* (Cambridge, 2002)

Cole, Hubert, *Laval: A Biography* (London, 1963)

Colton, Joel, *Léon Blum: Humanist in Politics* (Cambridge, MA, 1966)

Cooper, John Milton, *Breaking the Heart of the World: Woodrow Wilson and the Fight for the League of Nations* (Cambridge, 2001)

Cooper, Russell M., *American Consultation in World Affairs for the Preservation of Peace* (New York, 1934)

Cooper, Sandi, *Patriotic Pacifists: Waging War on War in Europe, 1815–1914* (New York, 1991)

Costigliola, Frank, *Awkward Dominion: American Political, Economic, and Cultural Relations with Europe, 1919–1933* (Ithaca, NY, 1984)

Crosby, Gerda Richards, *Disarmament and Peace in British Politics, 1914–1919* (Cambridge, MA, 1957)

Dahl, Robert A., *Who Governs? Democracy and Power in an American City* (New Haven, CT, 1961)

Dallek, Robert, *Franklin D. Roosevelt and American Foreign Policy, 1932–1945* (New York, 1995)

Davis, Calvin DeArmond, *The United States and the First Hague Peace Conference* (Ithaca, NY, 1962)

——, *The United States and the Second Hague Peace Conference* (Durham, NC, 1975)

DeBenedetti, Charles, *Origins of the Modern American Peace Movement, 1915–1929* (Millwood, NY, 1978)

Deist, Wilhelm, *The Wehrmacht and German Rearmament* (London, 1981)

Delbreil, Jean-Claude, *Les catholiques français et les tentatives de rapprochement franco-allemand, 1920–1933* (Metz, 1972)

Della Porta, Donatella, Hanspeter Kriesi and Dieter Rucht (eds.), *Social Movements in a Globalizing World* (Basingstoke, 1999)

——, and Sidney Tarrow (eds.), *Transnational Protest and Global Activism* (Lanham, MD, 2004)

Diehl, James, and Stephen Ward, *The War Generation: Veterans of the First World War* (Port Washington, NY, 1975)

Dingman, Roger, *Power in the Pacific: The Origins of Naval Arms Limitation, 1914–1922* (Chicago, 1976)

Dockrill, Michael L., and J. Douglas Goold, *Peace Without Promise: Britain and the Peace Conferences, 1919–23* (London, 1981)

Doh, Jonathan P., and Hildy Teegen (eds.), *Globalization and NGOs: Transforming Business, Government and Society* (Westport, CT, 2003)

Doise, Jean, and Maurice Vaïsse, *Diplomatie et outil militaire, 1871–1969* (Paris, 1987)

Douglas, James, *Parliaments Across Frontiers: A Short History of the Inter-Parliamentary Union*, second edition (London, 1976)

Dupuy, Trevor N., and Gay M. Hammerman (eds.), *A Documentary History of Arms Control and Disarmament* (New York, 1973)

Duroselle, Jean Baptiste, *La Décadence, 1932–1939* (Paris, 1979)
——, *From Wilson to Roosevelt: Foreign Policy of the United States, 1913–1945* (London, 1964)
Dutton, David, *Austen Chamberlain: Gentleman in Politics* (Bolton, 1985)
——, *Simon: A Political Biography of Sir John Simon* (London, 1992)
Edwards, Michael, and Alan Fowler (eds.), *The Earthscan Reader on NGO Management* (London, 2002)
——, and John Gaventa (eds.), *Global Citizen Action* (London, 2001)
——, and David Hulme (eds.), *Making a Difference: NGOs and Development in a Changing World* (London, 1992)
Egerton, George W., *Great Britain and the Creation of the League of Nations: Strategy, Politics and International Organization, 1914–1919* (London, 1979)
Ekirch, Arthur A., *The Civilian and the Military* (New York, 1956)
Evangelista, Matthew, *Unarmed Forces: The Transnational Movement to End the Cold War* (Ithaca, NY, 1999)
Evans, Richard, *Comrades and Sisters: Feminism, Socialism and Pacifism in Europe, 1870–1945* (Brighton, 1987)
Fagerberg, Elliott Pennell, *The 'Anciens Combattants' and French Foreign Policy* (Annemasse, 1966)
Falk, Richard A., *On Humane Governance: Toward a New Global Politics* (Cambridge, 1995)
Fanning, Richard W., *Peace and Disarmament: Naval Rivalry & Arms Control, 1922–33* (Lexington, KY, 1995)
Fausold, Martin L., *The Presidency of Herbert C. Hoover* (Lawrence, KS, 1985)
Ferrell, Robert H., *American Diplomacy in the Great Depression: Hoover-Stimson Foreign Policy, 1929–1933* (Hamden, CT, 1969)
——, *Frank B. Kellogg, Henry L. Stimson* (New York, 1963)
——, *Peace in their Time: The Origins of the Kellogg-Briand Pact* (New Haven, CT, 1952)
Fleming, Denna Frank, *The United States and the League of Nations, 1918–1920* (New York, 1932)
Fletcher, Sheila, *Maude Royden: A Life* (Oxford, 1989)
Florini, Ann M., *The Coming Democracy: New Rules for Running a New World* (London, 2003)
—— (ed.), *The Third Force: The Rise of Transnational Civil Society* (Washington, DC, 2000)
Floto, Inga, *Colonel House in Paris: A Study of American Policy at the Paris Peace Conference, 1919* (Princeton, NJ, 1980)
Foster, Carrie A., *The Women and the Warriors: The US Section of the Women's International League for Peace and Freedom, 1915–1946* (Syracuse, NY, 1995)
Foster, Catherine, *Women for All Seasons: The Story of the Women's International League for Peace and Freedom* (Athens, GA, 1989)
Foster, William Z., *History of the Three Internationals: The World Socialist and Communist Movements from 1848 to the Present* (New York, 1955)
Fowler, Robert Booth, *Carrie Catt: Feminist Politician* (Boston, MA, 1986)
François-Poncet, André, *De Versailles à Potsdam: La France et le problème allemand contemporaine, 1919–1943* (Paris, 1948)
Gallo, Patrick, *Swords and Plowshares: The United States and Disarmament, 1898–1979* (Manhattan, KS, 1980)
Georges, Bernard, Denise Tintant and Marie-Anne Renauld, *Léon Jouhaux dans le mouvement syndical français* (Paris, 1979)
Gilpin, Robert, *War and Change in World Politics* (Cambridge, 1981)
Giugni, Marco, Doug McAdam, and Charles Tilly (eds.), *How Social Movements Matter* (Minneapolis, MN, 1999)
Goldberg, George, *The Peace to End Peace: The Paris Peace Conference of 1919* (New York, 1969)

Goldstein, Erik, *Winning the Peace: British Diplomatic Strategy, Peace Planning and the Paris Peace Conference, 1916–1920* (Oxford, 1991)

——, and John Maurer (eds.), *The Washington Conference, 1921–1922: Naval Rivalry, East Asian Stability and the Road to Pearl Harbor* (London, 1994)

Goslin, Rhylis A., *Church and State* (New York, 1937)

——, *Cooperatives* (New York, 1937)

Grayson, Richard S., *Austen Chamberlain and the Commitment to Europe: British Foreign Policy, 1924–29* (London, 1997)

Gruenewald, Guido, and Peter van den Dungen (eds.), *Twentieth Century Peace Movements: Successes and Failures* (Lewiston, 1994)

Guillen, Pierre, *Opinion Publique et Politique Extérieure en France, 1914–1940* (Milan, 1981)

Hall, Christopher, *Britain, America and Arms Control, 1921–1937* (London, 1987)

Hamann, Brigitte, *Bertha von Suttner: A Life for Peace* (Syracuse, NY, 1996)

Hamburger, Maurice, *Léon Bourgeois: La Politique Radicale Socialiste, la Doctrine de la Solidarité, l'Arbitrage International et la Société des Nations* (Paris, 1932)

Harris, Christina Phelps, *The Anglo-American Peace Movement in the Mid-Nineteenth Century* (New York, 1930)

Haslam, Beryl, *From Suffrage to Internationalism: The Political Evolution of Three British Feminists, 1908–1939* (New York, 1999)

Headlam-Morley, James, *Studies in Diplomatic History* (London, 1930)

Held, David, *Global Transformations: Politics, Economics and Culture* (Cambridge, 1999)

——, and Anthony McGrew (eds.), *The Global Transformations Reader: An Introduction to the Globalization Debate*, second edition (Cambridge, 2003)

Henig, Ruth B., *The League of Nations* (Edinburgh, 1973)

Herren, Madeleine, and Sacha Zala, *Netzwerk Aussenpolitik: Internationale Kongresse und Organisationen als Instrumente der schweizerischen Aussenpolitik, 1914–1950* (Zurich, 2002)

Hicks, John Donald, *Republican Ascendancy, 1921–1933* (New York, 1963)

Higham, Robin, *Armed Forces in Peacetime: Britain, 1918–1940: A Case Study* (London, 1962)

Hinsley, F. H., *Power and the Pursuit of Peace* (Cambridge, 1963)

Hoag, Charles Leonard, *Preface to Preparedness: the Washington Disarmament Conference and Public Opinion* (Washington, DC, 1941)

Hoefling, Beate, *Katholische Friedensbewegung zwischen zwei Kriegen: Freidensbund Deutscher Katholiken, 1917–1933* (Tuebingen, 1979)

Hoffmann, Stefan-Ludwig, *Civil Society, 1750–1914* (Basingstoke, 2006)

Holl, Karl, *Pazifismus in Deutschland* (Frankfurt, 1988)

——, and Wolfram Wette, *Pazifismus in der Weimarer Republik* (Paderborn, 1981)

Howard, Michael, *The Continental Commitment: the Dilemma of British Defence Policy in the Era of the Two World Wars* (London, 1972)

——, *War and the Liberal Conscience* (London, 1978)

Hubert, Don, *The Landmine Ban: A Case Study in Humanitarian Advocacy* (Providence, RI, 2000)

Hudson, Darril, *The Ecumenical Movement in World Affairs* (London, 1969)

Hughes, Judith M., *To the Maginot Line: The Politics of French Military Preparation in the 1920s* (Cambridge, MA, 1971)

Hyde, Charles L., *Charles Evans Hughes* (New York, 1929)

Ingram, Norman, *The Politics of Dissent: Pacifism in France, 1919–1939* (Oxford, 1991)

Iriye, Akira, *Global Community: The Role of International Organizations in the Making of the Contemporary World* (Berkeley, CA, 2002)

Israel, Gérard, *René Cassin, 1887–1976: la guerre hors la loi, avec de Gaulle, les droits de l'homme* (Paris, 1990)

Jacobson, Jon, *Locarno Diplomacy: Germany and the West, 1925–1929* (Princeton, NJ, 1972)

Jaffe, Lorna S., *The Decision to Disarm Germany: British Policy towards Postwar German Disarmament, 1914–1919* (Boston, MA, 1985)

Jeanneney, Jean-Noel, *François de Wendel en République: l'Argent et le Pouvoir, 1914–1940* (Paris, 1976)

Jessup, Philip, *Elihu Root* (New York, 1938)

Johnson, Claudius O., *Borah of Idaho* (Seattle, WA, 1936)

Johnson, Robert David, *The Peace Progressives and American Foreign Relations* (Cambridge, MA, 1995)

Jones, S. Sheperd, *The Scandinavian States and the League of Nations* (Princeton, NJ, 1939)

Jordan, W. M., *Great Britain, France and the German Problem* (London, 1943)

Josephson, Harold, *James T. Shotwell and the Rise of Internationalism in America* (Rutherford, NJ, 1975)

—— (ed.), *Biographical Dictionary of Modern Peace Leaders* (Westport, CT, 1985)

Josselin, Daphné, and William Wallace, *Non-State Actors in World Politics* (Basingstoke, 2001)

Joyce, James Avery, *Broken Star: The Story of the League of Nations, 1919–1939* (Swansea, 1978)

Kaldor, Mary, *Global Civil Society: An Answer to War* (Cambridge, 2003)

Kaltefleiter, Werner, and Robert Pfaltzgraff (eds.), *The Peace Movements in Europe and the United States* (London, 1985)

Kaufman, Robert Gordon, *Arms Control during the Pre-Nuclear Era: The United States and Naval Disarmament between the two World Wars* (New York, 1990)

Keane, John, *Global Civil Society?* (Cambridge, 2003)

Keck, Margaret, and Kathryn Sikkink, *Activists Beyond Borders: Transnational Advocacy Networks in World Politics* (Ithaca, NY, 1998)

Keeton, Edward, *Briand's Locarno Policy: French Economics, Politics and Diplomacy, 1925–1929* (New York, 1987)

Kempf, Beatrix, *Suffragette for Peace: The Life of Bertha von Suttner* (London, 1972)

Kennedy, Paul M., *The Realities Behind Diplomacy: Background Influences on British External Policy, 1865–1980* (London, 1981)

Keohane, Robert, and Joseph Nye (eds.), *Transnational Relations and World Politics* (Cambridge, MA, 1971)

Khagram, Sanjeev, James V. Riker and Kathryn Sikkink (eds.), *Restructuring World Politics: Transnational Social Movements, Networks and Norms* (Minneapolis, MN, 2002)

Khan, Azeez Mehdi, *Shaping Policy: Do NGOs Matter? Lessons from India* (New Dehli, 1997)

Kimmich, Christoph, *Germany and the League of Nations* (Chicago, IL, 1976)

Kitching, Carolyn, *Britain and the Geneva Disarmament Conference: A Study in International History* (Basingstoke, 2002)

—— *Britain and the Problem of International Disarmament, 1919–1934* (London, 1999)

Knock, Thomas J., *To End All Wars: Woodrow Wilson and the Quest for a New World Order* (Princeton, NJ, 1995)

Korten, David C., *Getting to the 21st Century: Voluntary Action and the Global Agenda* (Hartford, CT, 1990)

Krut, Riva, *Globalization and Civil Society: NGO Influence in International Decision-Making* (Geneva, 1997)

Kuehl, Warren F., *Seeking World Order: The United States and International Organization to 1920* (Nashville, TX, 1969)

—— (ed.), *Biographical Dictionary of Internationalists* (Westport, CT, 1983)

—— and Lynne Dunn, *Keeping the Covenant: American Internationalists and the League of Nations, 1920–1939* (Kent, OH, 1997)

Kyba, Patrick, *Covenants Without the Sword: Public Opinion and British Defence Policy, 1931–1935* (Waterloo, Ont., Canada, 1983)

Lambert, Robert W., *Soviet Disarmament Policy, 1922–1931* (Washington, DC, 1964)

Laxer, Gordon, and Sandra Halperin (eds.), *Global Civil Society and its Limits* (Basingstoke, 2003)

Leffler, Melvyn, *The Elusive Quest: America's Pursuit of European Stability and French Security, 1919–1933* (Chapel Hill, NC, 1979)

Liddell Hart, B. H., *Deterrent or Defence: A Fresh Look at the West's Military Position* (London, 1960)

Liddington, Jill, *The Long Road to Greenham: Feminism and Anti-Militarism in Britain since 1820* (London, 1989)

Link, Arthur Stanley, *Wilson the Diplomatist: A Look at His Major Foreign Policies* (Baltimore, MD, 1957)

—— (ed.), *Wilson's Diplomacy: An International Symposium* (Cambridge, MA, 1973)

Lloyd, Lorna, *Peace through Law: Britain and the International Court in the 1920s* (Woodbridge, 1997)

——, and Nicholas Sims, *British Writing on Disarmament from 1914 to 1978: A Bibliography* (London, 1979)

Long, David, and Peter Wilson (eds.), *Thinkers of the Twenty Years Crisis: Inter-war Idealism Reassessed* (Oxford, 1995)

Loosli-Usteri, Carl, *Geschichte der Konferenz fuer die Herabsetzung und die Begrenzung der Ruestungen, 1932–1934: Ein Politischen Welzspiegel* (Zurich, 1940)

Lorwin, Lewis Levitzki, *The International Labor Movement: History, Politics, Outlook* (New York, 1953)

—— *Labor and Internationalism* (New York, 1929)

Luza, Radomir, *History of the International Socialist Youth Movement* (Leyden, 1970)

Lynch, Cecelia, *Beyond Appeasement: Interpreting Interwar Peace Movements in World Politics* (Ithaca, NY, 1999)

MacFarland, Charles Stedman, *Pioneers for Peace through Religion, Based on the Records of the Church Peace Union (Founded by Andrew Carnegie), 1914–1945* (New York, 1946)

Macmillan, Margaret, *Peacemakers: The Paris Conference of 1919 and its Attempt to End War* (London, 2001)

Maddox, Robert J., *William E. Borah and American Foreign Policy* (Baton Rouge, LA, 1969)

Marks, Sally, *The Illusion of Peace: International Relations in Europe, 1918–1933*, second edition (Basingstoke, 2003)

Marquand, David, *Ramsay MacDonald* (London, 1997)

Martin, James Joseph, *American Liberalism and World Politics, 1931–1941: Liberalism's Press and Spokesmen on the Road Back to War between Mukden and Pearl Harbor* (New York, 1964)

Martin, Laurence, *Peace Without Victory: Woodrow Wilson and the British Liberals* (New Haven, CT, 1958)

Mauermann, Helmut, *Das Internationale Friedensbuero, 1892 bis 1950* (Stuttgart, 1990)

McAdam, Doug, Sidney Tarrow, and Charles Tilly, *Dynamics of Contention* (Cambridge, 2001)

McCoy, Donald R., *Calvin Coolidge: The Quiet President* (New York, 1967)

McDougall, Walter A., *France's Rhineland Diplomacy, 1914–1924: The Last Bid for a Balance of Power in Europe* (Princeton, NJ, 1978)

McKercher, B. J. C. (ed.), *Anglo-American Relations in the 1920s: The Struggle for Supremacy* (Basingstoke, 1991)

——, *Arms Limitation and Disarmament: Restraints on War, 1899–1939* (Westport, CT, 1992)

Mendelson, Sarah E., and John K. Glenn (eds.), *The Power and Limits of NGOs: A Critical Look at Building Democracy in Eastern Europe and Eurasia* (New York, 2002)

Meynaud, Jean, *Les Groupes de Pression en France* (Paris, 1958)

Micaud, Charles Antoine, *The French Right and Nazi Germany, 1933–1939: A Study of Public Opinion* (Durham, 1943)

Michalka, Wolfgang, and Marshall Lee, *German Foreign Policy, 1918–1933: Continuity or Break?* (New York, 1987)
Middlemas, Keith, and John Barnes, *Baldwin: A Biography* (London, 1969)
Milhaud, Edgard, *La France Avait Raison: Sécurité Collective* (Neuchâtel, 1945)
Miller, David Hunter, *The Drafting of the Covenant*, volumes 1–2 (New York, 1928)
Miquel, Pierre, *La Paix de Versailles et l'Opinion Publique Française* (Paris, 1972)
Monnet, François, *Refaire la République: André Tardieu, une dérive réactionnaire, 1876–1945* (Paris, 1993)
Mouton, Marie-Renée, *La Société des Nations et les intérêts de la France, 1920–1924* (Lille, 1989)
Munch, P., *Les origines et l'oeuvre de la Société des Nations* (Copenhagen, 1923–4)
Muukkonen, Martti, *Ecumenism of the Laity: Continuity and Change in the Mission View of the World's Alliance of Young Men's Christian Associations, 1855–1955* (Joensuu, 2002)
Myers, William Starr, *The Foreign Policies of Herbert Hoover* (New York, 1940)
Nadolny, Sten, *Abruestungsdiplomatie, 1932/3: Deutschland auf der Genfer Konferenz im Uebergang von Weimar zu Hitler* (Munich, 1978)
Néré, J., *The Foreign Policy of France from 1914 to 1945* (London, 1975)
Nicolson, Harold, *Peacemaking, 1919* (London, 1933)
Noble, George Bernard, *Policies and Opinions at Paris, 1919: Wilsonian Diplomacy, the Versailles Peace and French Public Opinion* (New York, 1935)
Northedge, F. S., *The League of Nations: Its Life and Times, 1920–1946* (Leicester, 1986)
Notter, Harley A., *The Origins of the Foreign Policy of Woodrow Wilson* (Baltimore, MD, 1937)
Nye, Joseph S., *The Paradox of American Power: Why the World's Only Superpower Can't Go It Alone* (Oxford, 2002)
O'Brien, Robert, Anne Marie Goetz, Jan Aart Scholte and Marc Williams, *Contesting Global Governance: Multilateral Economic Institutions and Global Social Movements* (Cambridge, 2000)
O'Connor, Raymond G., *Perilous Equilibrium: The United States and the London Naval Conference of 1930* (Lawrence, KA, 1962)
Orde, Anne, *Great Britain and International Security, 1920–1926* (London, 1978)
Ostrower, Gary B., *Collective Insecurity: The United States and the League of Nations during the Early Thirties* (London, 1979)
———, *The League of Nations from 1919 to 1929* (Garden City, NY, 1995)
Peck, Mary G., *Carrie Chapman Catt: A Biography* (New York, 1944)
Petrie, Charles, *The Life and Letters of the Right Hon. Sir Austen Chamberlain, K.G., P.C., M.P.*, second edition (London, 1940)
Pickard, Bertram, *The Greater United Nations: An Essay Concerning the Place and Significance of International Non-Governmental Organizations* (New York, 1956)
Pimlott, Ben, *Hugh Dalton* (London, 1985)
Piper, Nicola, and Anders Uhlin (eds.), *Transnational Activism in Asia: Problems of Power and Democracy* (London, 2004)
Playne, Caroline E., *Bertha von Suttner and the Struggle to Avert the World War* (London, 1936)
Polasky, Janet L., *Emile Vandervelde, le patron* (Brussels, 1995)
Potter, Philip, and Thomas Wieser, *Seeking and Serving the Truth: The First Hundred Years of the World's Student Christian Federation* (Geneva, 1997)
Potter, Pitman B., *An Introduction to the Study of International Organization*, fourth edition (New York, 1935)
Potts, Archie, *Zilliacus: A Life for Peace and Socialism* (London, 2002)
Pratt, Julius W., *Cordell Hull, 1933–44*, volume one (New York, 1964)
———, Vincent P. de Santis, and Joseph M. Siracusa, *A History of United States Foreign Policy*, fourth edition (Englewood Cliffs, NJ, 1980)
Princen, Thomas, and Matthias Finger (eds.), *Environmental NGOs in World Politics: Linking the Local with the Global* (London, 1994)

Prost, Antoine, *Les anciens combattants et la société française, 1914–1945* (Paris, 1977)
——, *In the Wake of War: 'Les Anciens Combattants' and French Society, 1919–1939* (Oxford, 1992)
Randall, Mercedes M., *Improper Bostonian: Emily Greene Balch* (New York, 1964)
Ranshofen-Wertheimer, Egon Ferdinand, *The International Secretariat: A Great Experiment in International Administration* (Washington, DC, 1945)
Rappaport, Armin, *The Navy League of the United States* (Detroit, MI, 1962)
Rappard, William E., *The Quest for Peace since the World War* (Cambridge, MA, 1940)
Réau, Elizabeth du, *Edouard Daladier, 1884–1970* (Paris, 1993)
Rice, Anna, *A History of the World's Young Women's Christian Association* (New York, 1947)
Richardson, Dick, *The Evolution of British Disarmament Policy in the 1920s* (London, 1989)
——, and Glyn Stone (eds.), *Decisions and Diplomacy: Essays in Twentieth Century International History: In Memory of George Grun and Esmonde Robertson* (London, 1995)
Richter, Ingo K., Sabine Berking, and Ralf Mueller-Schmid, *Building a Transnational Civil Society: Global Issues and Global Actors* (Basingstoke, 2007)
Riddell, Walter A., *World Security by Conference* (Toronto, 1947)
Riesenberger, Dieter, *Geschichte der Friedensbewegung in Deutschland: von den Anfaengen bis 1933* (Goettingen, 1985)
Risse-Kappen, Thomas (ed.), *Bringing Transnational Relations Back In: Non-State Actors, Domestic Structures and International Institutions* (Cambridge, 1995)
Robins, Dorothy, *Experiment in Democracy: The Story of U.S. Citizen Organizations in Forging the Charter of the United Nations* (New York, 1971)
Roessler, H. (ed.), *Locarno und die Weltpolitik, 1924–1932* (Goettingen, 1969)
Rosenau, James N., *Turbulence in World Politics: A Theory of Change and Continuity* (Princeton, NJ, 1990)
Roskill, Stephen, *Hankey: Man of Secrets*, volumes 1–3 (London, 1970–4)
——, *Naval Policy Between the Wars* (London, 1968–76)
Rothwell, Victor S., *British War Aims and Peace Diplomacy, 1914–1918* (Oxford, 1971)
Rouse, Ruth, *The World's Student Christian Federation: A History of the First Thirty Years* (London, 1948)
——, and Stephen Charles Neill, *A History of the Ecumenical Movement, 1517–1948* (London, 1954)
Rupp, Leila J., *Worlds of Women: The Making of an International Women's Movement* (Princeton, NJ, 1997)
Salomon, Lester M., Helmut K. Anheier, Regina List, Stefan Toepler, S. Wojciech Sokolowski and Associates, *Global Civil Society: Dimensions of the Nonprofit Sector* (Baltimore, MD, 1999)
Santi, Rainer, *100 Years of Peacemaking* (Geneva, 1991)
Scholte, Jan Aart, *Globalization: A Critical Introduction* (Basingstoke, 2000)
——, and Albrecht Schnabel (eds.), *Civil Society and Global Finance* (London, 2002)
Schott, Linda K., *Reconstructing Women's Thoughts: The Women's International League for Peace and Freedom before World War II* (Stanford, CA, 1997)
Schulte Nordholt, J. W., *Woodrow Wilson: A Life for World Peace* (Berkeley, CA, 1991)
Scott, George, *The Rise and Fall of the League of Nations* (London, 1973)
Scott, James Brown, *The Hague Peace Conferences of 1899 and 1907: A Series of Lectures Delivered Before the Johns Hopkins University in the Year 1908* (Baltimore, MD, 1909)
Sharp, Alan, *The Versailles Settlement: Peacemaking in Paris, 1919* (Basingstoke, 1991)
Shedd, Clarence Prouty, *History of the World's Alliance of Young Men's Christian Associations* (London, 1955)
Shirer, William L., *The Collapse of the Third Republic: An Inquiry into the Fall of France in 1940* (London, 1970)
Shotwell, James T., and Marina Salvin, *Lessons on Security and Disarmament from the History of the League of Nations* (Westport, CT, 1949)

Shoup, Lawrence H., and William Minter, *Imperial Brain Trust: The Council on Foreign Relations and United States Foreign Policy* (New York, 1977)

Siegel, Mona, *The Moral Disarmament of France: Education, Pacifism, and Patriotism, 1914–1940* (Cambridge, 2004)

Sloutzski, N. M., *The World Armaments Race, 1919–1939* (Geneva, 1941)

Smith, Jackie, Charles Chatfield and Ron Pagnucco (eds.), *Transnational Social Movements and World Politics: Solidarity beyond the State* (Syracuse, NY, 1997)

——, and Hank Johnston (eds.), *Globalization and Resistance: Transnational Dimensions of Social Movements* (Lanham, MD, 2002)

Soulié, Michel, *La vie politique d'Edouard Herriot* (Paris, 1962)

Sprout, Harold and Margaret, *Toward a New Order of Sea Power: American Naval Policy and the World Scene, 1918–1922* (Princeton, NJ, 1940)

Steiner, Zara, *The Lights that Failed: European International History, 1919–1933* (Oxford, 2005)

Stevenson, David, *French War Aims Against Germany, 1914–1919* (Oxford, 1982)

Stienstra, Deborah, *Women's Movements and International Organisations* (Basingstoke, 1994)

Stromberg, Roland N., *Collective Security and American Foreign Policy: From the League of Nations to NATO* (New York, 1963)

Suarez, Georges, *Briand: sa vie, son oeuvre, avec son journal et de nombreux documents inédits*, volume six (Paris, 1952)

Swartz, Marvin, *The Union of Democratic Control in British Politics during the First World War* (Oxford, 1971)

Tansill, Charles Callan, *Back Door to War: The Roosevelt Foreign Policy, 1933–41* (Chicago, IL, 1952)

Tarrow, Sidney, *The New Transnational Activism* (Cambridge, 2005)

——, *Power In Movement: Social Movements, Collective Action and Politics* (Cambridge, 1994)

Tate, Merze, *The Disarmament Illusion: The Movement for a Limitation of Armaments to 1907* (New York, 1942)

——, *The United States and Armaments* (Cambridge, MA, 1948)

Taylor, A. J. P., *The Origins of the Second World War* (London, 1961)

——, *The Troublemakers: Dissent over Foreign Policy, 1792–1939* (London, 1993)

Taylor, Rupert (ed.), *Creating a Better World: Interpreting Global Civil Society* (Bloomfield, CT, 2004)

Temperley, Harold William Vazeille, *A History of the Peace Conference of Paris* (London, 1920–4)

Thomas, Alan, Susan Carr and David Humphreys (eds.), *Environmental Policies and NGO Influence: Land Degradation and Sustainable Resource Management in Sub-Saharan Africa* (London, 2001)

Tilly, Charles, *Social Movements, 1768–2004* (Boulder, CO, 2004)

Toynbee, Arnold Joseph, *Survey of International Affairs* (London, 1920–35)

Tyrrell, Ian, *Woman's World/Woman's Empire: The Woman's Christian Temperance Union in International Perspective, 1880–1930* (Chapel Hill, NC, 1981)

United Nations Centre for Disarmament Affairs, *The United Nations and Disarmament since 1945* (New York, 1996)

United Nations Library, *The League of Nations in Retrospect: Proceedings of the Symposium organized by the United Nations Library and the Graduate Institute of International Studies, Geneva, 6–9 November 1980* (Berlin, 1983)

Université des Sciences Sociales de Grenoble: Centre de Recherche d'Histoire de l'Italie et de Pays Alpines, *La France et l'Italie pendant la Première Guerre Mondiale: Actes du colloque tenu à l'Université des Sciences Sociales de Grenoble les 28, 29 et 30 septembre 1973* (Grenoble, 1976)

University Group on Defence Policy, *The Role of the Peace Movements in the 1930s* (London, 1959)

Vaïsse, Maurice, *Sécurité d'abord: la politique française en matière de désarmement, 9 décembre 1930–17 avril 1934* (Paris, 1981)

———, and Anthony Adamthwaite (eds.), *Le pacifisme en Europe des années 1920 aux années 1950* (Brussels, 1993)

Valentin, J. M., J. Bariéty and A. Gruth (eds.), *La France et l'Allemagne entre les deux Guerres Mondiales: Actes du colloque tenu en Sorbonne (Paris IV), 15–16–17 janvier 1987* (Nancy, 1987)

van der Linden, Wilhelmus Hubertus, *The International Peace Movement, 1815–1874* (Amsterdam, 1987)

Van Voris, Jacqueline, *Carrie Chapman Catt: A Public Life* (New York, 1987)

Waley, Daniel, *British Public Opinion and the Abyssinian War, 1935–6* (London, 1975)

Wallis, Jill, *Valiant FoR Peace: A History of the Fellowship of Reconciliation, 1914 to 1989* (London, 1991)

Walters, F. P., *A History of the League of Nations* (London, 1960)

Walworth, Arthur, *Wilson and His Peacemakers: American Diplomacy at the Paris Peace Conference, 1919* (New York, 1986)

Walzer, Michael (ed.), *Toward a Global Civil Society* (Oxford, 1995)

Wank, Solomon (ed.), *Doves and Diplomats: Foreign Offices and Peace Movements in Europe and America in the Twentieth Century* (Westport, CT, 1978)

Werth, Alexander, *The Twilight of France, 1933–1940* (New York, 1942)

Weygand, Jacques, *Weygand, Mon Père* (Paris, 1970)

Wheeler-Bennett, John W., *Disarmament and Security since Locarno, 1925–1931, Being the Political and Technical Background of the General Disarmament Conference, 1932* (London, 1932)

———, *The Disarmament Deadlock* (London, 1934)

———, *Information on the Problem of Security, 1917–1926* (London, 1927)

———, *Information on the Reduction of Armaments* (London, 1925)

———, *The Pipe Dream of Peace: The Story of the Collapse of Disarmament* (London, 1935)

Whitaker, John Thompson, *And Fear Came* (New York, 1936)

White, Hope Costley, *Willoughby Hyett Dickinson, 1859–1943* (Gloucester, 1956)

White, Lyman Cromwell, *The Structure of Private International Organizations* (Philadelphia, PA, 1933)

———, and Marie Ragonetti Zocca, *International Non-Governmental Organizations: Their Purposes, Methods and Accomplishments* (New Brunswick, 1951)

Whittaker, D. J., *Fighter for Peace: Philip Noel-Baker, 1889–1982* (York, 1989)

Whittick, Arnold, *Woman Into Citizen: The World Movement towards the Emancipation of Women in the Twentieth Century with Accounts of the Contributions of the International Alliance of Women, the League of Nations and the Relevant Agencies of the United Nations, 1902–78* (London, 1979)

Willetts, Peter (ed.), *Pressure Groups in the Global System: The Transnational Relations of Issue-Oriented Non-Governmental Organisations* (London, 1982)

Williams, Benjamin H., *The United States and Disarmament* (New York, 1931)

Wilson, Florence, *The Origins of the League Covenant: Documentary History of its Drafting* (London, 1928)

Winkler, Henry R., *The League of Nations Movement in Great Britain, 1914–1919* (New Brunswick, 1952)

Wittner, Lawrence, *Rebels Against War: The American Peace Movement, 1933–1983* (Philadelphia, PA, 1984)

———, *The Struggle Against the Bomb*, volumes 1–3 (Stanford, CA, 1993–2003)

Wolfers, Arnold, *Britain and France between Two Wars: Conflicting Strategies of Peace from Versailles to World War II* (New York, 1966)

———, *Discord and Collaboration: Essays on International Politics* (Baltimore, MD, 1962)

Wootton, Graham, *The Politics of Influence: British Ex-Servicemen, Cabinet Decisions, and Cultural Change, 1915–57* (London, 1963)

Wright, Quincy, *Public Opinion and World Politics* (Chicago, IL, 1933)

Young, Robert J., *France and the Origins of the Second World War* (Basingstoke, 1996)

——, *French Foreign Policy, 1918–1945: A Guide to Research and Reasearch Materials* (Wilmington, DE, 1981)

Zarjevski, Yéfime, *The People Have the Floor: A History of the Inter-Parliamentary Union* (Aldershot, 1989)

Theses and Dissertations

Abbot, Frank Winchester, *From Versailles to Munich: The Foreign Policy Association and American Foreign Policy* (DPhil, Texas Tech University, 1972)

Adams, Jenny, *Toward Permanent Peace: The Women's International League for Peace and Freedom, 1915–1933* (BA, University of Oxford, n.d.)

Ardalan, Farajollah, *The League of Nations and Disarmament: National Policies and Concepts of Sovereignty, Security and Peace, 1919–1934* (PhD, University of Akron, 1980)

Bowen, Adelphia Dane, *The Disarmament Movement, 1918–1935* (PhD, Columbia University, 1956)

Burch, Elisabeth Helen, *The United Nations Special Sessions on Disarmament, 1978 and 1982* (MLitt, University of Oxford, 1990)

Buzan, Barry Gordon, *The British Peace Movement from 1919 to 1939* (PhD, London School of Economics and Political Science, 1973)

Chirouf, Lamri, *The French Approach to Disarmament, 1920–1930: Policy Making Process, Principles and Methods* (PhD, Southampton University, 1989)

Chung, Donna E., *Transnational Advocates, Norm Advancement, and US Corporate Self-Regulation in China, 1993–2003* (DPhil, University of Oxford, 2004)

Coyle, William E., *President Hoover and World Disarmament* (MA, Georgetown University, 1953)

Davenport-Hines, Richard Peter Treadwell, *The British Armaments Industry During Disarmament, 1918–36* (PhD, University of Cambridge, 1979)

Davies, Thomas Richard, *The Possibilities of Transnationalism: The International Federation of League of Nations Societies and the International Peace Campaign, 1919–1939* (MPhil, University of Oxford, 2002)

——, *Transnational Activism and its Limits: The Campaign for Disarmament between the Two World Wars* (DPhil, University of Oxford, 2005)

Deboe, David Cornelius, *The United States and the Geneva Disarmament Conference, 1932–1934* (PhD, Tulane University, 1969)

Eagleton-Pierce, Matthew, *You've Got Protest! Exploring Transnational Activism and Hacktivism* (MPhil, University of Oxford, 2004)

Hogge II, John L., *Arbitrage, Sécurité, Désarmement: French Security and the League of Nations, 1920–1925* (DPhil, New York University, 1994)

Howlett, Gareth, *The Croix de Feu, the Parti Social Français and Colonel de la Rocque* (DPhil, University of Oxford, 1985)

Irvin, Thomas Casey, *Norman H. Davis and the Quest for Arms Control, 1931–1938* (PhD, Ohio State University, 1963)

Kyba, John Patrick, *British Attitudes toward Disarmament and Rearmament, 1932–1935* (PhD, London School of Economics and Political Science, 1967)

Leung, Stephanie Hoi-Ying, *Haunting the Hallways of Power: The Influence of Non-Governmental Organizations on the Negotiation Process at the Rome Conference for the Establishment of the International Criminal Court* (MPhil, University of Oxford, 2004)

Marabell, George Peter, *Frederick Libby and the American Peace Movement, 1921–1941* (PhD, Michigan State University, 1975)

Miller, Carol Ann, *Lobbying the League: Women's International Organizations and the League of Nations* (DPhil, University of Oxford, 1992)

Mouton, Marie-Renée, *La Société des Nations et les Intérêts de la France, 1920–1924* (Doctorat d'Etat, Université de Paris I, 1988)

Silverlock, Gerard Anthony, *The Impact of Pacifism on British Defence and Foreign Policy, 1931–37* (MLitt, Bristol University, 1986)

——, *Issues of Disarmament in British Defence and Foreign Policy, 1918–1925* (PhD, King's College, London, 2000)

Shorney, David S., *Britain and Disarmament, 1916–1931* (PhD, University of Durham, 1980)

Skidmore, Ellen Towne, *Pierre Cot: Apostle of Collective Security, 1919–1939* (DPhil, University of Tennessee, Knoxville, 1980)

Turner, Arthur S., *British Policies towards France with Special Reference to Disarmament and Security, 1926–1931* (DPhil, University of Oxford, 1978)

Waring, Stephen P., *Herbert Hoover and the Promotion of Disarmament, 1929–1932* (MA, University of Iowa, 1985)

Webster, Andrew Goodwin, *Anglo-French Relations and the Problems of Disarmament and Security, 1929–1933* (PhD, University of Cambridge, 2001)

Winkler, Fred Herbert, *The United States and the World Disarmament Conference, 1926–1935: A Study of the Formulation of Foreign Policy* (PhD, Northwestern University, 1957)

INDEX

a indicates an appendix; n indicates a footnote; t indicates a table

History of International Relations, Diplomacy, and Intelligence

History of International Relations, Diplomacy, and Intelligence is a peer-reviewed book series which seeks to publish high-quality, pioneering works in the history of international relations, broadly conceived. In addition to disseminating original research in traditional areas addressed by this field, including diplomacy, national security, economic conflict, and the role of individuals, this series also embraces the ongoing expansion of the study of international relations into such areas as culture, race, gender, sexuality, and the environment. Its books will encompass as well the often-overlooked role of intelligence and intelligence agencies in shaping foreign relations.

History of International Relations, Diplomacy, and Intelligence actively intends to further engagement between the scholarly community and the policy-making one, by demonstrating the continued importance of past patterns, practices, and policies for today's pressing debates.

1. Berridge, G.R. *Gerald Fitzmaurice (1865-1939), Chief Dragoman of the British Embassy in Turkey*. 2007. ISBN 978 90 04 16035 4
2. Davies, Thomas Richard. *The Possibilities of Transnational Activism: the Campaign for Disarmament between the Two World Wars*. 2007. ISBN 978 90 04 16258 7